TOKYO
ENCOUNTER

D0958802

BRANDON PRESSER
WENDY YANAGIHARA

Tokyo Encounter

Published by Lonely Planet Publications Pty Ltd
ABN 36 005 607 983

Australia (Head Office)	Locked Bag 1, Footscray, Vic 3011 ☎ 03 8379 8000 fax 03 8379 8111
USA	150 Linden St, Oakland, CA 94607 ☎ 510 250 6400 toll free 800 275 8555 fax 510 893 8572
UK	2nd fl, 186 City Rd London EC1V 2NT ☎ 020 7106 2100 fax 020 7106 2101
Contact	talk2us@lonelyplanet.com lonelyplanet.com/contact

The 3rd edition of Lonely Planet's *Tokyo Encounter* was written and researched by Brandon Presser. Wendy Yanagihara wrote the previous two editions. This title was commissioned in Lonely Planet's Oakland office, and produced by the following: **Commissioning Editor** Emily Wolman **Coordinating Editor** Victoria Harrison **Coordinating Cartographer** Xavier di Toro **Layout Designer** Wibowo Rusli **Assisting Editors** Pat Kinsella, Cathryn Game **Senior Editor** Susan Paterson **Managing Editor** Annelies Mertens **Managing Cartographer** Shahara Ahmed **Cover Research** Naomi Parker **Internal Image Research** Sabrina Dalbesio **Managing Layout Designer** Jane Hart **Thanks to** Laura Crawford, Heather Dickson, Chris Girdler, Nora Gregory, Liz Heynes

All images are copyright of the photographers unless otherwise indicated. Many of the images in this guide are available for licensing from Lonely Planet Images: lonelyplanetimages.com.

10 9 8 7 6 5 4 3 2 1   3rd edition
ISBN: 978 1 74179 819 7   Printed in China

MIX
Paper from
responsible sources
FSC® C021741
www.fsc.org

Paper in this book is certified against the Forest Stewardship Council™ standards. FSC™ promotes environmentally responsible, socially beneficial and economically viable management of the world's forests.

HOW TO USE THIS BOOK
Colour-Coding & Maps

Colour-coding is used for symbols on maps and in the text that they relate to (eg all eating venues on the maps and in the text are given a green knife and fork symbol). Each neighbourhood also gets its own colour, and this is used down the edge of the page and throughout that neighbourhood section.

Shaded yellow areas on the maps denote areas of interest – for their historical significance, their attractive architecture or their great bars and restaurants. We encourage you to head to these areas and just start exploring!

Prices

Multiple prices listed with reviews (eg €10/5 or €10/5/20) indicate adult/child, adult/concession or adult/child/family.

Although the authors and Lonely Planet have taken all reasonable care in preparing this book, we make no warranty about the accuracy or completeness of its content and, to the maximum extent permitted, disclaim all liability arising from its use.

Send us your feedback We love to hear from travellers – your comments keep us on our toes and help make our books better. Our well-travelled team reads every word on what you loved or loathed about this book. Although we cannot reply individually to postal submissions, we always guarantee that your feedback goes straight to the appropriate authors, in time for the next edition. Each person who sends us information is thanked in the next edition, and the most useful submissions are rewarded with a free book.

Visit **lonelyplanet.com** to submit your updates and suggestions or to ask for help. Our award-winning website also features inspirational travel stories, news and discussions.

Note: We may edit, reproduce and incorporate your comments in Lonely Planet products such as guidebooks, websites and digital products, so let us know if you don't want your comments reproduced or your name acknowledged. For a copy of our privacy policy visit lonelyplanet.com/privacy.

BRANDON PRESSER

Tokyo has held a special place in Brandon's heart for as long as he can remember. While studying at Harvard University he wrote his senior thesis on the city's fascinating array of retail architecture, and has since collaborated with many Japanese architects throughout his professional career. These days, Brandon has joined the glamorous ranks of eternal nomadism – he travels the world, pen in hand – and has contributed to over 25 Lonely Planet titles from Iceland to Thailand and many lands in between.

BRANDON'S THANKS

First and foremost, I'd like to thank my dear friend Misa – I could not have done this without you! A very special thank you to Ariel, Naomi, Taro, Makoto, Cecile, Marissa, Aiko, BAPE, the JNTO, my three local voices, Kikuchi Rinko, Shimizu Takashi and Terrie Lloyd, and everyone else who took time out of their busy schedules to help me piece together this guide.

Our Readers Many thanks to the travellers who wrote to us with helpful hints, useful advice and interesting anecdotes, including Ching-Li Tor and Evi de Maeyer.

Cover photograph Woman standing in front of the Keisen Hama sculpture *Garyu no mon* in the lobby of the Peninsula Hotel, Will Robb/Lonely Planet Images.

Neon signs along busy Yasukuni-dōri, Shinjuku

CONTENTS

THE AUTHOR   3
THIS IS TOKYO   7
HIGHLIGHTS   8
TOKYO DIARY   29
ITINERARIES   35
NEIGHBOURHOODS   40
>MARUNOUCHI, GINZA &
  CENTRAL TOKYO   44
>ROPPONGI   66
>EBISU & MEGURO   82
>SHIBUYA   90
>HARAJUKU   102
>SHINJUKU   118
>IKEBUKURO   132
>UENO   138
>ASAKUSA   146
>ODAIBA   154
SNAPSHOTS   160
>ACCOMMODATION   162
>ANIME & MANGA   164
>ARCHITECTURE   165
>FOOD   166
>GALLERIES   168
>GAY & LESBIAN   169
>KIDS   170
>LIVE MUSIC   171
>MARKETS   172
>MUSEUMS   173
>NIGHTLIFE   174
>PARKS & GARDENS   175

>SENTŌ & ONSEN   176
>SHRINES & TEMPLES   177
>SHOPPING   178
>SPECTATOR SPORTS   180
BACKGROUND   181
DIRECTORY   191
INDEX   208

>THIS IS TOKYO

Life in Tokyo moves at a well-oiled clip, with an energy that borders on mania and an obsession with newness that seems to make all ideas quickly obsolete. Fashions begin to fade almost as soon as they are plucked from clothes hangers, and *keitai* (mobile phones) are traded up for each latest technological advancement. But even while throngs of tech-savvy, smartly styled Tokyoites trot through subway stations, there is a traditional side to this hyperurban cosmopolis, which may not be immediately evident.

Beneath the conspicuous consumption of its shopping districts and shiny façades of the latest architectural achievement, Tokyo throws out unexpected glimpses of its cultural core. At a Shintō shrine across town, a young man purchases a fortune and, after reading it, ties it to a strung frame whose many paper fortunes rustle like leaves in a breeze. In a neighbourhood *sentō* (public bath) in Asakusa, an old woman bathes with her tiny granddaughter, much as she once did with her own grandmother.

Tokyo's unique vitality springs from this intertwining of the new with the time-honoured old. While it's the wellspring of Japanese pop culture, it is also a place where the patrilineage of its imperial family is a tightly held institution. It's the city to which Japanese nonconformists flee but where individuality is often linked to an older form of small-group identity. It's a metropolis where the pressure cooker of traditional societal mores and expectations explodes into cutting-edge art, music and inventions like the 'boyfriend's arm pillow'. Even pop culture like manga, as it takes the world by storm, is rooted in the tradition of Edo-period ukiyo-e (wood-block prints from the 'floating world'). And so, as its modern gears keep turning, the basic machinery of this intriguing city remains true to its origins.

Top left A traditional wedding at Meiji-jingū-gyoen (p103) **Top right** Traditional straw sandals and hat
Bottom School kids tie their fortunes at Sensō-ji temple (p149)

7

>HIGHLIGHTS

>1 Enjoy the ritualistic display of athletic prowess
that is *sumō*   10

>2 Become a fashion voyeur in Ura-Hara, where
sartorial appreciation is a serious spectator sport   12

>3 Dodge flying fish at Tokyo's world-famous
seafood market   13

>4 Drink at dusk in the narrow alleys of the
Golden Gai   14

>5 Get spirited away to *anime* master Hayao
Miyazaki's charming museum   15

>6 The sky is the limit as Tokyo stretches its limbs to
take out another tower record   16

>7 Explore the captivating exhibits detailing
Edo-era life at the Edo-Tokyo Museum   17

>8 Window-shop with the ladies who lunch along
the Ginza boulevards   18

>9 Soak up the synthetic Edo-era atmosphere at an
honest-to-goodness onsen   19

>10 Take in the magnificence of Meiji-jingū, Tokyo's
shrine for all seasons   20

>11 Drop in and chill out in a low-key urban haven   21

>12 Take in temples and national treasures at
Ueno-kōen and Tokyo National Museum   22

>13 Explore what makes youth culture tick in Shibuya 24

>14 Take a leisurely ride down the Sumida River   25

>15 Experience the modern life of an ancient temple 26

>16 Root, root root for the home team amid rabid fans,
then loiter with the cosplay crew outside   28

ANTHONY PLUMMER / LONELY PLANET IMAGES ©
Looking up through the spidery legs of *Maman*, by Louise Bourgeois, to the Roppongi Hills tower (p72)

>1 THE BIG BOYS

ENJOY THE RITUALISTIC DISPLAY OF ATHLETIC PROWESS THAT IS SUMŌ

Highly ritualistic and more athletic than initial appearances may imply, sumō is a stunning, charged spectacle that you cannot miss if you're in Tokyo at tournament time. Linked with the rituals of Shintōism, sumō probably originated about 2000 years ago, but became a popular sporting event in its own right only in the 17th century. Sumō's whole visual vocabulary is infused with Shintōist motifs and ideas, from the scattering of salt to the structure and embellishments of the sumō *dōyō* (wrestling ring).

The rules are simple: the *rikishi* (wrestler) who causes any part of his opponent's body other than his feet to touch the ground inside the *dōyō*, or pushes him outside the *dōyō*, wins. Although *rikishi* may look like infants on steroids, those prodigious amounts of flesh conceal some very powerful muscle.

The action during the Tokyo tournaments, or *bashō*, takes place at the green-roofed Ryōgoku Kokugikan (p64) in January, May and September. Although the best ringside seats are bought up by those with the right connections, box seats accommodating up to four people are a great way to watch sumō in style. Attendees in box seats can order food and tea from servers dressed smartly in *happi* (half-coats) and straw sandals.

RITUALS OF THE RING

It begins with the victor of the last match offering a wooden ladle of water to the incoming *rikishi* (wrestler), in order to perform a symbolic cleansing. Before entering the *dōyō*, each *rikishi* takes a handful of coarse salt to scatter before him to purify the ring. Then squatting, facing each other from opposite ends of the *dōyō*, they stretch their arms out to their sides, palms raised, to signify their intentions for a fair fight. Several minutes of false starts – in which they both slap their thighs and bellies in an intimidating manner – usually precede the final stare down as the *rikishi* settle into squats. Only when both *rikishi* have put both fists to the ground does the match officially begin, at which point the opponents will suddenly charge.

ANTONY GIBLIN / LONELY PLANET IMAGES ©

11

>2 HARAJUKU & OMOTE-SANDŌ

BECOME A FASHION VOYEUR IN URA-HARA, WHERE SARTORIAL APPRECIATION IS A SERIOUS SPECTATOR SPORT

Pop icon Gwen Stefani once described Tokyo's vibrant, fashion-hungry vibe as 'a pedestrian paradise where the catwalk got its claws', and her observation pretty much holds true. Shopping is a national pastime – a competitive sport, even – where Gucci purses and Chanel sunglasses are both a snazzy accessory and a souvenir from a whirlwind day of high-speed purchasing. Chaotic as they may seem, outfits are assembled with the utmost seriousness, from the pattern of safety pins in one's schoolgirl tartan to the zig-zagging streak of fuchsia accenting a Mohawk coiffure. The result of this fashion fixation is a magnificent parade of sculpture-like stores – monuments to the brand names that inhabit them. While established houses of haute couture such as Vuitton, Dior and Prada line Omote-sandō, Ura-Hara (p102; the Harajuku backstreets) is where the small boutiques and studios represent the indie spirit. Wander the alleys snaking off either side of Omote-sandō and check out the boutiques and secondhand shops. Further south, Aoyama (Map pp104–5) caters to more sophisticated mainstream (and expensive) tastes.

MARK HEMMINGS / LONELY PLANET IMAGES ©

>3 TSUKIJI MARKET
DODGE FLYING FISH AT TOKYO'S WORLD-FAMOUS SEAFOOD MARKET

Come for the tuna auctions, stay for the sushi breakfast. After it's been fished from the sea and before it turns up on a sashimi platter, most of Tokyo's seafood transits through Tsukiji Market (p51). This gigantic pulsating hub of Tokyo's gastronomic system pumps at a frenetic, fish-fuelled pace. Watching the rough-and-ready, hardworking market men and women of Tsukiji, you can imagine the massive creative, communal energy that allowed Tokyo to rise, in less than 200 years, from riverside swamp to one of the world's greatest cities. But you'll have to catch this market atmosphere while you can, as the market is expected to move to Toyosu in 2012.

You'll have to trundle out here early to see the predawn arrival of fish and its wholesale auctioning, but even around 7am there's still some good market bustle and seafood slinging going on. Slicks of wet muck cover the floor, so don't wear your party shoes, and watch out for the electric carts zipping around the narrow aisles.

After poking around the market, move out to the nearby alleys of the external market, where hundreds of little stalls sell pottery, cooking equipment, cutlery and packaged foods for a fraction of the prices charged at department stores. Then top it all off with melt-in-your-mouth bluefin sushi as another morning winds down in Tsukiji.

KRZYSZTOF DYDYNSKI / LONELY PLANET IMAGES ©

HIGHLIGHTS

>4 GOLDEN GAI

DRINK AT DUSK IN THE NARROW ALLEYS OF THE GOLDEN GAI

Tenaciously hanging on in the shadow of the skyscrapers surrounding it, the narrow alleys of the Golden Gai are a stubborn anomaly in a city relentlessly obsessed with making the old new. Filled with tiny, eccentric drinking establishments, some so small that they can fit only a few patrons at a time, these alleys come to life as dusk settles and the lights of the city begin to glow. Wandering into this little maze at this witching hour feels like walking into a time warp.

But as the keepers of older bars retire, many spots are being turned over by a new generation who are remaking them with their own creative style while honouring the spirit of these small watering holes. While it's true that some bars in the Golden Gai do not welcome foreigners, or even nonregulars, those that do are an intriguing and unique venue for a drink.

See also p128.

GREG ELMS / LONELY PLANET IMAGES ©

>5 GHIBLI MUSEUM

GET SPIRITED AWAY TO *ANIME* MASTER HAYAO MIYAZAKI'S CHARMING MUSEUM

Fall under the spell of a Hayao Miyazaki film and you'll never be one of the philistines who liken him to a Japanese Walt Disney. Surreal landscapes, anthropomorphic objects and spirit-characters form the enticing worlds of Miyazaki's animated movies, in which the storytelling is as compelling as the phenomenally rendered animation. And though the storylines may be directed at children, they aren't saccharine or condescending, instead acknowledging the world of children as complicated yet hopeful.

A real-life testament to this way of thinking, the Ghibli Museum delights fans with its Cat Bus (pictured below), tiny rooms and towers, cosy movie theatre and artist's studio that looks as though the animator had just stepped out and left his work on the table. Walls are papered with actual Miyazaki drawings, while paints, toys and antique film projectors make up the captivating clutter of the studio. Each ticket even contains an original animation cel from a Studio Ghibli film.

See p121 for ticketing information.

TWPHOTO / CORBIS

>6 TOKYO SKY TREE

THE SKY IS THE LIMIT AS TOKYO STRETCHES ITS LIMBS TO TAKE OUT ANOTHER TOWER RECORD

And Tokyo's at it again…trying to insert itself into yet another of the world's superlative lists. After Tokyo Tower trumped the Eiffel Tower in the late '50s, the city's newest challenge is taking things to new heights, so to speak. At 634m, the Tokyo Sky Tree (www.tokyo-skytree.jp/english/), designed by Nikken Sekkei, will technically be the world's highest tower (though not the highest structure, an honour that Dubai's Burj Khalifa still holds) when it opens in the spring of 2012. There are two observation decks (at 350m and 450m) and plans are underway to create a commercial complex at its base that will include dozens of shops, an aquarium and a planetarium. The main motive behind the venture is to put Tokyo back on the map after a stint spent in the shadows while other Asian capitals progressed, but civically the tower will reorient the city, giving the sleepy districts of *shitamachi* a new sense of life and vitality as it rises above old wooden homes and hidden temples.

IPPEI NAOI / GETTY IMAGES

>7 EDO-TOKYO MUSEUM

EXPLORE THE CAPTIVATING EXHIBITS DETAILING EDO-ERA LIFE AT THE EDO-TOKYO MUSEUM

The oddly modern, tradition-inspired exterior of the Edo-Tokyo Museum (p64) both belies and reflects what's inside – exhibits illustrating Tokyo's rise from the humble riverside origins of Edo (the eastern capital) to today's futuristic megalopolis. The museum's layout is imaginatively designed, with a full-size replica of the bridge at Nihombashi dividing the vast display into recreations of Edo-period and Meiji-period Tokyo.

Life-size reconstructions of typical wooden homes and workshops depict scenes from everyday living; these are outdone only by the intricately assembled scale models of the riverside near Nihombashi, the market and the residence compound of a *daimyō* (feudal lord). Examples of the wooden wells and water pipes that made up Edo's first waterworks system bring to life the more quotidian underpinnings of Edo infrastructure, while displays of the gorgeously made kimonos worn by style-setting courtesans capture the more glamorous aspects of its culture. Don't miss the miniature animated model of a kabuki theatre, showing how special effects were cleverly created.

Meiji-period displays trace the influence of international culture on Tokyo, with photographs, models and multimedia presentations, and there's a detailed exhibit on the Great Kantō Earthquake of 1923.

While you're out here, consider checking out the Ryōgoku Kokugikan (p64) and taking a self-guided tour of the local sumō *beya* (sumō stable).

GLOWIMAGES / GETTY IMAGES

>8 SHOPPING IN GINZA

WINDOW-SHOP WITH THE LADIES WHO LUNCH ALONG THE GINZA BOULEVARDS

Ginza is classic glam, Tokyo's parallel to New York City's Fifth Avenue. With some of the priciest real estate on this planet, the boulevards are lined with serious contenders such as Chanel, Tiffany, Hermès and the big-in-Japan Louis Vuitton. Ginza is not shy about showing off its status, nor are the ladies who shop here, displaying designer-label shopping bags on delicately crooked forearms.

Shopping here is not the exclusive domain of the elite; nestled along with the purveyors of *haute couture* are wonderful stationery shops carrying fountain pens and hand-dyed handkerchiefs, Japan's department store heavies with their heavenly *depachika* (basement food halls) and handicraft shops that carry Japanese goods befitting Tokyo's traditional roots.

Nor is Ginza only about material consumption – sumptuous eye candy fills the many art and photography galleries scattered about, and restaurants here live up to the high expectations of those who haunt the neighbourhood.

Weekends in Ginza are particularly pleasant, when Chūō-dōri and some smaller cross-streets are closed to vehicles, allowing kimono-clad ladies and toddlers alike to meander peacefully in the middle of the crowded boulevard.

See also p52.

ATLANTIDE PHOTOTRAVEL / CORBIS

>9 ŌEDO ONSEN MONOGATARI

SOAK UP THE SYNTHETIC EDO-ERA ATMOSPHERE AT AN HONEST-TO-GOODNESS ONSEN

Modelled after a town from Edo times, this honest-to-goodness *onsen* actually pipes in sourced mineral waters from 1400m beneath Tokyo Bay. If you're new to the *onsen* experience, this is a great place to start. As you enter, you'll be given the choice of several *yukata* prints – be sure to grab a brochure that explains how to properly wear and tie your robe. Afterwards you'll quickly discover a wooden wonderland with hundreds of costume-clad visitors where you can enjoy comedians, a dedicated TV lounge space, and a noodle-stocked food court between soaks in the various tubs (separated by gender, of course). There's a coed footbath stream outside, which truly transports romantics to a bygone world in the evening. Jagged stones placed in the stream have been carefully positioned for maximum health benefits according to the foundations of reflexology.

In all, it's a great place for couples, friends and families. And even if *onsen* aren't your thang, it offers a Disney-fied glimpse of what leisure life was like several centuries ago. See also p159.

ANTHONY PLUMMER / LONELY PLANET IMAGES ©

>10 MEIJI-JINGŪ

TAKE IN THE MAGNIFICENCE OF MEIJI-JINGŪ, TOKYO'S SHRINE FOR ALL SEASONS

No doubt about it – Meiji-jingū (p103) is Tokyo's, if not Japan's, most splendid Shintō shrine. Passing under each majestic *torii* (shrine gate) takes you further into the muffled, green temple grounds to the symbolic domain of the *kami* (gods). Completed in 1920, Meiji-jingū was constructed in honour of Emperor Meiji and Empress Shōken, under whose rule Japan ended its long isolation from the outside world. Unfortunately, like much of Tokyo, it was obliterated by WWII incendiary bombing, but up it sprang again in 1958 next to Yoyogi-kōen (p107). It might be a reconstruction of the original, but it was rebuilt with all the features of a Shintō shrine preserved: the main building with Japanese cypress, and the huge *torii* with cypress from Taiwan.

On many weekends you have a fair chance of catching the striking yet subdued wedding proceedings of couples in full-on, kimono-clad regalia at Meiji-jingū. Spring brings a burst of pink when the cherry blossoms come into season, while June and July mean that the purple irises are in bloom at the adjacent Meiji-jingū-gyoen (p103), the tranquil, shaded park that was formerly an imperial garden. The one time of the year you're guaranteed not to be alone here is at New Year's and the few days thereafter, when throngs (as in millions) of people come to celebrate in Shintō style.

ANTHONY PLUMMER / LONELY PLANET IMAGES ©

>11 SHIMO-KITAZAWA

DROP IN AND CHILL OUT IN A LOW-KEY URBAN HAVEN

The times they are a-changin' – especially in Tokyo, where it seems as though skyscrapers vanish in dust clouds and new ones sprout in their stead overnight. Sometimes this happens to entire neighbourhoods, or landmarks one would think had historical value apart from collective nostalgia.

Sadly, the meandering alleys and low-slung buildings of Shimo-kitazawa (p95) may be going the way of countless Tokyo neighbourhoods before it. The charm of Shimo-kita, a favourite of artists and hip young things, comes from its hodgepodge of tiny secondhand shops, cafés, bars and live houses. It's a world apart from the cosmopolitan centre of Tokyo precisely because of the distinct lack of skyscrapers, traffic and generic urban shininess. Street life here is pedestrian-ruled, open air, funky and human, the maze of alleys organic. The independently owned shops on either side of the station secrete incense-scented dens filled from floor to ceiling with indie designer clothing to art books and local music. In the cafes and bars, students and artists mingle with the designers and architects who have lived in this quiet haven for decades.

Trek out to Shimo-kitazawa on the Keiō Inokashira line from Shibuya or the Odakyū line from Shinjuku and see if it's still humming along quietly.

ROBERT GILHOOLY / ALAMY

>12 UENO-KŌEN & TOKYO NATIONAL MUSEUM

TAKE IN TEMPLES AND NATIONAL TREASURES AT UENO-KŌEN AND TOKYO NATIONAL MUSEUM

Expansive Ueno-kōen is one of those parks where Tokyo comes to unwind, date, have illicit encounters, busk and hone hip-hop moves. But aside from the usual attractions for relaxation, Ueno-kōen is also the place where you can coo over the pandas at Ueno Zoo, take a paddleboat for two to view the giant lotuses covering Shinobazu Pond, look in on the latest Dalí or Matisse exhibition at the National Museum of Western Art (p140) or roam around its many temples and shrines. And then there is the National Science Museum (p140), the Tokyo Metropolitan Museum of Art (p141) and the magnificent Tokyo National Museum (p141). The park packs a cultural punch.

Ueno Hill was the site of a last-ditch defence of the Tokugawa Shōgunate by about 2000 Tokugawa loyalists in 1868. They were duly dispatched by the imperial army and the new Meiji government decreed that Ueno Hill would become one of Tokyo's first parks. It's now home to these major museums and is a big destination for *hanami* (cherry-blossom viewing) in the spring.

At the park's northern end is the Tokyo National Museum, established in 1872. Comprising of five buildings, this is unquestionably the museum of choice if a gallery stroll figures in your Ueno-kōen plans. The Honkan (Main Gallery) is the most important, with an awe-inspiring collection of art from the Jōmon period to the Edo. The Gallery of Hōryū-ji Treasures displays masks, scrolls and gilt Buddhas from Hōryū-ji – in Nara Prefecture, said to be the first Buddhist temple in Japan (founded 607) – in a spare, elegant box of a contemporary building, built in 1999 and designed by Taniguchi Yoshio, who also designed New York's Museum of Modern Art (MoMA). The Heiseikan (Heisei Hall) opened in 1993 to commemorate the marriage of Crown Prince Naruhito, and it is used for exhibitions of Japanese archaeology as well as special exhibits.

Hyōkeikan (Hyōkei Hall) was built in 1909, with Western-style architecture that is reminiscent of a museum you might find in Paris, though inside it shows works from across East Asia and South Asia and the Middle East. Normally these are in a fifth building, Tōyōkan (Gallery of Eastern Antiquities), which is closed for earthquake retrofitting and is due to reopen in 2012.

BRENT WINEBRENNER / LONELY PLANET IMAGES ©

>13 SHIBUYA

EXPLORE WHAT MAKES YOUTH CULTURE TICK IN SHIBUYA

Schlep in any direction across Shibuya's six-way intersection for a rush of youth culture – this is *the* spot for people-watching and prime shopping. Hip *gyaru* ('gals' identifiable by their big hair, fake tans and exaggerated white eyeshadow) and their male counterparts travel in packs around Center-gai and the department stores that cater to their fast-forward fashion trends.

Leave the JR station via the Hachikō exit and you'll get an eyeful of moving images flashing across the buildings looming over Shibuya Crossing, notably the several-storeys-high screen of the Q-Front Building. Don't forget to say hello to the Hachikō statue (p92) before joining the timed tide across Shibuya Crossing.

From Hachikō exit head to the right of Shibuya 109 (p95), the streets between Bunkamura-dōri and Jingū-dōri are full of excellent youth-oriented department stores for the knee-high pink boots or vinyl micro-mini you covet. If you seek vinyl of a different groove, you'll hit a cluster of record shops in Udagawachō, specialising in everything from Motown to Japanese hip-hop. Also, Shibuya stays up late, and the streets between Bunkamura-dōri and Dōgenzaka are covered with clubs, bars and love hotels, so soak it up as long as you please.

GREG ELMS / LONELY PLANET IMAGES ©

>14 SUMIDA-GAWA

TAKE A LEISURELY RIDE DOWN THE SUMIDA RIVER

Travelling by *suijo-bus* (water bus; see p196) down the Sumida River not only gets you a faceful of fresh air but also brings you closer to Tokyo's riverborne heritage, showing off a more home-grown perspective of the city than a subway spin will. When you're hemmed in by concrete and glass, it's easy to forget that Tokyo's vibrant river systems are the arteries through which its commerce has traditionally flowed, from the Edo period to the present day.

Down at water level, you see the huge timber- and landfill-hauling barges, the occasional lone fisherman and the *yakata-bune* – floating restaurants where, traditionally, customers seated on tatami (woven-floor matting) eat *ayu* (sweet fish) washed down with sake. Redevelopment schemes are slowly changing the face of the riverfront, but as you pass beneath the dozen colourful bridges on your journey, you'll continue to spy the hanging laundry drying on the apartment blocks of regular Tokyo folk, as well as some prime riverfront encampments of Tokyo's more down-at-heel inhabitants.

The best way to work in a river cruise is to travel between Asakusa (p146) and Hama-rikyū-teien (p48), the lovely waterfront garden near Ginza. Consider taking in a walking tour of Asakusa sights, then catching the *suijo-bus* for a stroll through Hama-rikyū-teien. Alternatively, you could cruise across Tokyo Bay to travel from old-fashioned Asakusa out to the modern amusements of the artificial island of Odaiba (p154).

GREG ELMS / LONELY PLANET IMAGES ©

>15 SENSŌ-JI & THE TEMPLES OF SHITAMACHI

EXPERIENCE THE MODERN LIFE OF AN ANCIENT TEMPLE

The grand old temple Sensō-ji (p149) may attract millions of tourists annually, but it is still very much a living, working temple for the people of working-class Asakusa.

Indeed, Sensō-ji's very origins are intertwined with the history of the local people. Legend has it that a golden image of Kannon, the goddess of compassion, was fished out of the nearby Sumida-gawa by two fishermen in AD 628. In time, a temple was built to house the image, which has remained on the same spot ever since, giving it its alternative name, Asakusa Kannon-dō. Whether the ancient image of Kannon actually exists inside is a secret. Not that this stops a steady stream of worshippers making their way up the stairs to the temple, where they cast coins, clap ceremoniously and bow in a gesture of respect.

When approaching Sensō-ji from the Asakusa subway stations, enter through Kaminarimon (Thunder Gate) between the scowling protective deities: Fūjin, the god of wind, on the right; and Raijin, the god of thunder, on the left. Near Kaminari-mon, you'll probably be wooed by *jinrikisha* (people-powered rickshaw) drivers in traditional dress with gorgeous lacquer rickshaws; these energetic, fit guides will cart you around the temple and neighbourhood, giving you the scoop on architecture and history in English or Japanese.

Straight on through the gate is Nakamise-dōri, a busy pedestrian shopping street set within the actual temple precinct. Everything from

---

THE TEMPLES OF YANAKA

After exploring the wondrous grounds of Senso-ji, branch out and discover the constellation of fascinating temples that dot the low-lying *shitamachi* district. Be sure to swing by the tourist information office in Asakusa and pick up their handy Yanaka brochure, which details a suggested walking tour and plots the location of several of the district's temples and shrines including Nezu-jinja with its radiant torii, and Tenno-ji (7-14-8 Yanaka), a relic from the 13th century with a giant Buddha and perfectly kept gardens. There are over 70 places of worship in the district. When you've worshipped up an appetite, visit Yanaka Ginza (p145), near Nippori station, a bustling pedestrian road with countless vendors peddling delicious street snacks.

GREG ELMS / LONELY PLANET IMAGES ©

tourist trinkets to genuine Edo-style crafts are sold here; there's even a shop selling the elaborate wigs that are worn with kimonos.

Nakamise-dōri leads to the main temple compound. In front of the temple is a large incense cauldron, whose smoke is said to bestow health. If any part of your body – modesty permitting, naturally – is giving you trouble, do as the locals do and fan some smoke your way, rubbing it through your clothes into the area that ails you.

>16 TOKYO DOME CITY

ROOT, ROOT ROOT FOR THE HOME TEAM AMID RABID FANS, THEN LOITER WITH THE *COSPLAY* CREW OUTSIDE

Tokyo's versatile Dome City (Map pp46–7) is the metropolis' ultimate one-stop-shop wonder. Home to Japan's favourite baseball team, the Yomiuri Giants, it's a haven for sports enthusiasts who gather in droves to root, root, root for the home team with a canon of impeccably performed chants, cheers and songs. So-called beer girls tote miniature kegs on their backs while pouring icy draughts with precocious grins.

The dome itself is an engineering marvel, especially considering that the Teflon roof is supported by nothing but air – the pressure is 0.3% higher indoors than out.

Also on the grounds of Dome City is the old-school Kōrakuen Amusement Park and Spa LaQua (www.laqua.jp), which offers an inner-city *onsen* experience, where you can bathe in spacious luxury while gazing out over the infinite expanse of concrete and neon. Of particular interest are the colour therapy suites (which supposedly help with rejuvenation) and the trippy aquarium room where you can sit and gaze at alien-like jellyfish pulsing around their blue-tinted world.

Tokyo Dome City (see p64) is best on Sundays – stop by to see some *cosplay* freaks (p62; it's their new favourite hangout), watch a rousing baseball match, swoosh around on the rollercoaster and relax at the *onsen*.

SOL NEELMAN / CORBIS

>TOKYO DIARY

As one of the brighter stars of Asia's constellation of cities, Tokyo plays host to many international festivals and events. Festivities across the city can be as humble as the neighbourhood *matsuri* (p26) to huge *anime* trade fairs, gay-and-lesbian film festivals and singularly Japanese holidays when it seems the entire population of Tokyo is converging all at once on its most famous shrines. The larger holidays celebrate auspicious ages and the turning of seasons, reconnecting Tokyoites to their roots and allowing visitors a chance to mingle with locals at their most traditional.

STEVE VIDLER / IMAGESTATE LTD / PHOTOLIBRARY

Smiling faces and bright kimonos celebrate Shichi-Go-San (7-5-3), a festival for these milestone ages (p34)

JANUARY

Shōgatsu

From 1 to 3 January people turn out in droves to shrines and temples such as Sensō-ji (p149) and Meiji-jingū (p20) to celebrate the New Year.

Seijin-no-Hi (Coming-of-Age Day)

Also at Meiji-jingū (p20), traditional archery displays are held on the second Monday in January to mark the move into adulthood.

FEBRUARY

Setsubun

At home and at temples such as Sensō-ji (p149), beans are thrown outside as people shout 'Oni wa soto! Fuku wa uchi!' ('Devils out! Fortune in!') to mark the first day of spring on 3 or 4 February.

MARCH

Hina Matsuri (Girls' Day)

On 3 March a doll festival is held near Azumabashi and *hina* (princess) dolls are displayed in homes and public spaces.

Tokyo International Anime Fair

www.tokyoanime.jp/en

Held in late March or early April, this huge trade fair is held at Tokyo Big Sight (p157) for *anime* fans and industry pros alike.

PHOTO JAPAN / ALAMY

Hina (princess) dolls are displayed for the 'princess' in every family on the annual Girls' Day

Seijin-no-Hi (Coming-of-Age Day) is celebrated across Tokyo

ADINA TOVY AMSEL / LONELY PLANET IMAGES ©

APRIL

Hanami

In late March and early April, *hanami* (cherry blossom) viewing parties (p175) take place day and night in parks across the city.

Art Fair Tokyo

www.artfairtokyo.com

Held at the appropriately innovative Tokyo International Forum (p51), this young fair showcases cutting-edge art from Japan, Asia and beyond. Artists and collectors meet here in mid-April.

MAY

Otoko-no-Hi (Boys' Day)

Family homes honour their sons by flying *koinobori* (banners in the shape of a carp) on 5 May.

Sanja Matsuri

Hundreds of *mikoshi* (portable shrines) are carried through the thronged streets around Sensō-ji (p149) over three days in mid-May.

Design Festa

www.designfesta.com

In mid-May a wide showcase of work from budding designers and artists is displayed at Design Festa, held at Tokyo Big Sight (p157).

A boat ride on the Kitanomaru-kōen moat during *hanami* (p31)

WIBOWO RUSLI / LONELY PLANET IMAGES ©

JUNE

Iris Viewing

The inner garden at Meiji-jingū (p20) is a favoured spot for viewing irises – most vibrant in June, when these flowers are in full bloom.

JULY

Fuji Rock Festival

http://fujirockfestival.com
This outdoor concert in late July draws international acts and thousands of fans to its beautiful woodland surroundings.

Tokyo International Lesbian & Gay Film Festival

www.tokyo-lgff.org
Check the website to see where screenings are held for this queer film festival, growing steadily into its second decade. Held in mid-July.

Sumida River Fireworks

On the last Saturday of July, *hanabi* (fireworks) over the Sumida River are the year's most popular.

AUGUST

Asakusa Samba Festival

The highlight of this festival is the parade down Kaminarimon-dōri, drawing half a million spectators and samba troupes from Tokyo to Rio. On the last Saturday of August.

Tokyo Pride Parade

http://parade.tokyo-pride.org

It's on again, off again, but come mid-August, the parade may be taking to the streets in Harajuku (p102). Check the website.

SEPTEMBER

Ningyō-kujō

Dolls are offered to Kannon (the Buddhist goddess of mercy) at Kiyomizu Kannon-dō (p140) by childless couples who wish to conceive. The dolls are ceremonially burned there on 25 September.

OCTOBER

Tokyo International Film Festival

www.tiff-jp.net

This festival lasts about 10 days and begins in late October. Although featured films focus on Asia, most are subtitled in English.

Kōyō

Autumn foliage-viewing season (p175) begins in mid-October or early November. As this colourful season is longer, the crowds are more low-key than for *hanami* (p175).

Two men pout, preen and pose for the Tokyo Pride Parade

HARUYOSHI YAMAGUCHI / CORBIS

A sea of fluttering white-and-red flags greet the Emperor of Japan on his birthday

PETER USBECK / ALAMY

NOVEMBER

Shichi-Go-San (Seven-Five-Three Festival)

On 15 November this festival celebrates these milestone ages, and parents in turn bring their traditionally clad little ones to temples and shrines to mark the occasion on the nearest weekend.

Design Festa

www.designfesta.com

Returning to Tokyo Big Sight (p157) for its biannual stint (see p107).

DECEMBER

Emperor's Birthday

On 23 December, this is one of only two days per year that the *Kōkyo* (Imperial Palace; Map pp46–7) is opened to the public; the other is 2 January.

ANTHONY PLUMMER / LONELY PLANET IMAGES

Admire the glass walls and open spaces of Tokyo International Forum (p51)

ITINERARIES

Don't be daunted by Tokyo's immensity. Taken in small bites you can get your fill of a thousand of the city's unique flavours. Pick a few must-do experiences and appealing neighbourhoods to explore. If your time is limited, use these itineraries as suggestions and customise according to your own tastes.

SOMETHING OLD

Savour that old shitamachi feel in Ueno (p138) and Asakusa (p146), then head down to Ginza (p52) to visit the district's collection of grand department stores – relics of a bygone era. Book ahead to tour the stately grounds of the Imperial Palace (p48), and in the evening uncover the cluster of well-worn hovel-bars in Shinjuku's Golden Gai (p128) district.

SOMETHING NEW

Scout out the latest designer trends in Harajuku (p102), peek at Meiji-jingū (p103), then march between the luxury boutique monuments on Omote-sandō-dōri (p103). Walk down to Shibuya (p90) to find Tokyo's teens – the city's freshly minted fashion victims – frenetically bouncing between shops.

SOMETHING BORROWED

Rummage through other people's closets at some of city's top second-hand shops in the trendy satellite district of Shimokitazawa (p95). Later in the day, head to Tokyo Dome City (p28) to witness Japan's favourite American import – baseball. Afterwards, wander the backstreets of Kagurazaka (p45) and choose between traditional eats or exceptional French fare.

SOMETHING BLUE

Start the day early with a trip to Tsukiji Market (p51), then walk off your sushi breakfast at the manicured grounds of Hama-rikyū-teien (p48). Hop on a river bus (p196) bound for Ryōgoku (p64) to check out the Edo-Tokyo Museum (p64), or a rousing sumō match if a tournament is in session. Then sail over to the artificial island of Odaiba (p154) for a Vegas-like shopping experience and a quick trip back in time at the Edo-themed Ōedo Onsen Monogatari (p19).

Top left Take to the streets on a rickshaw (p26) ride in Asakusa **Top right** Ornate doorways at Meiji-jingū Shrine (p103) **Bottom** The busy Shibuya Crossing (p93) at night

ONE DAY

Capitalise on your jetlag and start the day before the sun rises at Tsukiji Market (p51) – don't miss the opportunity to savour a scrumptious sushi breakfast at one of the main stalls clustered around the chaos. Walk off the calories at nearby Hama-rikyu-teien (p48), then board a river bus for a scenic ride up to the Ryogoku district and step back in time at the Edo-Tokyo Museum (p64). Next, cross the river into old Asakusa to wander around the fascinating temple district. Shoot straight across town and zip through time as you emerge among the pulsing lights of Shinjuku (p118). Climb to the Tokyo Metropolitan Government Offices (p121) and, later on, indulge in a drink in Golden Gai (p128).

SUNDAYS

If you're looking for the *cosplay* crowd, make a beeline for Tokyo Dome City (p28) where you'll get some serious exercise for your camera-clicking finger. Catch a baseball game if one is on, and witness the wrath of thousands of rabid fans. Then wander the cobbled streets of Kagurazaka (p45), being sure to grab a bite at one of the area's splendid French restaurants or traditional soba houses. If time allows, hop on the metro for a spirited evening amid fashionistas-in-training at their home base, Shibuya (p90), where gaggles of gals fill the retail stores scooping up carts-ful of clothing before school starts the following day.

THREE DAYS

Follow the one-day itinerary and start day two in Harajuku (p102). Pay your respects at Meiji-jingu (p103), then strut your stuff on the concrete catwalks of Omote-sando-dori (p103), Takeshita-dori (p102) and Cat Street (p108) as you weave in and out of the district's back alleys. For day three make your way to Ueno. While away an hour gazing at the lazy lily pads in the grand pond, then head to the Tokyo National Museum (p141) to explore the nation's most cherished artifacts from the last 10,000 years. Wander down Ameya-yokocho (p143), snacking on curious seafood, then arrive in Akihabara (p50) to explore the nexus of geek culture amid strange cafes and overflowing electronics boutiques. Move along to Ginza (p18), stroll down the elegant boulevards, and dine among businessmen. Then down shooters at one of the bars huddled under the JR train tracks nearby.

FIVE DAYS

After three long days, reward yourself with a soak and a splash at Ōedo Onsen Monogatari (p159) on artificial island Odaiba. Then buck the tour-

---

FORWARD PLANNING

Two to three months before you go Book an appointment for the Ghibli Museum (p121); reserve a table at Beige (p58) to sweep your date off their feet with fancy French or at Ukai Tofu-ya (p76) for memorable *kaiseki* (multicourse traditional Japanese).

One month before you go Find out what holidays (p29) will be in swing during your visit, like *hanami* (cherry-blossom viewing) in spring, Asakusa's Sanja Matsuri in May and *hanabi* (fireworks) over the Sumida River in July.

One week before you go Check *Metropolis* online (p199) for current goings-on and concert listings.

One day before you go Reconfirm your flight, review the Japanese names of your favourite sushi and pack some comfortable (and stylin') shoes.

---

ist trend with visits to some of Tokyo's lesser-known neighbourhoods, such as Shimo-Kitazawa (p21), Nakano (p164) or Kichijoji (p122). With a little advance planning, a tour to the Imperial Palace grounds (p48) or the Ghibli Museum (p15) could be on the cards. Don't forget to save Friday or Saturday for pulling an all-nighter at a club in Roppongi (p76). Prep your lyrics – this is your chance to be a karaoke star!

RAINY DAY

It's wet, but this doesn't have to dampen your mood as there's lots to do indoors. Hole up in one of Tokyo's megamalls for the day. Or, better yet, seize the opportunity to wander around a few of Ginza's department stores and their basement *depachika* (p57). Museums are plentiful in Tokyo – check out the Mori Art Museum (p67) in Roppongi, the Hara Museum (p92) near Shinagawa, the Nezu Museum near Harajuku, or perhaps the Mitsubishi Ichigokan (p49) in the Marunouchi area. Endless shopping malls await in Odaiba as do the many virtual-reality rides at Tokyo Joypolis (p159). In the evening try for a bar with a view of the glittering lights below – Maduro (p78) in Roppongi is a great choice.

FOR FREE

If Tokyo's prices have you eating too many beef bowls and 7-Eleven snacks, you'll be pleased to discover there are plenty of free things to do, including guided tours (p107) of the city organised by volunteers. Window shopping isn't a pastime here, it's a national sport; wander the backstreets of Harajuku (p102), or meander through Ginza (p18) if you have more expensive tastes. And remember, all Tokyo's temple and shrines are free; you'll find the motherlode sprinkled around Ueno (p138) and Asakusa (p146).

>NEIGHBOURHOODS

>1	Marunouchi, Ginza & Central Tokyo	44
>2	Roppongi	66
>3	Ebisu & Meguro	82
>4	Shibuya	90
>5	Harajuku	102
>6	Shinjuku	118
>7	Ikebukuro	132
>8	Ueno	138
>9	Asakusa	146
>10	Odaiba	154

ANTHONY PLUMMER / LONELY PLANET IMAGES
View from Tokyo Tower (p72), Central Tokyo

NEIGHBOURHOODS

All perceptive visitors must first resign themselves to Tokyo's infiniteness before mounting their assault on the city. But don't let its seemingly chaotic nature fool you; despite the skyscrapers and mazelike webbing depicted on subway maps, Tokyo isn't as hard to navigate as one might expect. Think of its various districts as smaller villages within the bigger megalopolis, for this is how Tokyo evolved and how its neighbourhoods are organised.

An above-ground rail loop known as the JR Yamanote line cuts its way through the conurbation unofficially marking the extent of the city centre, with the Imperial Palace, or 'empty centre', acting as Tokyo's incongruously verdant core. A trip around the loop makes a good introduction to the city, as it links most of Tokyo's major neighbourhoods.

We start with the districts surrounding the Imperial Palace, including the upscale commercial district of Ginza and the business centre of Marunouchi near Tokyo Station. Moving in a clockwise fashion, you'll find the *gaijin*-teeming area of Roppongi sandwiched between the Yamanote and the palace grounds. Further on, a refined but relaxed vibe prevails in the stylish neighbourhoods orbiting Ebisu and Meguro, then all hell breaks loose amid the trend-obsessed youngsters of Shibuya. Street fashion and high-end brands blur the lines of the concrete catwalks in Harajuku, then, Shinjuku marks the western edge of the city centre with its majestic skyscrapers. There's retro Ikebukuro to the north, and completing the circle of Tokyo's central districts is the area knows as *shitamachi* in the city's northeast corner. 'Low town' is filled with an array of museums and temples peppering Ueno and Asakusa. It's forgivable to forget that Tokyo is a seaside city, but a visit to Odaiba, an artificial island in Tokyo Bay, makes an excellent reminder.

>MARUNOUCHI, GINZA & CENTRAL TOKYO

Central Tokyo is rooted in the location of the Imperial Palace, where the imperial family resides today, and the outer garden in which visitors can stroll. Just across the moat is the business district of Marunouchi, where salarymen busily power the banks, communications and big businesses lining these streets. To the east of Marunouchi is the hub that is Tokyo Station, and still eastward is Nihombashi and its commerce. South of Tokyo Station lies the upscale shopping district of Ginza, whose Western architecture was once the pinnacle of modernity and now provides a stately backdrop to conspicuous consumption. Further southeast of Ginza you'll find the seafood-trading bustle of Tsukiji Market and the revital-

MARUNOUCHI, GINZA & CENTRAL TOKYO

🜨 SEE
Advertising Museum Tokyo	(see 11)	
Bridgestone Museum	1	E6
Ginza Graphic Gallery	2	D7
Hama-Rikyū-Teien	3	D8
Idemitsu Art Museum	4	D5
Imperial Palace East Garden	5	C4
Jinbōchō	6	C2
Kite Museum	7	F4
Koishikawa Kōrakuen	8	C1
Mitsubishi Ichigokan	9	D5
National Museum of Modern Art	10	C3
Shiodome	11	D8
Sony Building	12	D6
Tokyo International Forum	13	E5
Tsukiji Market	14	E8
Yasukuni-jinja	15	B3

🛍 SHOP
Akihabara Gachapon Kaikan	16	E1
Haibara	17	F5
Hakuhinkan Toy Park	18	D7
Hashi Ginza Natsuno	19	D6
Itōya	20	E6
Jinbōchō	21	D2
Kudan Kaikan	22	C2
Laox	23	E2
Maruzen	24	E4
Matsuya	25	E6
Mikimoto Pearl	(see 41)	
Mitsukoshi	26	E6
Muji	27	E6
Sofmap	28	F2
Takashimaya	29	F5
Takumi Handicrafts	30	D7
Tora-no-Ana	31	F2
Uniqlo	32	E6
Yodobashi Akiba	33	F2

🍴 EAT
Beige	34	E6
Birdland	35	D6
Daiwa Sushi	36	E8
Kiji	37	E5
Lugdunum Bouchon Lyonnais	38	A1
Marugo	39	E2
Meal MUJI	40	E6
Mikimoto Lounge	41	E6
Opippi	42	C7
Rengatei	43	E6
Robata	44	D6
Sushi Kanesaka	45	D7
Ten-Ichi	46	D6

🍸 DRINK
300 Bar	47	D7
Aux Amis des Vins	48	E6
Ginza Lion	49	D7

🎭 PLAY
AKB48 Theatre	50	F2
National Film Centre	51	E6
National Theatre	52	B5
Session House	53	A1
Shinbashi Enbujō	54	E7
Tokyo Dome	55	C1
Tokyo Takarazuka Gekijō	56	D6

Please see over for map

ised commercial district of Shiodome, with its luxury hotel-and-dining complexes. The core of central Tokyo is fringed with sights worth the walk or extra subway stop, such as the Yasukuni-jinja war memorial and Tokyo Dome for sports-mad fans, as well as speciality neighbourhoods such as Jimbōchō with its bookshops, and Akihabara for manga and electronics.

SEE

BRIDGESTONE MUSEUM

www.bridgestone-museum.gr.jp; 1-10-1 Kyobashi, Chiyoda-Ku; admission ¥800; 10am-8pm Tue-Sat, 10am-6pm Sun; JR Yamanote line to Tokyo, Yaesuguchi exit

Tokyo has a love affair with all things French, so it shouldn't be a surprise that French impressionist art looms large in the civic imagination. The tyre company's collection, which was previously a private collection by its founder Ishibashi Shōjiro, features all the big names – Renoir, Ingres, Monet, Matisse, Picasso – and an interesting selection of works by Japanese impressionists as well.

GINZA GRAPHIC GALLERY

ギンザグラフィックギャラリー

3571 5206; www.dnp.co.jp/gallery; 1F, DNP Ginza Bldg, 7-7-2 Ginza, Chūō-ku; admission free; 11am-6pm Mon-Fri,

---

WORTH THE TRIP

Nestled just above central Tokyo but seemingly from another decade, **Kagurazaka** (Chūō line to Iidabashi, east exit, Nambuku, Tōzai, Yūrakuchō & Toei Ōedo lines to Iidabashi, exit B3) is a formerly vibrant geisha quarter, whose local residents are attempting to preserve its old-fashioned integrity. Before WWII the alleys here, many still cobbled, saw steady foot traffic to the many traditional, exclusive restaurants called *ryotei*. Nowadays, the slope is looking almost as modern as other low-scale Tokyo neighbourhoods, with the addition of convenience stores and a few small high-rise apartment buildings. But these narrow, winding alleys still hide small temples and shrines, tiny old-fashioned bars, atmospheric restaurants and its inherent, abundant charm. Kagurazaka-dōri leads uphill from Iidabashi Station, leaving behind the canal that was formerly the outermost moat of the Imperial Palace grounds. Walking uphill, the street is lined with shops selling *geta* (wooden sandals worn with kimono), kitchen wares and old-fashioned *wagashi* (sweets). The best way to explore the neighbourhood is to simply lose yourself on some of the backstreets that are worth checking out – Kakurenbo-yokochō ('hide and seek' alley) is particularly charming and features several high-end dining options, including several French establishments and old soba houses. Stop by **Akagi-jinja** (http://akagi-jinja.jp), which puts an interesting spin on the traditional shrine with mod decor that feels undeniably sleek. There's a welcoming cafe on the grounds, or you could continue down the hill and pause at Canal Café for a snack along the river. At weekends the buffet brunch attracts large crowds of chilled-out trendsetters.

to 7pm Sat; ⓜ Ginza, Hibiya & Maru-nouchi lines to Ginza (exits A1 & A2); ♿ Excellent exhibitions with an emphasis on graphic design are this gallery's forte. The gallery also hosts workshops and talks by visiting artists, covering every-thing from tiny typography to monumental architecture.

ⓒ HAMA-RIKYŪ-TEIEN
浜離宮庭園
☎ 3541 0200; admission ¥300/150; ⏱ 9am-5pm; ⓜ Toei Ōedo line to Tsukiji-shijō (exit A2); ♿

The shōguns used to have this magnificent place to themselves when it was Hama Rikyū, the 'beach palace'. Now mere mortals can enjoy this wonderful garden, one of Tokyo's best. Sometimes known as the Detached Palace Garden, it is impossibly elegant and a must for garden aficionados. Con-sider approaching it from Asakusa via the Sumida-gawa cruise (p25).

ⓒ IDEMITSU ART MUSEUM
出光美術館
☎ 3213 9402; 9F, Teigeki Bldg, 3-1-1 Marunouchi, Chiyoda-ku; admission ¥1000/700/200; ⏱ 10am-5pm Sun-Thu, 10am-7pm Fri ⓜ Chiyoda & Toei Mita lines to Hibiya (exits A1 & B3); ♿

Most famous for its collection of work by the Zen monk Sengai, this superb, eclectic collection of Chi-nese and Japanese art is brought to you courtesy of a petroleum zillionaire. There are also lovely views of the Imperial Palace from the museum, which is next to the Imperial Theatre.

ⓒ IMPERIAL PALACE EAST GARDEN 皇居東御苑
☎ 3213 2050; admission free; ⏱ 9am-4.30pm Tue-Thu, Sat & Sun Mar-Oct, 9am-4pm Nov-Feb; ⓜ Chiyo-da, Hanzōmon, Marunouchi & Tōzai lines to Ōtemachi (exits C10 & C13b); ♿

One of the nearest emergency exits from Ginza street chaos, this garden (known as the Kōkyo Higashi Gyoen) is the only quarter of the palace proper that is open to the public. The Edo-period watchtower, Fujimi-yagura, was designed to pro-vide the aristocracy with a handy view of Mt Fuji. The store inside the garden sells a good map for ¥150.

ⓒ KITE MUSEUM
凧の博物館
☎ 3271 2465; www.tako.gr.jp/eng /museums_e/tokyo_e.html; 5F, Taimeikan

---

VISITING THE IMPERIAL PALACE

The palace is closed to the public for all but two days of the year, 2 January and 23 December (the emperor's birthday). It is possible to tour the **imperial grounds** (http://sankan.kunaicho.go.jp; ⏱ Mon-Fri 10am & 1.30pm, closed late Jul-late Aug & public holidays), but you must book ahead through the Imperial House-hold Agency's website. Slots become available on the first day of each month.

A tranquil pond in the Imperial Palace East Garden

PETER HORREE / ALAMY

Bldg, 1-12-10 Nihombashi, Chūō-ku; admission ¥200/100; ⏱ 11am-5pm Mon-Sat; Ⓜ Ginza, Tōzai & Toei Asakusa lines to Nihombashi (exit C5); ♿
This unusual little museum feels like a kitemaker's store cupboard, with everything crammed in tight (and not much explanatory material). But the kites are wonderful, especially the vintage ones depicting folk tales and kabuki (stylised Japanese theatre). Made of bamboo and *washi* (handmade paper), the kites for sale make beautiful souvenirs.

Ⓒ KOISHIKAWA KŌRAKUEN
小石川後楽園
☎ 3811 3015; 1-6-6 Kōraku, Bunkyō-ku; admission ¥300/free; ⏱ 9am-5pm; Ⓜ Namboku, Tōzai, Yūrakuchō & Toei Ōedo lines to Iidabashi (exits C3 & 6); ♿
A beautiful amalgam of Japanese and Chinese landscape design, this mid-17th-century garden is left off most tourist itineraries. That's a shame, because it's one of Tokyo's best gardens; but then again, it's also a blessing, since you'll be far from the madding crowds. You can buy an excellent English map at the garden's entrance.

Ⓒ MITSUBISHI ICHIGOKAN
http://mimt.jp/english; 2-6-2 Maru-nouchi, Chiyoda-ku; admission varies; ⏱ 10am-8pm Wed-Fri, 10am-6pm Tue, Sat & Sun; Ⓜ Hibiya & Chiyoda line Hibiya exit B7)

AKIHABARA

Akihabara began its evolution into 'Denki-gai' (Electric Town) after WWII when the area around the station became a black market for radio parts. In more recent decades, Akihabara has been widely known as *the* place to hunt for bargains on new and used electronics. Nowadays, you're more likely to hear it referred to as **Akiba** (http://akiba-guide.com), the more common nickname among the manga and *anime* fans, who are drawn by its gravitational pull, as Akihabara has morphed into the centre of the known *otaku* (geek) universe. Even if you aren't interested in electronics, it's well worth embarking on a subculture safari.

The Mitsubishi Ichigokan was the area's first office building, designed shortly after the Meiji Restoration by controversial architect Josiah Conder. Though the first structure was destroyed long ago, the current structure (completed in 2009) is an exact replica of the original. Today, the building is one of Tokyo's most inviting gallery spaces. The concept behind the museum is simple: to create a convivial place where local businessfolk could stop by on their lunch break to unwind and enjoy the exhibits. International exhibitions rotate regularly, meaning that the area's workforce could ostensibly stop by several times a year.

NATIONAL MUSEUM OF MODERN ART
国立近代美術館
☎ 5777 8600; www.momat.go.jp /english; 3-1 Kitanomaru-kōen, Chūō-ku; admission ¥420/130/70; ⏰ 10am-5pm Tue-Thu, Sat & Sun; 10am-8pm Fri; Ⓣ Tōzai line to Takebashi (exit 1a); ♿ The National Museum of Modern Art has a magnificent collection of Japanese art from the Meiji period onwards. Your ticket (hold on to the stub) gives you free admission to the nearby Crafts Gallery, which houses ceramics, lacquerware and dolls.

Ⓒ SHIODOME
Ⓣ Toei Oedo line to Shiodome
Built with similar aspirations as Roppongi Hills, Shiodome is complex of multipurpose towers stuffed with the usual spread of offices and restaurants. This 'future-city' hasn't quite hit its stride like its Roppongi counterpart, which means that it's thankfully never too crowded, but there also isn't much to see or do. The **Advertising Museum Tokyo** (www .admt.jp; B1F-B2F Caretta Shiodome Bldg 1-8-2 Higashi-shinbashi, Chūō-ku; ⏰ 11am-6.30pm Tue-Fri, 11am-4.30pm Sat; Ⓣ Toei Oedo line to Shiodome, JR Shinbashi exit) recounts the history of product marketing in Japan. None of the displays have English signage, but the appealing visuals (both images and video) offer plenty of stimuli for a short visit.

MARUNOUCHI, GINZA & CENTRAL TOKYO

☺ SONY BUILDING
ソニービル

☎ 3573 2371; www.sonybuilding.jp;
5-3-1 Ginza, Chūō-ku; admission free;
⏰ 11am-7pm; ⊕ Ginza, Hibiya,
Marunouchi line to Ginza (exit B9)
Although essentially a Sony
showroom, this place has fascinating hands-on displays
of Sony's latest gizmos and
gadgets – some that have yet
to be released. There's often
a bit of a wait, but it's a good
place to test-drive Sony's latest
digital cameras, laptops and idiosyncratic electronic 'pets'.

☺ TOKYO INTERNATIONAL FORUM
東京国際フォーラム

☎ 5221 9000; www.t-i-forum.co.jp
/english; 3-5-1 Marunouchi, Chiyoda-ku;
admission free; ⏰ 8am-11pm; 🚉 JR
Yamanote line to Yūrakuchō (main exit),

⊕ Yūrakuchō line to Yūrakuchō (exit
A4b); ♿
Designed by architect Rafael
Viñoly, the Tokyo International
Forum looks like a fantastic glass
ship plying the urban waters of
central Tokyo. Largely used for
conventions and meetings, the
cantilevered spaces and plaza also
house a library, art gallery, cafes
and shops.

☺ TSUKIJI MARKET 築地市場
☎ 3541 2640; www.tsukiji-market.or.jp;
5-2 Tsukiji, Chūō-ku; ⏰ closed some Mon
& Wed, Sun & public holidays; ⊕ Toei
Ōedo line to Tsukiji-Shijō (exits 1 & 2)
Tsukiji has the honour of being
the world's biggest seafood
market. 'Japan's kitchen' moves
at a frenetic pace as thousands of
fish are processed, purchased and
carted off. The infamous tuna auction starts at 5am and peters out
by 8am when the day's catch has

MORE ON TSUKIJI
To access the tuna auction, it is best to arrive at 4.30am and queue in front of the **Fish
Information Center** (Osakana Fukyu Center) located at the Kachidoki Gate. The first 140
individuals are granted admission – the first shift of 70 visitors is from 5am to 5.40am, the
second shift is from 5.40am to 6.15am.

If you aren't keen to wake up before dawn, you can show up later in the morning and still
get a flavour of the frenetic atmosphere (especially when the tuna auction is off limits) and
glimpse Japan's seafood obsession. The intermediate wholesalers area opens up to visitors
at 9am, while other areas of the market are open even earlier, including the Jogai Sijou.

For the last few years, rumours have been flying about Tsukiji's uncertain future – it is
expected to move to Toyosu at the end of 2012.

WORTH THE TRIP

Pop quiz: what's the most visited sight in Japan? Kyoto's temples? Nope. Harajuku? Not quite. Ten points if you guessed **Tokyo Disneyland** (www.tokyodisneyresort.co.jp; 1-1 Maihama, Urayasu-shi, Chiba; 1-day ticket adult/child ¥5800/3900; 🚃 JR Keiyō line to Maihama). As tragic (or as telling) as it may be, it's been a smashing success, offering visitors two theme parks: Tokyo Disneyland, modelled after the California original, and Tokyo DisneySea, a clever add-on that caters more to adults. A Fast Pass will reduce time lost waiting in lines; it's also worth packing a *bentō*, as on-site restaurants are almost always overrun with diners.

been purchased by middlemen and sold off to gawking retailers.

🔵 YASUKUNI-JINJA
靖国神社

☎ 3261 8326; www.yasukuni.or.jp /english; 3-1-1 Kudan-kita, Chiyoda-ku; admission free; ⏰ 9.30am-5.30pm Mar-Oct, 9.30am-5pm Nov-Feb; 🚇 Hanzōmon, Tōzai & Toei Shinjuku lines to Kudanshita (exits 1 & 2); ♿

Yasukuni-jinja, the perennial fly-in-the-Chardonnay in Japan-Asia relations, is the 'Peaceful Country Shrine' and a memorial to Japan's victims of war. No wonder it invites controversy. Politics aside, it has a beautiful, contemplative inner sanctum in the style of ancient Ise shrines – a stark contrast to the *uyoku* (right-wing activists) shouting their rhetoric outside.

🛍 SHOP

North of the Marunouchi business district is the Kanda neighbourhood, which holds little of interest to travellers other than for bookworms. Jimbōchō is famous for its bookshops, serving all sorts of special-interest readers, from manga maniacs to collectors of antique maps. Northeast of Jimbōchō across the Kanda River is even more manga, and electronics, in Akihabara (Electric Town). But the most famous shopping mecca in central Tokyo is glittery Ginza, its snob value still holding sway.

🛍 AKIHABARA GACHAPON KAIKAN 秋葉原 *Toys*

☎ 5209-6020; www.akibagacha.com; 1F, MN Bldg, 3-15-5 Soto-Kanda, Chiyoda-ku; ⏰ 11am-8pm; 🚃 JR Yamanote line to Akihabara (west exit)

Come with pockets full of 100-yen coins, as this shop houses hundreds of *gachapon* (capsule-vending machines) dispensing manga character toys, keychain and mobile-phone mascots and some-assembly-required figurines – perfect, pre-packaged Tokyo souvenirs.

Kikuchi Rinko
Internationally recognised actress and Tokyo native, and nominated for an Academy Award for her performance in Babel *(2006).*

If a movie were being made about Tokyo, and each neighbourhood was a character, which neighbourhood would you want to play? I'd want to be Shibuya (p90). There's an amazing overflow of spirit and vigour that the neighbourhood cannot digest! It's seedy, sloppy and reckless – it's filled with tonnes of energy to waste. Seems like it could be a very colourful role. **Is there a place in the city that you find particularly inspiring?** Of the places I've resided in Tokyo, the place I lived at the longest was close to Arisugawa Park. Throughout the year, while filming a movie, I would go and take walks to gather my thoughts. **For visitors interested in Japanese theatre and performance, what would you recommend they check out?** The Honda Theatre in Shimo-Kitazawa (p21) is where I often go to watch theatrical plays.

HAIBARA はいばら

Stationery

☎ 3272 3801; 2-7-6 Nihombashi, Chūo-ku; ⏱ 9.30am-6.30pm Mon-Fri, 9.30am-5pm Sat; ⊕ Ginza, Tōzai, Toei Asakusa lines to Nihombashi (exits B8 & C3)

Even Haibara's business cards are made from exquisite paper. Find high-quality *washi* and tiny treasures such as wallets, hand mirrors and mobile-phone accessories made from printed paper in this jewellery box of a paper shop.

HAKUHINKAN TOY PARK

博品館 *Toys*

☎ 3571 8008; www.hakuhinkan.co.jp; 8-8-11 Ginza, Chūo-ku; ⏱ 11am-8pm; 🚇 JR Yamanote line to Shimbashi (Ginza exit), ⊕ Ginza & Toei Asakusa lines to Shimbashi (exits 1 & 3)

One of Tokyo's most famous toy stores, this 'toy park' is crammed to the rafters with dolls, action figures, squawking video games, seas of colourful plastic and the softest plush toys ever. Hakuhinkan also harbours child-friendly restaurants and even a theatre in this huge children's attention-deficit paradise.

HASHI GINZA NATSUNO

箸銀座夏野 *Handicrafts*

☎ 3569 0952; www.e-ohashi.com in Japanese; 1F & 6F, Ginza Takahashi Bldg, 6-7-4 Ginza, Chūo-ku; ⏱ 10am-8pm Mon-Sat, 10am-7pm Sun; ⊕ Ginza, Hibiya & Marunouchi lines to Ginza (exit B3)

Look out for this narrow shopfront in Ginza if you'd like to add some *hashi* (chopsticks) to your stash of souvenirs. Ginza Natsuno stocks a staggering array of *hashi*, from inexpensive, colourful children's sets to hand-carved pairs costing thousands of yen. Lovely chopstick rests, ceramics and decorations fill out every other corner of usable space.

ITŌYA 伊東屋 *Stationery*

☎ 3561 8311; 2-7-15 Ginza, Chūo-ku; ⏱ 9.30am-7pm Mon-Sat, 9.30am-6pm Sun; ⊕ Ginza, Hibiya & Marunouchi lines to Ginza (exits A12 & A13)

Nine floors of stationery-shop love await paper (and paperclip) fanatics at Itōya. In addition to a comprehensive collection of *washi*, there are Italian leather agendas, erasable pens in the season's coolest hues and even *tenugui* – beautifully hand-dyed, all-purpose traditional handkerchiefs.

JINBŌCHŌ *Books*

Kanda-jinbōchō, Chiyoda-ku; ⊕ Tozai & Hanzomon line to Jinbocho (exits A1, A6 or A7)

Definitely worth a visit, if only to witness the incredible feats of hoarding, Jinbocho's fascinating neighbourhood of over 170 secondhand booksellers stretches far across Yasukuni-dōri. Start with **Isseido Books** (www.isseido-books.co.jp; 1-7

CHOPSTICK TIPS

Although foreigners will be forgiven most dining faux pas, remember this basic *hashi* (chopstick) etiquette:

> As anywhere in Asia, never leave chopsticks upright in your rice bowl; this is done only at funerals.

> Don't pass food from one set of chopsticks to another, as this is associated with another funereal ritual.

> Use the other end of your chopsticks when picking up food from a shared plate, so as not to use the ends that go in your mouth.

> It's considered rude to gesture with or point at anyone with chopsticks; when you're not using them to eat, it's best to lay them on the table in front of you.

> If you must resort to stabbing your food rather than picking it up with your chopsticks, consider requesting a fork and knife.

Kanda-jinbōchō) to pick up a copy of the neighbourhood booksellers map, then wander down the main drag and up into the backstreets north of Yasukuni-dōri for more.

⌂ LAOX ラオックス
Cameras & Electronics
☎ 3253 7111; 1-2-9 Soto-Kanda, Chiyoda-ku; ⏱ 10am-9pm, closing hours vary at end of month; 🚇 JR Sōbu & Yamanote lines to Akihabara (Electric Town exit)

The multilingual staff at this duty-free Laox will help you figure out whether the voltage on your new superjuicer is compatible with your home voltage before you lug it onto the plane. This huge chain, selling discounted electrical equipment, has very competitive prices. There's another duty-free Laox nearby.

⌂ MARUZEN 丸善 *Books*
☎ 5288 8881; 1F-4F, Oazo Bldg, 1-6-4 Marunouchi, Chiyoda-ku; ⏱ 9am-9pm; 🚇 JR Yamanote line to Tokyo (Marunouchi north exit)

Based in the curvy Oazo Building just across from Tokyo Station's Marunouchi exit, Maruzen boasts a satisfyingly wide selection of English-language books and magazines. The 4th floor is where you'll find the foreign-language material, a stationery shop and a cafe. Maruzen's original branch, accessible via exit B3 at Nihombashi Station, has foreign-language books on the 3rd floor.

⌂ MATSUYA 松屋
Department Store
☎ 3567 1211; 3-6-1 Ginza, Chūō-ku; ⏱ 10.30am-7.30pm; 🚇 Ginza, Hibiya, Marunouchi lines to Ginza (exits A12 & A13)

A boon for foreign visitors, Matsuya offers the works with packaging and international shipping service, tax-exemption assistance and useful, if haphazard, in-store English-speaking guides. Don't forget to take a peek at Matsuya's art gallery on the 7th floor and, in the summer, the rooftop beer garden.

🛍 MIKIMOTO PEARL ミキモト真珠
Jewellery & Accessories
www.mikimoto.co.jp; 2-4-12 Ginza, Chūō-ku; 🔘 Ginza, Hibiya & Marunouchi lines to Ginza (exit B2)
No one can touch Mikimoto when it comes to pearls, so it's no surprise that this luxury slugger has joined its fellow name brands and created a memorable boutique facade. This eye-catching endeavour looks like the work of a futuristic spider that has woven trapezoidal crystals into its elaborate web.

🛍 MITSUKOSHI 三越
Department Store
☎ 3562 1111; 4-6-16 Ginza, Chūō-ku; 🕙 10am-8pm, closed occasional Mon; 🔘 Ginza, Hibiya, Marunouchi lines to Ginza (exits A7 & A11)
One of Ginza's grande dames, Mitsukoshi embodies the essence of Tokyo's department stores and gleams after a recent renovation. Treasures include the 2nd floor's outpost of Ladurée, the Parisian *macaron* monolith, decked out like a giant pastel Easter egg. The Mitsukoshi lion at the corner entrance is a popular local meeting spot.

🛍 MUJI 無印良品
Fashion, Homewares
☎ 5208 8241; 2F & 3F, 3-8-3 Marunouchi, Chiyoda-ku; 🕙 10am-9pm ; 🚃 JR Yamanote line to Yūrakuchō (main exit), 🔘 Yūrakuchō line to Yūrakuchō (exit A4b)
Mujirushi Ryōhin (literally, 'no name brand') has taken the world by storm with its signature line of simple lifestyle goods. At the flagship store, things are taken to the next level – customers can tour a full-sized 'MUJI House' fully constructed within the shop. Yes, this do-it-yourself abode is for sale in three different sizes.

🛍 SOFMAP ソフマップ
Cameras & Electronics
☎ 3253 1111; 4-1-1 Soto-Kanda, Chiyoda-ku; 🕙 11am-9pm; 🚃 JR Sōbu & Yamanote lines to Akihabara (Electric Town exit)
Crafty marketing, ruthless discounting and a staff of tech geeks have helped Sofmap sprout more than a dozen branches within Akihabara alone. The gigantic main shop has seven floors of electronics of all types, games, and new and used PCs, and is as overwhelmingly cacophonous as you would expect.

🛍 TAKASHIMAYA 高島屋
Department Store
☎ 3211 4111; 2-4-1 Nihombashi, Chūō-ku; 🕙 10am-7.30pm; 🔘 Ginza, Tōzai, Toei Asakusa lines to Nihombashi (exit B1 & B2)

DEPACHIKA DECODED

Department stores (depāto) have long been a staple of Japan's modern consumerism. Popularised in the early boom years, these capitalist bastions offered elegant one-stop shopping for the hurried Tokyoite. Tucked in the basement, the depachika (デパ地下) was the department store's supermarket avatar, where locals could tick off a wide array of items on their grocery list. Today, the depachika has evolved into a destination in its own right, boasting a veritable library of domestic and international products.

For the uninitiated, a trip to the vast, bustling depachika can be overwhelming. Here's a short list of picnic-prone items to help you navigate the seemingly endless array of stalls. Oh, and don't forget to pick up disposable chopsticks (waribashi; 割り箸).

> **Cakes and pastries** (スイーツ) Be prepared to spend around ¥500 per cake slice (ケーキ); don't worry – it's worth it. Look out for signs touting 'limited time only' confections (期間限定), which usually incorporate seasonal fruits and flavours.

> **Souvenirs** (お土産) Depachika are busiest during the perfunctory holiday gift-giving season, but stalls sell meticulously packaged cookies, rice crackers, teas and traditional Japanese desserts all year.

> **Sashimi** (刺身) The best place to snag the freshest and most affordable sashimi is at a depachika after 6pm when crowds begin to dwindle and prices are slashed. Platters come with packets of wasabi, but rarely soy sauce; 解凍 indicates previously frozen, while 天然 indicates fresh (never frozen).

> **Souzai** (総菜) Multiple stalls offer souzai – side dishes inspired by diverse cuisines (stick to the Japanese preparations). While rubbing elbows with the older folks ordering items for dinner, take note of their selections to get your hands on the tastiest items.

> **Bentō** (弁当) Look for artfully crafted bentō with meat, fish, flavoured rice and seasonal vegetables. Some booths steam giant vats of traditional sticky rice with vegetables (おこわ; okowa). Pair these with various souzai to create a personalised bentō.

In Nihombashi Takashimaya is one of the more venerable establishments with palatial architecture. Primly dressed, white-gloved attendants operate the old-fashioned lifts and bow demurely as you arrive and depart; take the lift to the rooftop patio, where you can bring your bentō (boxed meal). There's another branch in Ginza and the enormous Takashimaya Times Square complex in Shinjuku.

🏠 TAKUMI HANDICRAFTS
たくみ *Handicrafts*
☎ 3571 2017; www.ginza-takumi.co.jp, in Japanese; 8-4-2 Ginza, Chūō-ku; ⏰ 11am-7pm Mon-Sat; 🚇 JR Yamanote line to Shimbashi (Ginza exit)
Takumi carries an elegant selection of toys, textiles, ceramics and other traditional folk crafts from around Japan. The shop also thoughtfully encloses information detailing

the origin and background of any pieces you purchase.

📖 TORA-NO-ANA
とらのあな *Books*
☎ 5294 0123; www.toranoana.co.jp;
4-3-1 Soto-Kanda, Chiyoda-ku;
🕙 10am-10pm; 🚃 JR Sōbu & Yamanote
lines to Akihabara (Electric Town exit)
Keep your eyes up and look for the cute illustrated tiger-girl on the top of this building, which has seven floors of manga and *anime*. Tora no Ana has other branches in Shinjuku and Ikebukuro.

👕 UNIQLO ユニクロ
Fashion
☎ 3569 6781; 5-7-7 Ginza, Chūō-ku;
🕙 11am-9pm; 🚃 Ginza, Hibiya &
Marunouchi lines to Ginza (exit A2 & A3)
Clothe yourself in brilliant basics at this low-cost hegemony. There are dozens of branches around the city, but the Ginza location is the flagship behemoth with an entire building devoted to each gender.

📷 YODOBASHI AKIBA
ヨドバシアキバ
Cameras & Electronics
☎ 5209 1010; 1-1 Kanda-Hanaokachō,
Chiyoda-ku; 🕙 9.30am-10pm; 🚃 JR
Sōbu & Yamanote lines to Akihabara
(Electric Town exit)
This megalith of a discount store is located on the east side of Aki-habara Station, with a whopping

nine floors of cameras, computer equipment and enough electronics for the most hardcore geek.

🍴 EAT

Ginza is a great place to splash out on a quality Japanese dinner, at one of its classic establishments. For lunch there are heaps of excellent traditional *soba* (buckwheat noodle) shops around less-pretentious Kanda, while the must-do sushi breakfast should be taken in Tsukiji, naturally.

For *yakitori* (skewers of grilled chicken) in the most atmospheric spot in the neighbourhood, try Yūrakuchō Yakitori Alley, a conglomeration of simple *yakitori* stalls beneath the JR tracks just south of Yūrakuchō station. It's noisy, smoky and convivial; sit yourself down and wash down your *yakitori* with some cold beer.

🍴 BEIGE *Fusion* ¥¥¥
☎ 5159-5500; www.beige-tokyo.com;
3-5-3 Ginza, Chūō-ku; 🕙 lunch & dinner;
🚃 Ginza, Hibiya & Marunouchi lines to
Ginza (exits A9 & A13)
Beige is the love child of fashion headliner Chanel and celebrity chef Alain Ducasse, and the menu is decadence defined: locally raised beef, fresh-from-the-sea lobster, hand-selected vegetables and expertly blended marinades. A wine list of encyclopaedic proportions and swish, East-meets-West decor

rounds out the perfect top-end To-kyo experience. **Jardin de Tweed** (lunch ¥2500), nesting on the building's rooftop, is a bit more affordable to those with luxe aspirations.

🍴 BIRDLAND バードラン
Yakitori ¥¥

☎ 5250 1081; B1F, Tsukamoto Sozan Bldg, 4-2-15 Ginza, Chūō-ku; 🕙 5-9pm Tue-Sat; Ⓜ Ginza, Hibiya & Marunouchi lines to Ginza (exits C6 & C8)

Who knew Gewürztraminer went so well with skewered chicken hearts? Birdland does. Before said hearts are set aflame, they belong to free-range chickens so pure that they can be ordered as sashimi. Upscale and in demand, Birdland limits your dinner to two hours and takes only same-day reservations (from noon) for its famous *yakitori*.

🍴 DAIWA SUSHI 大和寿司
Sushi & Sashimi ¥¥

☎ 3547 6807; 5-2-1 Tsukiji, Chūō-ku; 🕙 5am-1.30pm Mon-Sat, closed 2nd Wed of the month; Ⓜ Toei Ōedo line to Tsukiji-shijō (exit A2); ♿ Ⓥ 👶

Lines are unavoidable at Tsukiji's famed sushi bar, but once your first piece of sushi hits the counter gratification is inevitable. The sushi sets are a good bet if you're not comfortable ordering in Japanese and, though staff will be too polite to say so, you're expected to eat without wasting time and then give up your seat.

Watch expert sushi chefs cut loose on your dinner at Daiwa Sushi, Tsukiji Market

GREG ELMS / LONELY PLANET IMAGES ©

🍴 KIJI きじ *Okonomiyaki* ¥

☎ 3216-3123; www.o-kiji.jp; B1 Tokia Bldg 2-7-3 Marunouchi, Chūō-ku; ⏱ lunch & dinner; 🚃 JR Yamanote line to Tokyo (Marunouchi South exit)

Fresh off the bullet train from Osaka, Kiji brings expertly crafted *okonomiyaki* to the legions of businessmen in bustling Marunouchi. Slide down the escalator to sample some seriously scrumptious soul food. Perfect for neophytes, these pancake, omelette, noodle mash-ups come ready to eat (rather than DIY).

🍴 LUGDUNUM BOUCHON LYONNAIS *French* ¥¥¥

☎ 6426-1201; www.lyondelyon.com; 4-3-7 Kagurazaka, Chiyoda-ku; ⏱ lunch & dinner; 🚇 Tozai line to Kagurazaka (exit 1)

Bringing the proud culinary heritage of Lyon to the backstreets of Kagurazaka, this welcoming outpost of French fare does everything imaginable to transport the senses across continents. The emphasis here is on simple, back-to-nature recipes accompanied by one of the best wine lists in town.

🍴 MARUGO 丸五 *Tonkatsu* ¥

☎ 3255-6595; 1-8-14 Soto Kanda, Chiyoda-ku; ⏱ lunch & dinner; 🚇 Tozai & Hanzomon lines to Jinbocho (exit A6)

Marugo's succulent slices of slow-cooked pork and chicken cutlets are served with generous mounds of shredded cabbage, miso soup and pickled vegies. Dine among a cast of regulars who tuck into their meals amid old clocks upstairs or sit side-by-side at the bar on the ground level. Marugo's been around for over 35 years, so you know they're doin' something right.

🍴 MEAL MUJI *Cafe* ¥

☎ 5208-8241; www.muji.net; 2F 3-8-3 Marunouchi, Chūō-ku; ⏱ lunch & dinner; 🚇 Yurakuchō line to Yurakuchō (exit D9)

Those who subscribe to the Muji lifestyle will be delighted to know that the 'no name brand' experience goes beyond neutral-toned notebooks, containers and linens. Meal Muji follows the 'simpler is better' mantra with fresh deli fare uncluttered by chemicals and unpronounceable ingredients.

🍴 MIKIMOTO LOUNGE *Cafe* ¥

www.mikimoto.co.jp; 3F 2-4-12 Ginza, Chūō-ku; 🚇 Ginza, Hibiya & Marunouchi lines to Ginza (exit B2)

Elegantly positioned behind the futuristic pastel webbing of the pearl magnate's flagship boutique, Mikimoto Lounge is one of Ginza's premiere dessert parlours. Tuck into your artisanal treat – made from fairy-tale ingredients like cloud ear compote and wolfberry – while dining upon ivory-smooth tabletops.

🍴 OPIPPI おぴっぴ
Rāmen ¥

1-20-11 Shinbashi, Chūō-ku; 🕑 lunch & dinner; 🚇 Ginza & Asakusa lines to Shinbashi (exit 8)

Quietly lost amid Shinbashi's urban grid, this family-run soup shop whips up slurp-worthy udon with a twist – instead of factory-line fare and vats of broth, each bowl is individually assembled from fresh ingredients.

🍴 RENGATEI 煉瓦亭
Yoshoku ¥

☎ 3882-7258; www.ginza-rengatei.com; 3-5-16 Ginza, Chūō-ku; 🕑 dinner; 🚇 Ginza, Hibiya & Marunouchi lines to Ginza (exit A12)

Dating back to the early days of the Meiji period, Rengatei is credited with inventing the katsu cutlet and the omelette – Japan's first stab at Western cuisine, which quickly became its own culinary category called *yōshoku*. Wonderfully outdated decor (think clanging cash register, faded waitress uniforms and well-worn chequered tablecloths) hint at the restaurant's lengthy history.

🍴 ROBATA 爐端
Izakaya ¥¥

☎ 3591 1905; 1-3-8 Yūrakuchō, Chiyoda-ku; 🕑 5-11pm Mon-Sat; 🚇 Hibiya & Chiyoda lines to Hibiya (exit A4)

Back near the railway tracks, this is one of Tokyo's most celebrated *izakaya* (Japanese-style pubs). A little Japanese language ability is helpful here, but the point-and-eat method works just fine. It's hard to spot the sign, even if you can read Japanese; better to look for the rustic, weathered façade.

🍴 SUSHI KANESAKA
Sushi & Sashimi ¥¥¥

☎ 5568-4411; B1 8-10-3 Ginza, Chūō-ku; 🕑 lunch & dinner; 🚇 Ginza & Asakusa line to Shinbashi (exit 5)

Tucked away below street level, this sushi superstar is the workshop of the eponymous master chef – a prodigy by culinary standards – who slices through premium pieces of fresh fish with a surgeon's precision. If you're contemplating a sushi splurge during your time in Tokyo, this is the place to do it. But book ahead – there's only a dozen seats.

🍴 TEN-ICHI 天一
Tempura ¥¥¥

☎ 3571 1949; www.tenichi.co.jp; 6-6-5 Ginza, Chūō-ku; 🕑 11.30am-9.30pm; 🚇 Ginza, Hibiya, Marunouchi lines to Ginza (exits A1, B3 & B6)

One of Tokyo's oldest and best tempura restaurants, the refined and gracious Ten-Ichi is where one should go to experience tempura the way it's meant to be: light, airy and crispy. You'll find several branches elsewhere in Tokyo, but the distinguished Ginza original is the smartest. Reservations are recommended.

☽ DRINK
☽ 300 BAR *Bar*

☎ 3571 8300; www.300bar-8chome.com, in Japanese; B1F, No 2 Column Bldg, 8-3-12 Ginza Chūō-ku; ☾ 5pm-2am Mon-Sat, 5-11pm Sun; ◎ JR Yamanote line to Shimbashi (Ginza exit)

One of the few places in Ginza that can truthfully say it offers a bargain, the 300 Bar charges ¥300 for everything – cocktails, snacks and all. There's no cover, and it's a fun place to stand around with a few drinks after some Ginza window-shopping.

☽ AUX AMIS DES VINS
オザミデヴァン *Bar*

☎ 3567 4120; www.auxamis.com/desvins, in Japanese; 2-5-6 Ginza, Chūō-ku; ☾ 5.30pm-2am Mon-Fri & noon-midnight Sat; ◎ Yūrakuchō line to Ginza-itchōme (exits 5 & 8)

Both the informal indoor and a small outdoor seating area at this wine bar feel welcoming in all seasons. A solid selection of mostly French wines comes by the glass (¥800) or by the bottle. You can also order snacks to go with your wine, or full prix-fixe dinners; lunch is served only on weekdays.

☽ GINZA LION *Bar*

www.ginzalion.jp; 7-9-20 Ginza, Chūō-ku; ◎ Ginza, Hibiya & Marunouchi lines to Ginza (exit A4)

An institution more than anything else, the Lion was one of Japan's first beer halls when Yebisu rose to popularity during the early Meiji Period. Come for the atmosphere – skip the food.

★ PLAY
★ AKB48 THEATRE *Live Music*

www.akb48.co.jp; 8F Don Quijote 4-3-3 Soto-kanda, Chiyoda-ku; JR Yamanote line to Akihabara (Main exit)

Tokyo's biggest pop phenomenon takes the girl group prototype and

---

MAID CAFES

Where *cosplay* (costume-play) culture and *otaku* (geeks; see p164) intersect, Akihabara would seem the obvious crux. This collision of subcultures results in a new iteration of an old game, with Tokyo's uniquely modern twist: maid cafes. This is master-slave role-playing as above-board commercial service, where young waitresses dressed in cartoonish French maid outfits serve the Akiba geeks who love them. Variations on the theme abound, with cafes employing women in drag playing slender, spiky-haired *anime* heroes, and even nun (!) cafes for those with Catholic fetishes. Look out for flyers and costumed touts, luring customers to the dozens of maid cafes that have set up shop in Akihabara.

expands it far beyond the five-girl quorum that proved successful for the Spice Girls. AKB48 has not 10, not 20, but over 50 members in the lot, and they perform in shifts at their very own workhouse… er…theatre right in the heart of Akihabara.

⭐ NATIONAL FILM CENTRE
フィルムセンター *Cinema*
☎ 5777 8600; 3-7-6 Kyōbashi, Chūō-ku; cinema ¥500/300/100, gallery ¥200/70/40; ⏱ cinema 3-10pm Tue-Fri, 1-7pm Sat & Sun, gallery 11am-6.30pm Tue-Sat; Ⓜ Ginza line to Kyōbashi (exit 2) or Toei Asakusa line to Takarachō (exit A3)
The third arm of the National Museum of Modern Art (p50), this centre shows tremendous film series on a range of subjects, from the history of Japanese animation to the masterpieces of Cuba's film tradition. The centre also houses a library and a gallery that includes a permanent collection of antique cinematic equipment.

⭐ NATIONAL THEATRE
国立劇場 *Theatre*
☎ 3230 3000; www.ntj.jac.go.jp/english /index.html; 4-1 Hayabusachō, Chiyoda-ku; admission ¥1500-12,000; ⏱ reservations 10am-6pm, performances 11.30am & 5pm; Ⓜ Namboku & Yūrakuchō lines to Nagatachō (exit 4)
Otherwise known as Kokuritsu Gekijō, this theatre features

astonishingly lifelike bunraku puppets, which are half to two-thirds life-size and each operated by three hooded, visible puppeteers. A single narrator, standing on a dais to one side, intones the story using a different voice for each character. Performances take place in Tokyo in February, May, September and December.

⭐ SESSION HOUSE
セッションハウス *Theatre*
☎ 3266 0461; 158 Yaraichō, Shinjuku-ku; admission varies; ⏱ performances 7pm; Ⓜ Tōzai line to Kagurazaka (exit 1)
Dance aficionados consider Session House one of the best traditional, folk and modern dance spaces in the city. The theatre seats only 100 people, ensuring an intimate feel for all performances. Exit right from Kagurazaka Station, make a right into the first narrow alley, and turn left where it dead-ends. Session House is a few metres to your right.

⭐ SHINBASHI ENBUJYŌ
Theatre
www.shochiku.co.jp/play/enbujyo; 6-18-2 Ginza, Chūō-ku; Ⓜ Ginza & Asakusa lines to Shinbashi
While Tokyo's famous Kabuki-za theatre hides under rubble, Shinbashi Enbujō returns to its roots to act as the city's main kabuki venue. A full performance of traditional kabuki comprises three or four acts (usually from different

NEIGHBOURHOODS

MARUNOUCHI, GINZA & CENTRAL TOKYO

WORTH THE TRIP

On the east bank of the Sumida River, Ryōgoku is akin to a sumō village. Because the sumō stadium is located here, so too are the sumō *beya* (wrestling stables) that train and house *rikishi* (wrestlers).

During Grand Tournament time at **Ryōgoku Kokugikan** (☎ 3622 1100; www.sumo .or.jp; 1-3-28 Yokoami, Sumida-ku; ☼ 10am-4pm; ⧠ JR Sōbu line to Ryōgoku, west exit, ◉ Toei Ōedo line to Ryōgoku, exit A4), nonreserved seats at the back sell for as little as ¥1500 and standing-room-only tickets are a meagre ¥500. Simply turn up on the day you'd like to attend, but get there early as keen punters start queuing the night before. Only one ticket is sold per person to foil scalpers, so come with your entire entourage.

When tournaments aren't in session you can visit a local *beya*. Try **Arashio** (www.arashio .net; 2-47-2 Nihonbashi-hamamchi; ☼ 6.30-10.30am; ◉ Hibiya line to Ningyochō), which is one of the more welcoming sumō stables. Complete silence is expected during the practice session, but afterwards guests are invited to eat *chanko* and chat with the wrestlers. Visit the website for additional information and pricing.

Just behind Ryōgoku Kokugikan is the superb **Edo-Tokyo Museum** (☎ 3626 9974; www.edo-tokyo-museum.or.jp; 1-4-1 Yokoami, Sumida-ku; admission ¥600/300-480/free; ☼ 9.30am-5.30pm Tue-Fri & Sun, 9.30am-7.30pm Sat; ⧠ JR Sōbu line to Ryōgoku, west exit, ◉ Toei Ōedo line to Ryōgoku, exit A4). Offering a fascinating view into Edo-era life, this museum is highly accessible by wheelchair, fun for kids and even has volunteers who give free tours in English (and other languages). Call ahead to confirm availability of such tour guides.

For more information on sumō see p10.

plays) over an afternoon or an evening (typically 11am to 3.30pm or 4.30pm to 9pm), with long intervals between the acts. If four-plus hours sounds too long, you can usually purchase last-minute tickets for a single act.

⭐ TOKYO DOME
東京ドーム *Spectator Sports*
☎ 5800 9999; www.tokyo-dome.co.jp/e; 1-3-61 Kōraku, Bunkyō-ku; from ¥1000; ⧠ Chūō, Sōbu lines to Suidobashi (west exit), ◉ **Marunouchi & Namboku lines to Kōrakuen (Kōrakuen exit)**

A trip to a Japanese ballpark is truly a cultural experience in baseball-mad Japan. Fans in matching *happi* (half-coats) perform synchronised cheers, and entire sections of the extremely well-mannered crowd often wind up singing in unison. Tokyo Dome is the home turf of Japan's most popular team, the Yomiuri Giants.

GREG ELMS / LONELY PLANET IMAGES ©
Home-run hype hits Tokyo Dome

⭐ TOKYO TAKARAZUKA GEKIJŌ 東京宝塚劇場
Theatre

☎ 5251 2001; http://kageki.hankyu.co.jp/english; 1-1-3 Yūrakuchō, Chiyoda-ku; admission ¥3500-10,000 🕙 times vary; 🚇 Chiyoda, Hibiya & Toei Mita lines to Hibiya (exits A5 & A13)

Kabuki kicked women out of the tradition, but the ladies have taken the ball and run with it at the Takarazuka Revue, founded in 1913. The extensively trained, all-female cast puts on an equally grand – if drastically different – show. These musical productions tend towards the soap-operatic and attract a disproportionate percentage of swooning female fans.

>ROPPONGI

Exiting the subway station at Roppongi Crossing is like entering the world of Blade Runner, where throngs of the galaxy's most unscrupulous citizens gather to engage in a host of unsavoury activities under the sizzling neon lights. Over the last decade, however, Roppongi has really started to clean up its act – and it shows. Perhaps just as famous as Roppongi itself is the enormous complex of Roppongi Hills. It took developer Mori Minoru no less than 17 years to acquire the land and construct his labyrinthine microcosm of a city. Roppongi's other anchor, the newer Tokyo Midtown, has its own set of intriguing dining and shopping options. The area's three major museums – the Mori Art Museum, the Suntory Museum of Art and the National Art Center Tokyo – are collectively known as the Roppongi Art Triangle. It's well worth spending the day connecting the dots – finish with the Mori Art Museum and take in the morphing cityscapes during sunset.

ROPPONGI

◉ SEE
21_21 Design Sight	1	D4
Hie-jinja	2	F2
Mori Art Museum	3	D5
Musée Tomo	4	F4
National Art Center Tokyo	5	C4
National Diet Building	6	F2
Nogi-jinja	7	C3
Ōkura Shūkokan	8	F4
Sōgetsu Kaikan	9	D2
Suntory Museum of Art	10	D4
Tokyo Tower	11	G6

◎ SHOP
Japan Sword	12	G4
Kurofune	13	D4
Tolman Collection	14	H6

🍴 EAT
Eat More Greens	15	D6
Gonpachi	16	C5
Inakaya	(see 34)	
Jomon	17	D5
Kikunoi	18	D3
L'Atelier de Joël Robuchon	19	D5
Ninja Akasaka	20	E1
Nirvanam	21	G4
Seryna	22	D4
Tokyo Curry Lab	23	G5
Ukai Tofu-ya	24	G6

▼ DRINK
Agave	25	D4
Bernd's Bar	26	E5
Geronimo	27	D4
Heartland	(see 19)	
Mado Lounge	(see 3)	
Maduro	28	C5

★ PLAY
Abbey Road	29	D4
Alfie	30	D5
Billboard Live	31	D4
Blue Note	32	A5
BuL-Let's	33	C5
Cavern Club	34	D5
Club 328	35	C5
Egbok Azabu Oriental Clinic	36	E5
eleven	37	C5
Festa Iikura	38	F5
Lovenet	39	D4
Muse	40	B5
New Lex-Edo	41	D5
STB 139	42	D5
Vanity	43	E5

Please see over for map

SEE

21_21 DESIGN SIGHT
www.2121designsight.jp; 9-7-6 Akasaka, Minato-ku; admission ¥1000; ⏰ 11am-8pm Wed-Sun; ⓜ Chiyoda line to Nogizaka (exit 3)

More of a workshop than a museum, 21_21 Design Sight raises design awareness by acting as a beacon for local art enthusiasts, whether they are designers themselves or simply onlookers. Frequent exhibits and group discussions are the norm. Visit the iTunes store to download 21_21's curious iPhone app.

HIE-JINJA 日枝神社
☎ 3581 2471; www.hiejinja.net/jinja/english/index.html; 2-10-5 Nagatachō, Chiyoda-ku; admission free; ⏰ dawn-dusk; ⓜ Ginza & Namboku lines to Tameike-sannō (exits 5 & 7)

A casualty of WWII bombing, Hie-jinja dates back to 1659 in its present location. Although the shrine isn't a major attraction, the highlight is the walk up, through a 'tunnel' of red *torii* (shrine gate). It's also the site of one of Japan's most spectacular *matsuri* (festivals). Look for the concrete plaza-style entrance on Sotobori-dōri.

MORI ART MUSEUM
森美術館

☎ 5777 8600; www.mori.art.museum; 53F, Mori Tower, Roppongi Hills, 6-10-1 Roppongi, Minato-ku; admission ¥1500; ⏰ 10am-10pm Wed-Mon, 10am-5pm Tue, closed btwn exhibitions; ⓜ Hibiya & Toei Ōedo lines to Roppongi (exits 1c & 3)

Past exhibitions at this well-curated contemporary-arts museum have ranged from a comprehensive exhibition of contemporary African art to a huge, walk-through installation by

Get your fill of contemporary art at Mori Art Museum, Roppongi Hills

ANTHONY PLUMMER / LONELY PLANET IMAGES ©

NEIGHBOURHOODS

ROPPONGI

Kusama Yayoi. Museum admission also gets you into the spectacular 360-degree city views of Tokyo City View (and vice versa).

MUSÉE TOMO 智美術館
☎ www.musee-tomo.or.jp; 4-1-35 Toranomon, Minato-ku; admission ¥1300; ⏰ 10am-4.30pm Tue-Sun; ⊕ Hibiya line to Kamiyachō (exit 4b)
This is one of the most elegant and best curated museums in the city. The collection features a stunning assortment of ceramics displayed in spaces that are themselves a work of art – the walls are coated in *washi* paper; even the crystalline banister leading down to the galleries is an original commission.

NATIONAL ART CENTER TOKYO 国立新美術館
☎ 5777 8600; www.nact.jp; 7-22-2 Roppongi, Minato-ku; admission varies; ⏰ 10am-6pm Wed & Sat-Mon, 10am-8pm Fri; ⊕ Chiyoda line to Nogizaka (exit 6), Hibiya & Toei Ōedo lines to Roppongi (exits 4a & 7); ♿
The undulating glass exterior of this newer museum (the third point in the Roppongi Art Triangle) is alone worth a walk-by, and if the current exhibitions don't interest you, the museum shop is a treasure-trove of exquisite gifts.

NATIONAL DIET BUILDING 国会議事堂
☎ 5521 7445; www.sangiin.go.jp; 1-7-1 Nagatachō, Chiyoda-ku; ⏰ 8am-5pm

For a taste of government life take a tour of the National Diet Building

Mon-Fri; ⓜ Hanzōmon, Namboku & Yūrakuchō lines to Nagatachō (exit 1) or Marunouchi & Chiyoda lines to Kokkai-gijidōmae (exit 1)

When the Diet is not in session, you can take free 60-minute tours of the home of Japan's parliament, completed in 1936. Its architecture was meant to combine modern Asian and European styles.

ⓒ NOGI-JINJA 乃木神社

8-11-27 Akasaka, Minato-ku; ⏱ 8.30am-5pm; ⓜ Chiyoda line to Nogizaka (exit 1)

A shrine honouring General Nogi, hero of the Russo-Japanese War. Hours after Emperor Meiji's funeral, Nogi and his wife committed ritual suicide, following their master into death. Their blood spatter can still be seen on the tatami floors if you peek through the window.

ⓒ ŌKURA SHŪKOKAN 大倉集古館

☎ 3583 0781; www.okura.com/tokyo /info/shukokan.html; 2-10-3 Toranomon, Minato-ku; admission ¥800/500/ free; ⏱ 10am-4.30pm Tue-Sun; ⓜ Hibiya line to Kamiyachō (exit 4b) or Ginza & Namboku lines to Tameike-sannō (exit 13)

Surrounded by a small but well-populated sculpture garden, this museum has an impressive collection of lacquer writing boxes, scrolls, ancient sculptures and

---

RENDEZVOUS SPOTS EVERYONE KNOWS...

> *Hachikō* statue (p92); Shibuya
> Studio Alta building (p118); Shinjuku
> Mitsukoshi lion (p56); Ginza
> *The Spider* (Maman sculpture; pp8-9); Roppongi
> *Takamori Saigō* statue (p138); Ueno

---

several national treasures. The two-storey museum – with a collection that's rotated seasonally – is definitely worth a look if you're on this side of town.

ⓒ SŌGETSU KAIKAN 草月会館

☎ 3408 1151; www.sogetsu.or.jp/eng lish/index.html; Sōgetsu Kaikan Bldg, 7-2-21 Akasaka, Minato-ku; ⏱ 10am-5pm Mon-Thu & Sat, 10am-8pm Fri; ⓜ Ginza, Hanzōmon & Toei Ōedo lines to Aoyama-itchōme (exit 4)

The avant-garde Sōgetsu School of Ikebana, whose philosophy is that ikebana (Japanese flower arrangement) can go beyond its traditional roots, offers ikebana classes in English. Stop by the Sōgetsu Kaikan building for a look at current ikebana exhibits or to enquire about classes.

ⓒ SUNTORY MUSEUM OF ART サントリー美術館

www.suntory.co.jp/sma; 4F 9-7 Akasaka, Minato-ku; admission varies; ⏱ 10am-6pm Sun-Mon, to 8pm Wed-Sat; ⓜ Namboku line to Roppongi 1-chome (exit 1)

MARTIN MOOS / LONELY PLANET IMAGES ©

Watch the city sparkle from Tokyo Tower

This regal exhibition hall draws from its rich collection of artefacts to create regularly changing shows that accentuate different elements of the spectrum of Japanese arts. Architect Kuma Kengō has imbued the space with an uncanny Zen quality that should definitely be experienced, even if you aren't particularly fond of the current exhibition's theme.

TOKYO TOWER
東京タワー
☎ 3433 5111; www.tokyotower
.co.jp/english; 4-2-8 Shiba-kōen, Minato-ku; main observation deck ¥310-820, special observation deck extra ¥350-600; 🕙 9am-10pm; 🚇 Hibiya line to Kamiyachō (exits 1 & 2); ♿
Although it might play second fiddle to Roppongi Hills' 52nd-floor Tokyo City View, Tokyo Tower still affords a great 360-degree view of the city, best appreciated at night. It retains a sort of oldster charm next to the architectural wonders that have succeeded it. Catch live music on the main observatory, Wednesday and Thursday nights.

🛍 SHOP

Roppongi Hills lit up the neighbourhood when it opened as a much-vaunted microcosm within the greater megalopolis. The high-end shops based within the sexy architectural curves of the Hills still do a brisk business, but the smaller development of Tokyo Midtown down the way has established itself as a sophisticated, design-oriented shopping centre. You'll also find small shops around Akasaka and Roppongi selling antiques and handicrafts.

🛍 JAPAN SWORD 日本刀剣
Art & Antiques
☎ 3434 4321; www.japansword.co.jp; 3-8-1 Toranomon, Minato-ku; 🕙 9.30am-6pm Mon-Fri, 9.30am-5pm Sat; 🚇 Ginza line to Toranomon (exit 2)
If *Kill Bill* revived a long-dormant childhood attraction to swords,

this highly respected dealer has a beautiful showroom and lots of experience helping foreigners choose the right *katana* (sword) for their taste and budget. Priciest are the macabre *tameshi-giri* blades that have been 'used on humans'.

KUROFUNE 黒船
Art & Antiques

☎ 3479 1552; www.kurofuneantiques .com; 7-7-4 Roppongi, Minato-ku; ⏰ 10am-6pm Mon-Sat; ⊙ Toei Ōedo line to Roppongi (exit 7)

Kurofune, run for the past quarter-century by a friendly American collector, carries an awesome treasure trove of Japanese antiques. Correspondingly awesome amounts of cash are necessary for acquiring some of these items, such as painstakingly constructed Edo-period *tansu* (Japanese chests of drawers), but serious antique connoisseurs are well advised to have a look.

TOLMAN COLLECTION
Art & Antiques

☎ 3434 1300; www.tolmantokyo.com; 2-2-18 Shiba-Daimon, Minato-ku; ⏰ 11am-7pm Wed-Mon; ⊙ Toei Asakusa & Toei Ōedo lines to Daimon (exits A3 & A6)

For collectors keen on picking up some contemporary art, this well-established, estimable gallery represents a strong stable of printmakers, both Japanese and foreign. Although the artists exhibit a fairly broad range of styles ranging from abstract to representative, all of the work has a distinctly Japanese feel.

🍴 EAT

It's only logical that there's an abundance of international options in Tokyo's capital of *gaijin*-dom. In general, however, the prices are skewed a bit higher here, as they are largely geared towards tourists and moneyed ex-pats. Stacks of restaurants can be found in the modern complexes of Roppongi Hills and Tokyo Midtown (see Map pp68–9, D4 and D5).

Further north you'll find the district of Akasaka, which acts like a buffer between raucous Roppongi and the quiet garden-scapes of the imperial palace. Once a prominent geisha area, Akasaka is now a bustling business centre – great lunch deals and after-work *izakaya* can be scouted here.

🍴 EAT MORE GREENS
Vegetarian   ¥

www.eatmoregreens.jp; 2-2-5 Azabu-Jūban, Minato-ku; ⏰ lunch & dinner; ⊙ Toei Oedo line to Azabu-jūban, exit 4 & 5a

Inspired by the greengrocers and farmers markets of NYC, this shop holds its own farmers market on Saturdays. Choose the airy interior or outdoor patio to enjoy a delicious assortment of vegetarian and vegan dishes – the mushroom rice is divine.

GONPACHI 権八
Izakaya ¥¥

☎ 5771 0170; www.gonpachi.jp; 1-13-11 Nishi-Azabu, Minato-ku; ☷ 11.30am-5am; ⊖ Hibiya, Toei Ōedo lines to Roppongi (exit 2); ♿

The Edo-village décor and festive buzz in the air makes Gonpachi a great place for celebratory dinners, but do you really need a reason to thrill your palate with half-a-dozen exotic and untried Japanese morsels? Upstairs, you can order everything on the menu, plus sushi. Book ahead.

INAKAYA 田舎家
Robatayaki ¥¥¥¥

☎ 3408 5040; www.roppongiinakaya.jp; 5-3-4 Roppongi, Minato-ku; ☷ 5-11pm; ⊖ Hibiya & Toei Ōedo lines to Roppongi (exit 3)

Inakaya has gained fame as a top-end *robatayaki* (grilled-to-order seafood and meat). It does raucous, bustling, don't-stand-on-ceremony *robatayaki* with gusto. Point at what you'd like to eat and they'll grill it for you and serve it with a boisterous flourish. You'll pay for the privilege and have a rocking good time doing so.

JOMON ジョウモン
Yakiniku ¥

☎ 3405-2585; www.teyandei.com /tenpo_jomon.htm; 5-9-17 Roppongi, Minato-ku; ☷ dinner; ⊖ Hibiya & Toei Ōedo lines to Roppongi (exit 3)

Slide the stable door open to find a cosy kitchen with bar seating and rows of ornate *shochu* jugs lining the wall. Hundreds of freshly prepared skewers lie splayed in front of the patrons. Don't miss the *zabuton* beef stick (¥400).

KIKUNOI 菊乃井
Kaiseki ¥¥¥¥

☎ 3568 6055; http://kikunoi.jp/; 6-13-8 Akasaka, Minato-ku; ☷ 5-9pm Mon-Sat; ⊖ Chiyoda line to Akasaka (exit 6)

This Kyoto-based *kaiseki* restaurant has built its reputation over three generations, and its national fame has expanded to international recognition after being awarded with two Michelin stars in 2008. Exquisitely prepared seasonal dishes are as beautiful as they are delicious. If you don't speak Japanese, the bonus is that Kikunoi's Chef Murata has also written a book on *kaiseki*, and the staff helpfully uses the book to explain the dishes you are served.

L'ATELIER DE JOËL ROBUCHON ラトリエドゥ ジョエルロブション
French ¥¥¥

☎ 5772 7500; 2F Hillside, Roppongi Hills, 6-10-1 Roppongi, Minato-ku;

KAISEKI

Kaiseki (elegant, multicourse Japanese meals) grew as a complement to the traditions of the tea ceremony, with a similar ceremonial emphasis on attention to all of the senses during the dining experience. Each course is painstakingly prepared to bring out not only the flavours of the seasonally changing dishes but also the colours, textures and smells, which must be carefully presented to be aesthetically pleasing in every way. It's the height of Japanese cuisine and a singular experience. One of the more accessible places in Tokyo to sample *kaiseki* dining is at Kikunoi (p74) in Akasaka.

🕑 11.30am-2.30pm & 6-10pm; 🚇 Hibiya & Toei Ōedo lines to Roppongi (exits 1c & 3)
Another two-star Michelin standout, L'Atelier is an upscale French diner fashioned after a sushi bar. While the fantastic dishes are not overly fussy, everything is made to order, which can mean long waits in the queue and over your meal – leaving plenty of time for conversation and anticipation.

🍴 NATIONAL AZABU SUPERMARKET

ナショナル麻布
International groceries
☎ 3442 3181; 4-5-2 Minami-Azabu, Minato-ku; 🕑 9am-8pm; 🚇 Hibiya line to Hiro-o (exits 1 & 2)
Posher than posh can be, National Azabu is where the ambassadorial lackeys are sent to stock up on pâté de foie gras and truffles or their Japanese equivalents, *uni* (sea urchins) and *matsutake* (mushrooms). It's also got an awesome selection of imported wines and natural foods, and, importantly, has a pharmacy staffed with English speakers.

🍴 NINJA AKASAKA

Fusion   ¥¥¥
☎ 5157-3936; www.ninjaakasaka.com; 2-14-3 Nagatachō, Chiyoda-ku; 🕑 dinner; 🚇 Ginza & Marunouchi lines to Akasaka-mitsuke (Belle Vie exit)
Super-stealthy staff, trained in the deadly art of catering, escort you through a maze of trap doors and trick drawbridges before seating you at your private table. Savour tasty Japanese fare like 'cloaked chicken' or 'crouching salmon' and, at the end of the meal, a saucy senior ninja swings by to perform some impressive close magic. But perhaps the biggest trick of all is the food's swift disappearing act – portions are extremely small so, if you're sharing, be sure to order more plates than there are people (if you're dining à la carte). Reservations are a must.

🍴 NIRVANAM *Indian*   ¥¥
☎ 3433-1217; www.nirvanam.jp; 2F 3-19-7 Toranomon, Minato-ku; 🚇 Hibiya line to Kamiyachō (exit 3)
Skip the pomp and circumstance of the city's celebrity-run *dhabas*

and head to Nirvanam, the culinary sweetheart of Tokyo's expat Indian community. Although dinner can feel slightly overpriced, the all-you-can-eat lunch – loaded up with spicy curries and pillowy *naan* – is undoubtedly the city's best deal from the subcontinent.

¶ SERYNA 瀬里奈
Sukiyaki & Shabu-shabu　　　¥¥¥

☎ 3402 1051; 3-12-2 Roppongi, Minato-ku; ⏰ noon-11.30pm Mon-Fri, noon-10.30pm Sat & Sun; Ⓜ Hibiya & Toei Ōedo lines to Roppongi (exits 3 & 5); ♿
Although it feels a bit aged, like the high-quality Kōbe beef that draws expats and visiting guests here, Seryna provides a dignified backdrop for *shabu-shabu*, sukiyaki and *teppanyaki* (table-top grilling). The restaurant surrounds an attractive rock garden.

¶ TAJIMA 蕎麦たじま
Soba　　　¥¥

☎ 3445-6617; www.sobatajima.jp; 3-8-6 Nishi-azabu, Minato-ku; Ⓜ Hibiya line to Hiro-o (exit 3)
Slip behind the polished white wall to find Tajima – one of Tokyo's best *soba* houses. The understated decor lets senses focus exclusively on the flavours and aromas emanating from the freshly prepared dishes. Tease your tastebuds with a few appetisers, like daintily fried sweet potato wedges, then slurp your scrumptious soup and noodles.

¶ TOKYO CURRY LAB *Yoshoku* ¥
4-2-8 Shiba-kōen, Minato-ku; Ⓜ Hibiya line to Kamiyachō (exit 1)
The brainchild of local design powerhouse Wonderwall, this curry-wielding space station tucked under the soaring spires of Tokyo Tower sports personal TVs at each bar stool. The hilariously illustrated placemats (you'll see) make the perfect 'Tokyo is weird' souvenir.

¶ UKAI TOFU-YA *Kaiseki* ¥¥¥¥
☎ 3436-1028; www.ukai.co.jp; 4-4-13 Shiba-kōen, Minato-ku; Ⓜ Hibiya line to Kamiyachō (exit 4)
Make your reservations when you book your flights. You'll be glad you did; this is perhaps Tokyo's most gracious restaurant, in a former sake brewery moved from northern Japan and plunked down in an exquisite garden in the shadow of Tokyo Tower. Seasonal preparations of the namesake tofu and accompanying dishes are served in more ways than you may have thought possible.

🍸 DRINK

If, at the end of a long day, you need to unwind in a quiet corner nursing a single-malt Scotch, then the lobbies and high-rise bars of Akasaka hotels will serve nicely. But gearing up for a big night out means starting in Roppongi, where you can drink up for cheap in a dive bar, or kick off your evening with a stylish cocktail.

☿ AGAVE アガヴェ *Bar*

☎ 3497 0229; B1F, Clover Bldg, 7-15-10 Roppongi, Minato-ku; ⏱ 6.30pm-2am Mon-Thu, 6.30pm-4am Fri & Sat; Ⓜ Hibiya & Toei Ōedo lines to Roppongi (exit 2)

This amiable spot is for those more interested in savouring the subtleties of its 400-plus varieties of tequila than tossing back shots of Cuervo. Sip an *añejo* (aged tequila) or try one of their margaritas.

☿ BERND'S BAR バーンズバー *Bar*

☎ 5563 9232; www.berndsbar.com; 2F, Pure Roppongi Bldg, 5-18-1 Roppongi, Minato-ku; ⏱ 5pm-late Mon-Sat; Ⓜ Hibiya & Toei Ōedo lines to Roppongi (exit 3)

More a German *izakaya* (pub-eatery) than a bar, the very friendly Bernd's is slightly removed from the mad parade of Roppongi Crossing. Hearty, authentic German food goes with the German draught *bier*. Menus are in German, Japanese and English – languages that the owner speaks with aplomb.

☿ GERONIMO ジェロニモ *Bar*

☎ 3478 7449; www.geronimoshotbar .com; 2F, Yamamuro Bldg, 7-14-10 Roppongi, Minato-ku; ⏱ 6pm-6am Mon-Fri, 7pm-6am Sat & Sun; Ⓜ Hibiya & Toei Ōedo lines to Roppongi (exits 3 & 4)

Geronimo is poised over Roppongi Crossing, making it a logical place to start out a bar crawl through the neighbourhood. The place has a friendly vibe, and if you are feeling superfriendly you can bang on the drum that signals your intention to buy a round for everyone in the bar. *Kampai!*

☿ HEARTLAND ハートランド *Bar*

☎ 5772 7600; 1F, West Walk, Roppongi Hills, 6-10-1 Roppongi, Minato-ku; ⏱ 5pm-4am; Ⓜ Hibiya & Toei Ōedo lines to Roppongi (exits 1c & 3)

OK, so you're a grownup and don't feel like starting your evening in a rowdy, sloppy shot bar, but you have to start somewhere, so head over to Heartland and introduce yourself to Heartland beer and the world of Roppongi-style, Japanese-*gaijin* relations.

☿ MADO LOUNGE マドラウンジ *Lounge*

☎ 3470 0052; www.ma-do.jp; 52F, Mori Tower, 6-10-1 Roppongi Hills, Roppongi,

Minato-ku; cover Sun-Thu ¥500, Fri & Sat ¥2000; ⏱ 10am-11.30pm Sun-Thu, 10am-3am Fri & Sat; 🚇 Hibiya & Toei Ōedo lines to Roppongi (exits 1c & 3)
On the 52nd floor of Mori Tower, the views are indeed stunning from this very cool window lounge. To get in, you'll have to first pay admission to the Mori Art Museum (p67) and/or Tokyo City View, so it's worth the cover only if you're here already.

🍸 MADURO マデュロ *Lounge*
☎ 4333 8888; 4F, Grand Hyatt Tokyo, 6-10-3 Roppongi, Minato-ku; cover around ¥1500; ⏱ 6pm-2am Sun-Thu, 6pm-3am Fri & Sat; 🚇 Hibiya & Toei Ōedo lines to Roppongi (exits 1c & 3)
Make a dramatic entrance to Maduro from the 6th floor over the bridge and pond inside the labyrinthine Grand Hyatt Tokyo. Swanky and sleek, this is a chic spot to start your evening. There's live music nightly, but arrive before 9pm to avoid the cover.

⭐ PLAY

⭐ ABBEY ROAD
アビーロード *Live Music*
☎ 3402 0017; www.abbeyroad.ne.jp; B1F, Roppongi Annex Bldg, 4-11-5 Roppongi, Minato-ku; cover ¥1600-2100; ⏱ 6pm-midnight Mon-Thu, 6pm-1am Fri & Sat; 🚇 Hibiya & Toei Ōedo lines to Roppongi (exits 4a & 7)
Abbey Road is one of the two Roppongi clubs with uncannily good

live Beatles tribute bands. Pull up a chair and prepare to be flabbergasted by the house Beatles cover bands – all Japanese, all seriousness, and appearances aside, pretty dang impressive. Aside from the cover, there's a two-drink minimum. Book ahead if you can, especially at weekends.

⭐ ALFIE *Live Music*
http://homepage1.nifty.com/live/alfie; 5F 6-2-35 Roppongi Minato-ku; 🚇 Hibiya & Toei Ōedo lines to Roppongi (exit 1)
Not to be confused with Alife, this one of Roppongi's finest jazz venues. Soft amber lighting melts over the lounge singers while patrons nurse their cocktails.

⭐ BILLBOARD LIVE *Rock*
www.billboard-live.com; 4F Tokyo Midtown 9-7-4 Akasaka, Minato-ku; 🚇 Hibiya & Toei Ōedo lines to Roppongi, (exit 7)
This glitzy amphitheatre-like space in Tokyo Midtown plays host to foreign talent like Steely Dan, The Beach Boys and Arrested Development. Japanese jazz, soul and rock groups also shake the rafters. The service is excellent and the drinks reasonably priced.

⭐ BLUE NOTE ブルーノート
Live Music
☎ 5485 0088; www.bluenote.co.jp; Raika Bldg, 6-3-16 Minami-Aoyama, Minato-ku; cover ¥6000-10,000;

⏰ 5.30pm-1am Mon-Sat, 5pm-12.30am Sun; ⓜ Chiyoda, Ginza & Hanzōmon lines to Omote-sandō (exit B3)
Serious cognoscenti roll up at Tokyo's prime jazz spot, where you can get up close and personal with such greats as Maceo Parker and Chick Corea. From Roppongi-dōri, head up Kotto-dōri and hang a right at the 6th alley up.

⭐ BUL-LET'S ブレッツ *Club*
☎ 3401 4844; www.bul-lets.com; B1F, Kasumi Bldg, 1-7-11 Nishi-Azabu, Minato-ku; cover from ¥1500; ⓜ Hibiya & Toei Ōedo lines to Roppongi (exits 2 & 3)
This mellow basement space plays trance and ambient sounds for barefoot patrons. Beds and sofas await for those who need a soft spot. But don't get the wrong idea, it's not all lazy tranquillity. Get your groove on to live electronica and experimental rhythms.

⭐ CAVERN CLUB
キャヴァンクラブ
Live Music
☎ 3405 5207; www.cavernclub.jp; 1F, Saito Bldg, 5-3-2 Roppongi, Minato-ku; cover women/men ¥1575/1890; ⏰ 6pm-2.30am; ⓜ Hibiya & Toei Ōedo lines to Roppongi (exit 3)
Eerily flawless renditions of Beatles covers, sung by four Japanese mop-heads called the Silverbeats, have to be heard to be believed. This club is named for the place

where the Beatles first appeared in Liverpool. Reserve a table ahead.

⭐ CLUB 328 三二八 *Club*
☎ 3401 4968; www.3-2-8.jp; B1F, Kotsu Anzen Center Bldg, 3-24-20 Nishi-Azabu, Minato-ku; cover ¥2000-2500; ⏰ 8pm-5am; ⓜ Hibiya & Toei Ōedo lines to Roppongi (exits 1c & 3)
DJs at San-ni-pa (aka San-ni-hachi) spin a quality mix, from funk to reggae to R&B. With its refreshing un-Roppongi feel and a cool crowd of Japanese and *gaijin*, 328 is a good place to boogie 'til the break of dawn. Two drinks are included with the cover.

⭐ ELEVEN *Nightclub*
www.go-to-eleven.com; Thesaurus Nishiazabu B1/B2 1-10-11 Nishi-azabu, Minato-ku; ⓜ Hibiya & Toei Odeo lines to Roppongi (exit 2)
Notorious party box 'Yellow' is back with a vengeance as 'eleven' and it's still as hot as ever. Dive down to the lower basement and dance the night away to mostly house and techno beats.

⭐ FESTA IIKURA *Karaoke*
www.festa-iikura.com; 1F-2F Amerex Bldg 3-5-7 Azabudai, Minato-ku; 3hr room & set meal ¥4515-7350; ⏰ 5pm-5am Mon-Sat; ⓜ Toei Odeo line to Azabu-Juban
Kill two *tori* with one stone and savour some sushi while singing

your heart out. Excellent service and complimentary costume rentals make this one of the best places to perfect your rendition of 'My Sharona' – we know you've been practising…

⭐ LOVENET ラブネット

Karaoke

☎ 5771 5511; www.lovenet-jp.com; 3F, Hotel Ibis, 7-14-4 Roppongi, Minato-ku; private ste ¥4000-60,000; ⏰ 6pm-5am; 🚇 Hibiya & Toei Ōedo lines to Roppongi (exit 4a)

Over-the-top, imaginatively themed private karaoke rooms range from more modest Arabian Suite to the Aqua Suite, whose drawcard is the Jacuzzi tub from which guests can warble their favourite hits. This is karaoke as only Roppongi can make it. Lovenet also has a full menu and bar to fuel your vocal exertions.

⭐ MUSE ミューズ *Club*

☎ 5467 1188; www.muse-web.com; 4-1-1 Nishi-Azabu, Minato-ku; cover ¥3000; ⏰ 7pm-late Sun-Mon, 9pm-late Tue-Thu & Sat, 8pm-late Fri; 🚇 Hibiya & Toei Ōedo lines to Roppongi (exits 1b & 3)

With a friendly, international crowd, multilevel Muse has something for everyone – packed dance floor, several bar areas, cosy alcoves big enough for two, as well as pool tables, darts and karaoke. Women don't pay the

weekend cover, which includes two drinks.

⭐ NEW LEX-EDO

ニューレックス エドゥ

Club

☎ 3479 7477; www.newlex-edo.com; B1F, Gotō Bldg, 3-13-14 Roppongi, Minato-ku; cover women/men ¥3000/4000; ⏰ 8pm-5am; 🚇 Hibiya & Toei Ōedo lines to Roppongi (exit 3)

The Lex has forever been the club where visiting celebrities turn up, and though it's recently had a bit of a facelift, the scene retains its laid-back, fun atmosphere. Cover (waived if you've had your visage on the cover of *Vogue* or *Rolling Stone*) includes three free drinks.

⭐ STB 139 *Live Music*

☎ 5474 1395; http://stb139.co.jp; 6-7-11 Roppongi, Minato-ku; cover ¥3000-7000; ⏰ 6-11pm Mon-Sat; 🚇 Hibiya & Toei Ōedo lines to Roppongi (exit 3)

A two-minute walk south of Roppongi station, this is a large, lovely space that draws similarly big-name acts. Performances are predominantly jazz, covering the spectrum from acid to big band. Even if the act is unknown to you, the ambience will be wonderful and the standards high. Call for reservations between 11am and 8pm.

TOYLETS

Japan has long been number one when it comes to number twos. And now, Sega is taking things to a new level in the men's WC with a gaming console that partners peeing and points. These 'toylets' are making a splash with four programs including one that lifts a woman's skirt à la Marilyn Monroe. It's fairly straightforward – the longer you pee, the higher your score goes; and there's a USB port if you're keeping a running tally.

The best place to test these out is at the Sega Megastore in Akihabara (map pp46–7, F2). Displays are currently in kanji – if you can read Japanese, then urine luck.

⭐ **VANITY** *Nightclub*
www.vanitylounge.com; 13F 5-5-1 Roppongi, Minato-ku; ⓒ Hibiya & Toei Oedo lines to Roppongi (exit 3)
Perched high above the chaos, Vanity is a new name in Roppongi, blasting Top 40 tunes with amped up bass tracks. Coed go-go dancer teams take to the bar tops encouraging club-goers to drop their drinks and get down. There are the great views of the city when windows aren't fogged up.

>EBISU & MEGURO

There's a decidedly residential vibe in the neighbourhoods of Ebisu and Meguro. And though the area may not pack as much of a punch as, say, the skyscrapers of Shinjuku or the swarms of people in Shibuya, these quieter pockets are the perfect place for a relaxed stroll past chic boutiques and mod iterations of inventive city living.

Ebisu draws its name from the prominent beer manufacturer that once provided a lifeline for most of the neighbourhood's residents, but today the area is undoubtedly upscale. A short zip along the Skywalk from Ebisu station takes you to Yebisu Garden Place, another one of Tokyo's 'micro-cities' with a string of shops and restaurants, hundreds of offices and two museums. Further on, Daikanyama lures locals with its wonderland of swank retail havens in bite-sized form, while Naka-Meguro feels more organic with its parade of riverside hangouts that unfurl under thick cherry-tree trunks.

EBISU & MEGURO

⊙ SEE
Yebisu Beer Museum 1 C3
Meguro Parasitological
   Museum 2 A6
Naka-meguro 3 A3
Naka-Meguro 4 A3
National Institute for
   Nature Study (Shizen
   Kyōiku-en) 5 D4
Tokyo Metropolitan
   Museum of
   Photography 6 C4

🛍 SHOP
Daikanyama 7 A2
Kamawanu 8 A2
Limi Feu 9 A1
MISC 10 A6

🍴 EAT
Ebisu-yokochō 11 C2
Ippūdō 12 C2
Maison Paul Bocuse 13 A2
Tonki 14 C6

🍸 DRINK
Enjoy! House 15 B2
Tableaux Lounge 16 A2
What the Dickens 17 B2

★ PLAY
Air 18 A1
Blues Alley Japan 19 C5
Liquid Room 20 B2
Smash Hits 21 B2
Unit 22 A2
Yebisu Garden Cinema .. 23 C4
Yogajaya 24 A2

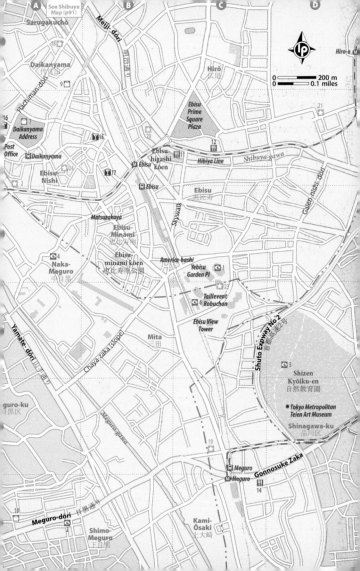

NEIGHBOURHOODS

EBISU & MEGURO

👁 SEE
👁 MEGURO PARASITOLOGICAL MUSEUM
目黒寄生虫館

☎ 3716 1264; http://kiseichu.org
/english.aspx; 4-1-1 Shimo-Meguro,
Meguro-ku; admission free; ⏱ 10am-5pm
Tue-Sun; 🚃 JR Yamanote line to Meguro
(west exit); ♿ 🚻

Some people will *not* find exhibits like the 9m-long tapeworm to their liking, but for others, this tiny museum is gruesomely fascinating. Though there isn't much English signage, kids will get a kick out of the rows of formaldehyde-preserved critters, which are labelled with their Latin names. Upstairs, the gift counter sells parasite-themed keychains and T-shirts.

👁 NAKA-MEGURO
中目黒

🚇 Hibiya line to Naka-meguro

To the untrained eye, 'Nakame' may seem like nothing more than another unholy mishmash of offices, shops and apartments clustered. But insiders know better – over the last few years this vibrant community has grown to become one of the most sought-after areas to live in. Trendy cafes have set up shop along the Meguro-gawa. You'll be spoilt for choice come dinnertime!

👁 NATIONAL INSTITUTE FOR NATURE STUDY
国立自然教育園

☎ 3441 7176; www.ins.kahaku.go.jp
/english/english.html; 5-21-5
Shirokanedai, Minato-ku; admission
¥300/free; ⏱ 9am-4.30pm Sep-Apr,
9am-5pm May-Aug; 🚃 JR Yamanote line
to Meguro (east exit), 🚇 Namboku line to
Shirokanedai (exit 1); ♿ 🚻

Prosaic in name but perfect in nature, this garden (known as Shi-zen Kyōiku-en in Japanese) is one of Tokyo's least known and most appealing getaways. It preserves the city's original flora in undisciplined profusion. Take a walk on Tokyo's wild side through woods and swamps, in this haven for bird-watchers, botanists and those overdosing on urban rhythms.

👁 TOKYO METROPOLITAN MUSEUM OF PHOTOGRAPHY
東京都写真美術館

☎ 3280 0099; www.syabi.com; 1-13-3
Mita, Meguro-ku; admission varies;
⏱ 10am-6pm Tue, Wed, Sat & Sun,
10am-8pm Thu & Fri; 🚃 JR Yamanote
line to Ebisu (east exit to Skywalk)

Japan's first large-scale museum devoted entirely to photography, this wonderfully curated space consists of several galleries. The emphasis is on Japanese photography, but international work is also well represented. As you enter Yebisu Garden Place, the museum

Shop in Euro-style amid the charming green spaces of Yebisu Garden Place

ANTHONY PLUMMER / LONELY PLANET IMAGES ©

is at the very back, towards the right.

YEBISU BEER MUSEUM

www.sapporobeer.jp; 4-20-1 Ebisu; tour (in Japanese) ¥500; 10am-6pm Tue-Sun; JR Yamanote to Ebisu (East exit to Skywalk)

This newly renovated museum details the 120-year history of Yebisu Beer through a series of photographs, artefacts and panels. The museum is free, but guided tours are available for ¥500, and include a drink and intense beer-drinking education session at the Communication Stage. Yes, the guide will teach you the rules of properly holding a beer glass while sipping.

SHOP
DAIKANYAMA 代官山
Boutiques

Tōkyū Tōyoko line to Daikanyama

The geometric wonderland of Daikanyama is a shopper's paradise set on a series of small, rolling hills. There's little to do here besides swiping your plastic and sitting in cafes – but we're not saying that's a bad thing…The neighbourhood eschews big brands in favour of unique boutiques, which means prices are high, but there are some wonderful treasures to be uncovered. Although the area is quite spread out compared to Tokyo's other nooks, the district's

85

NEIGHBOURHOODS

EBISU & MEGURO

core is located around **Daikanyama Address**, a commercial complex known throughout the city for its special evening illuminations.

🏠 KAMAWANU かまわぬ
Handicrafts

☎ 3780 0182; www.kamawanu.co.jp in Japanese; 23-1 Sarugakuchō, Shibuya-ku; ⏰ 11am-7pm; 🚃 JR Yamanote line to Ebisu (west exit) or Tōkyū Tōyoko line to Daikanyama (main exit)

This little shop specialises in beautifully dyed *tenugui*, those ubiquitous Japanese hand towels that you can use to genteelly pat the sweat off the back of your neck, or wrap your *bentō* (boxed meal) in to take with you for lunch.

🏠 MISC *Furniture, Homewares*

Meguro Interior Shops Community; www.misc.co.jp; Meguro-dōri, Meguro-ku; 🚃 JR Yamanote to Meguro (West exit)

Imagine not just one cool boutique but an entire district filled with funky furniture shops, car-boot sale bric-a-brac and hand-me-down treasures. Welcome to MISC – an inviting stretch of pavement linking dozens of interesting storefronts. Favourites include **Moody's** (www.moody-s.net; 4-26-3 Meguro), **Claska** (www.claska.com; 1-3-18 Nakatachō) and **Brunch** (http://brunchone.com; 3-12-7 Meguro). Several quaint cafes lurk about – perfect for your furniture-shopping snack break.

🏠 UNLIMITED BY LIMI FEU
リミフウ *Fashion*

☎ 3463 6324; www.limifeu.com; 7-4 Daikanyamachō, Shibuya-ku; ⏰ noon-9pm; 🚃 Tōkyū Tōyoko line to Daikanyama

Though she changed her surname from her famous father's (Yohji Yamamoto, that is), his deconstructionist influence certainly informs her designs. At the same time, Limi Feu has created her own distinct, streetwise style that appeals to women with a Daikanyama aesthetic.

🍴 EAT

🍴 EBISU-YOKOCHŌ *Street* ¥¥

www.ebisu-yokocho.com; 1-7-4 Ebisu, Shibuya-ku; 🚃 JR Yamanote line to Ebisu

Ebisu is full of upscale options, so this covered cluster of street-food stalls comes as a very welcome surprise. Inside you'll find everything from raw horsemeat to *okonomiyaki* – and it's all served up in quaint, sociable pods that overflow amid clanging pots and billowy smoke.

🍴 IPPŪDŌ 一風堂 *Rāmen* ¥

☎ 5420 2225; 1-3-13 Hiroo, Shibuya-ku; ⏰ 11am-4pm; 🚃 JR Yamanote line to Ebisu (east exit), 🚇 Hibiya line to Ebisu (exits 1 & 2); 🚼

Nationally famous, this *rāmen* shop specialises in *tonkotsu* (pork broth) noodles. While the *akamaru rāmen* (rich pork broth with red seasoning oil) is tailored towards the Tokyo palate, the *shiromaru* (milder, 'white' pork broth) is pure Kyūshū (grate fresh garlic over it for authenticity). You'll have to queue at peak periods and, as a courtesy, should take no more than 20 minutes to eat, but it's well worth it.

🍴 MAISON PAUL BOCUSE
French   ¥¥¥¥
☎ 5468-6324; www.paulbocuse.jp; B1F Daikanyama Forum 17-16 Sarugakucho, Shibuya-ku; ⬤ Tōkyū Tōyoko line to Daikanyama (Main exit)
Celebrity chef and Michelin star collector Paul Bocuse makes a splash in the heart of Daikanyama with his classic French fare. Try the truffle soup, said to have launched chef Bocuse's career. There's a second branch at the National Art Center (p70) in Roppongi.

🍴 TONKI とんき
Tonkatsu   ¥¥
☎ 3491-9928; 1-1-2 Shimo-Meguro, Meguro-ku; ⬤ dinner only Wed-Mon, closed 3rd Mon each month; 🚉 JR Yamanote to Meguro (West exit)
You know a place is doing something right when it offers only three choices – all different types of *tonkatsu*. The service is practically a science – the cooks

have the seating order memorised so hunker down on any of the benches behind the bar stools. After a wait, your perfectly prepared meal will arrive with rice, cabbage and miso soup.

🍸 DRINK
🍸 TABLEAUX LOUNGE *Bar*
www.lounge.tableaux.jp; B1 11-6 Sarugakucho, Shibuya-ku; 🚉 Tōkyū Tōyoko line to Daikanyama
If you love jazz, wine and cigars, Tableaux is the perfect spot to mix all three under chandeliers and stuffed bookshelves. Drinks start at ¥1000 and the band from 9.30pm. Oysters and Cohibas are also on offer. It's next door to the popular Tableaux restaurant.

🍸 WHAT THE DICKENS
ワットザディケンズ *Pub*
☎ 3780 2099; www.whatthedickens.jp; 4F, Roob 6 Bldg, 1-13-3 Ebisu-Nishi, Shibuya-ku; ⏰ 5pm-late Tue-Sat, 5pm-midnight Sun; 🚉 JR Yamanote line to Ebisu (west exit), ⬤ Hibiya line to Ebisu (exit 2)
One of Tokyo's better British-style pubs, this one has a pleasant, spacious feel, and there's usually a band in the corner playing mellow music. Good tunes, hearty pub food and Guinness on tap – what more could you want?

⭐ PLAY

⭐ AIR エアー *Club*

☎ 5784 3386; www.air-tokyo.com; B1F & B2F, Hikawa Bldg, 2-11 Sarugakuchō, Shibuya-ku; 🚃 Tōkyū Tōyoko line to Daikanyama (main exit) or JR Yamanote line to Shibuya (south exit)

DJs spin mostly house here, and the crowd tends to be happy and friendly – though not huge on dancing. Air is in an alley northwest of Hachiman-dōri, south of Shibuya station; there's a decent map on the website. The entrance to the basement is inside Frames restaurant. Remember to bring your ID.

⭐ BLUES ALLEY JAPAN ブルースアレイ日本 *Live Music*

☎ 5496 4381; www.bluesalley.co.jp, in Japanese; B1F, Hotel Wing International, 1-3-4 Meguro, Meguro-ku; cover from ¥3500; 🕐 2pm-midnight Mon-Sat; 🚃 JR Yamanote line to Meguro (west exit)

The name pretty well sums it up – this is the relaxed little place you want to come to if blues is more your speed than hip-hop. Most who appear here are highly regarded Japanese blues musicians, with the occasional jazz act thrown into the mix for good measure.

⭐ LIQUID ROOM リキッドルーム *Live Music*

☎ 5464 0800; www.liquidroom.net; 3-16-6 Higashi, Shibuya-ku; cover from ¥3000; 🕐 7pm-late; 🚃 JR Yamanote line to Ebisu (east exit)

Some of the world's greatest performers have graced the stage of the Liquid Room, from the Flaming Lips to Linton Kwesi Johnson. This spacious place in Ebisu is an excellent place to see an old favourite or find a new one.

⭐ SMASH HITS スマシヒッツ *Karaoke*

☎ 3444 0432; www.smashhits.jp; B1F, M2 Hiro-o Bldg, 5-2-26 Hiro-o, Shibuya-ku; admission ¥3500; 🕐 7pm-3am Mon-Sat; Ⓜ Hibiya line to Hiro-o (exit B2)

Watch your friends wince as you deafen them with the Sid Vicious version of 'My Way'. Smash Hits provides excruciating fun of the highest order, with 12,000 English-language songs to choose from for your 15 minutes of fame. There's no time limit, and the cover includes two drinks.

⭐ UNIT ユニット *Club*

☎ 5459 8630; www.unit-tokyo.com; B1F-B3F, Za House Bldg, 1-34-17 Ebisu-Nishi, Shibuya-ku; cover from ¥3000; 🕐 vary; 🚃 Tōkyū Tōyoko line to Daikanyama, Ⓜ Hibiya line to Naka-Meguro

This subterranean space contains a restaurant, club and bar on each descending floor. Shows are mostly big-name Japanese DJ events, but bands also play here. Be sure to bring ID to get in.

⭐ YEBISU GARDEN CINEMA
恵比寿ガーデンシネマ
Cinema

☎ 5420 6161; Yebisu Garden Place, 4-20-2 Ebisu, Shibuya-ku; tickets ¥1800/1000, on 1st day of month ¥1000; ⏰ 10am-11pm; 🚉 JR Yamanote line to Ebisu (east exit to Skywalk)

At Yebisu Garden Place, where you can have a bite beforehand and a cocktail afterwards, this cinema is a good place to catch a variety of films. Patrons are called into the theatre in groups according to ticket numbers (first come, first served), bypassing the usual mad rush for the best seats.

⭐ YOGAJAYA ヨガジャヤ
Yoga

☎ 5784 3622; www.yogajaya.com; 2F, 1-25-11 Ebisu-Nishi, Shibuya-ku; trial class/mat rental ¥1500/300; ⏰ 7am-9.30pm Mon-Fri, 11am-7.30pm Sat & Sun

Mainly Hatha, Ashtanga and Sivananda practices; classes in Japanese and English.

>SHIBUYA

Urban anthropologists will find much of interest in the field here in Shibuya, ground zero for Tokyo youth culture. You've probably seen scenes of Shibuya Crossing before, with the flood of humanity that the green light unleashes every few minutes, beneath the moving screens on buildings towering overhead. Shibuya department stores cater to the turnover of trends consumed by the subcultures cruising the street in packs. The more head-turning tribes include (but are certainly not limited to) *mamba,* the girls with the deep, fake tans, white eye makeup and bleached-blonde hair, who are usually decked out in microminis and tall boots. The *mamba* make up only a subset of *gyaru* (gal) culture, which is driven by consumerism, fashion and Shibuya-kei (Shibuya type) music. *Gyaru* culture splits into other variations, much like the alleys snaking off Shibuya Crossing – and these alleys form their natural habitat. You'll find them in its all-you-can-eat dessert cafes, specialised record shops, *izakaya* (pub-eateries) and clubs, discount shops selling accessories and a million boutiques selling the look of the moment.

SHIBUYA

◎ SEE
Hachikō Statue 1 C4
Love Hotel Hill 2 A4
Parco Factory ....(see 10)
Shibuya Crossing 3 C4
Tepco Electric Energy
    Museum 4 C2

🏠 SHOP
And A 5 C2
Disk Union 6 B3
Loft 7 B3
Mandarake 8 B3
Manhattan Records 9 B3
Parco I 10 B3
Parco II 11 B3
Parco III 12 B3
Ragtag 13 B3
Recofan ....(see 8)
Shibuya 109..............14 B4

Shibuya Publishing &
    Booksellers 15 A2
Three Minutes
    Happiness 16 B3
Tōkyū Hands 17 B3
Tower Records 18 C3

🍴 EAT
Den Rokuen-Tei ....(see 10)
Kaikaya 19 A4
Nabezo 20 B3
Sakana-tei 21 A4
Toriyoshi 22 B4
Tsukiji Honten 23 B3

▼ DRINK
Beat Café 24 A3
Chestnut & Squirrel ...25 D4
Nonbei-yokochō 26 C3
Pink Cow 27 D3

⭐ PLAY
Bunkamura Theatre
    Cocoon 28 A3
Cine Amuse East &
    West 29 A3
Cinema Rise 30 A3
Club Asia 31 A4
Club Quattro 32 B3
Harlem 33 A4
JZ Brat 34 B5
Kanze Nō-gakudō
    (Kanze Nō Theatre) ...35 A3
La.mama 36 B4
Ruby Room 37 B4
Shibuya O-East 38 A4
Shibuya O-West 39 A4
Tokyo Metropolitan
    Children's Hall 40 C3
Womb 41 A4

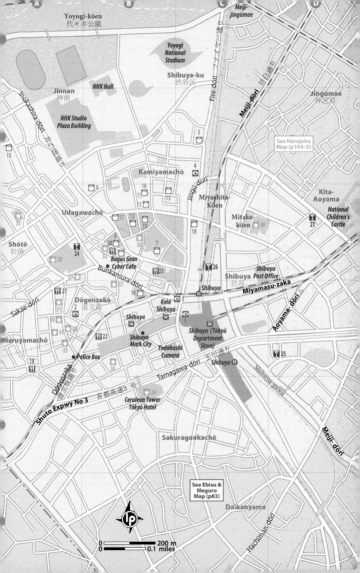

◉ SEE
◉ HACHIKŌ STATUE
ハチ公像

Outside the Hachikō exit of the Shibuya JR station is that exit's namesake and most famous meeting spot: the Hachikō statue (below). While the story behind it is poignant, its function as a meeting place is logical.

◉ LOVE HOTEL HILL

Around the top of Dōgenzaka is the highest concentration of love hotels in Tokyo. While it is ostensibly a place for amorous couples, you could keep it in mind as a good place to crash if you're out late in the area; rates are reasonable for overnight stays (see opposite).

◉ PARCO FACTORY
パルコファクトリー

☎ 3477 5873; www.parco-art.com; 6F, Parco Part 1, 15-1 Udagawachō, Shibuya-ku; admission; ⏱ 10am-9pm; 🚃 JR Yamanote line to Shibuya (Hachikō exit)

WORTH THE TRIP

A hipster's dream, **Hara Museum of Contemporary Art** (; 4-7-25 Kitashinagawa, Shinagawa-ku; admission ¥1000; ⏱ 11am-5pm Tue-Sun, to 8pm Wed; 🚃 JR Yamanote to Shinagawa, Takanawa exit) is a mansion turned unconventional art space, with rotating exhibits and a clutch of permanent wonders (including an installation by Morimura Yasumasa). As well as the fascinating architecture and exhibits, the building itself has a colourful history – in a former life it housed the Sri Lankan Embassy and American occupation soldiers. Explore all the nooks and crannies, then hit up the fantastic cafe and inspired gift shop.

In line with the neighbourhood vibe, this gallery favours contemporary art with a pop-culture flavour. Recent exhibitions have included a retrospective of *otaku* god Bome's figure sculptures, works inspired by the deceased 'Father of Anime' Osamu Tezuka and a toy exhibition.

A DOG'S LIFE

In the 1920s a professor who taught at what is now Tokyo University kept a small Akita dog named Hachikō. Hachikō accompanied the professor to Shibuya Station every morning, then returned in the afternoons to await the professor's arrival. One spring day in 1925, the professor died of a stroke while at the university and never came home. Hachikō continued to turn up at the station daily to wait for his master, until Hachikō's own death 10 years later. The dog's faithfulness touched the locals, who built a statue to honour his memory in the place where he died. Nowadays, Hachikō's statue is a favourite meeting spot so, fittingly, he's usually surrounded by people waiting for their someones.

LOVE HOTELS

These days, Japan's famous love hotels are more politely referred to as 'boutique' or 'fashion' hotels. There's a love hotel for everyone, from miniature Gothic castles to Middle Eastern temples…and these are just the buildings – some room themes can be even more outrageous. Some hotels are now catering more to Japanese women's tastes (think pink and cute). Although they're most highly concentrated on Love Hotel Hill (opposite), there are love hotels in most districts. Peek into a few of the entrances to check out the screen with illuminated pictures of available rooms; some lobbies even have vending machines selling sex toys. You can stay for a 'rest' of several hours, but if you want to stay overnight, check-in is usually after 9pm or 10pm and the rates are fairly inexpensive (around ¥8000). Same-sex couples might have trouble checking in, but insisting that you're *tomodachi* (friends) may get you in.

ⓒ SHIBUYA CROSSING

The first thing you'll notice in Shibuya is the astonishing amount of human traffic. Swarms of locals mill about at all times of the day – Shibuya Crossing, the area's centrepiece, is one of the world's busiest intersections with an estimated 100,000 people passing through every hour! It's worth pausing for a moment to take in a bird's-eye view of the crowds from the easily spotted Starbucks.

ⓒ TEPCO ELECTRIC ENERGY MUSEUM 電力館

☎ 3477 1191; 1-12-10 Jinnan, Shibuya-ku; admission free; ⓧ 10am-6pm Thu-Tue; 🚇 JR Yamanote line to Shibuya (Hachikō exit); ♿ 🚻
This is one of Tokyo's better science museums, offering seven floors of dynamic exhibitions on every conceivable aspect of electricity and its production. There are innumerable hands-on

displays and an excellent, free English handout that explains everything.

🛍 SHOP

There must be a hundred record shops in Udagawachō alone, many focusing on one genre of music. Their stacks usually include rare vinyl, releases available in Japan only and the standard fare you would expect to find in that reggae/Motown/fill-in-the-blank specialist.

🛍 DISK UNION

ディスクユニオン *Music*
☎ 3476 2627; http://diskunion.net, in Japanese; 30-7 Udagawachō, Shibuya-ku; ⓧ 11.30am-9pm; 🚇 JR Yamanote line to Shibuya (Hachikō exit)
The Disk Union chain sells used and new records here at its location on Center-gai. Each floor specialises in a different genre, including punk and jazz. There's

93

NEIGHBOURHOODS

SHIBUYA

another large branch in Shinjuku (p123) and smaller outposts elsewhere in Tokyo.

🏠 LOFT ロフト
Homewares & Novelties

☎ 3462 3807; 21-1 Udagawachō, Shibuya-ku; ⏰ 10am-9pm; 🚶 JR Yamanote line to Shibuya (Hachikō exit)
Insert expendable income here. Loft offers an enormous range of useful goodies such as silk washcloths, sleek furniture and brightly coloured kitchenware, but the best merchandise is the goofier stuff, such as shoe fresheners shaped like smiley-faced hedgehogs, mobile-phone charms and other seductive silliness. It has another branch in Ikebukuro (p132).

🏠 MANDARAKE まんだらけ
Books

☎ 3477 0777; www.mandarake.co.jp; B2F, Shibuya Beam Bldg, 31-2 Udagawachō, Shibuya-ku; ⏰ noon-8pm; 🚶 JR Yamanote line to Shibuya (Hachikō exit)
The Shibuya branch of Mandarake stocks a range of new manga and also boasts performances by real, live *cosplay* (costume-play) kids in full-on *anime* character drag. Avid fans should also make the trek to Mandarake's huge flagship store in Nakano, with three floors packed with all manner of new and used manga, *anime*, games and character-related collectibles.

🏠 MANHATTAN RECORDS
マンハッタンレコード
Music

☎ 3477 7737; 1F, 10-1 Udagawachō, Shibuya-ku; ⏰ noon-9pm; 🚶 JR Yamanote line to Shibuya (Hachikō exit)
Rifle through the records in Manhattan for hip-hop and a look at the flyers for local club schedules. There's also a cluster of record shops down the alleys on either side of the Manhattan building, so shop around a bit.

🏠 PARCO 1, 2 & 3
パルコパート1, 2&3
Department Store

☎ 3464 5111; 15-1 Udagawachō, Shibuya-ku; ⏰ 10am-8.30pm; 🚶 JR Yamanote line to Shibuya (Hachikō exit)
If you see it strutting across Shibuya Crossing, you'll find some version of it at Parco parts 1, 2 and 3. These interconnected department stores are mostly targeted toward fans of Vivienne Westwood and to other designers favouring the schoolgirl look. They also have art galleries that feature multimedia installations, avant-garde painting and fashion-oriented exhibitions.

🏠 RAGTAG *Fashion*

☎ 3476 6848; www.ragtag.jp; 1-17-7 Jinnan, Shibuya-ku; ⏰ noon-9pm; 🚶 JR Yamanote line to Shibuya (Hachikō exit)

SHOPPING IN SHIMO-KITAZAWA

'Shimokita' (www.shimokitazawa.org; Ⓜ Odakyū line to Shimo-kitazawa) is a trendy alternative to overexposed neighbourhoods such as Harajuku. Look closely and you'll find some hipster treasures hidden down crooked alleyways and crammed basements. Try:

Shimokita Garage Department (2-25-8 Kitazawa) An unconventional space putting an interesting spin on the department store with rentable cubbies for local artisans to sell their wares, be they jewellery or scarves. Secondhand clothes are also on sale.

Haight & Ashbury (2-37-2 Kitazawa) Like the forgotten closet of a chain-smoking drag queen, H&A provides all the costumes you'd need to re-enact almost any theatrical number, from the goatherd scene in *The Sound of Music* to the opening act of *Cabaret*.

Village Vanguard (2-10-15 Kitazawa) The hipster's answer to Don Quijote (p123) is crammed just as tight, but the collection is more offbeat and playful.

New York Joe Exchange (3-26-4 Kitazawa) Quality hand-me-downs line this converted *sentō*.

Hitting the secondhand shops of Tokyo is a great strategy for your wallet not to take such a hit. Ragtag is one reliable source for upmarket finds, particularly for Japanese-designer labels, for both men and women.

🏠 RECOFAN レコファン
Music

☎ 5454 0161; www.recofan.co.jp; 4F, Shibuya Beam Bldg, 31-2 Udagawachō, Shibuya-ku; 🕙 11.30am-9pm; 🚇 JR Yamanote line to Shibuya (Hachikō exit)

With several branches around town, this arm of Recofan stocks a wide variety of music, including folk, soul, J-pop and reggae. Between this store and the Mandarake (opposite) shop in the basement, you could lose several hours in here.

🏠 SHIBUYA 109 渋谷１０９
Department Store

☎ 3477 5111; 2-29-1 Dōgenzaka, Shibuya-ku; 🕙 10am-9pm Mon-Fri, 11am-10.30pm Sat & Sun; 🚇 JR Yamanote line to Shibuya (Hachikō exit)

Shibuya 109 is the department store selling the trends *du jour* of Shibuya's youth culture, whether it's the minidresses in blindingly saturated colours for the *gyaru* set or the bunched-up ankle socks the schoolgirls are so fond of pairing with their tiny skirts.

🏠 SHIBUYA PUBLISHING & BOOKSELLERS *Books*

www.shibuyabooks.net; 17-3 Kamiyamachō, Shibuya-ku; 🕙 noon-10pm; 🚇 JR Yamanote to Shibuya

The ultimate neighbourhood bookstore offering those difficult-to-find treasures, this eclectic

NEIGHBOURHOODS

SHIBUYA

bookseller also publishes its own volumes, offers editing and design workshops, and holds monthly thematic exhibits.

THREE MINUTES HAPPINESS
Homewares & Novelties

☎ 5459 1851; 3-5 Udagawachō, Shibuya-ku; ⏰ 11am-9pm; 🚇 JR Yamanote line to Shibuya (Hachikō exit)
Three minutes' worth is guaranteed, but your mileage may vary. This discount shop sells clothes out of decommissioned grocery-store freezers, and makes the shopping experience fun as well as cheap. Downstairs are clothes, shoes and accessories, while lurking upstairs are inexpensive homewares and kitchen knick-knacks.

TŌKYŪ HANDS
東急ハンズ
Homewares & Novelties

☎ 5489 5111; 12-18 Udagawachō, Shibuya-ku; ⏰ 10am-8.30pm; 🚇 JR Yamanote line to Shibuya (Hachikō exit)
Although this branch is a little more cramped than the one at Takashimaya Times Square, this detracts not at all from the appeal of the wonderful wares. Other stores can be found in Shinjuku (p124) and Ikebukuro (p136).

TOWER RECORDS
タワーレコード *Music*

☎ 3496 3661; 7F, Tower Records Bldg, 1-22-14 Jinnan, Shibuya-ku;

ANTHONY PLUMMER / LONELY PLANET IMAGES ©
Shop for shark suits and novelties at Tōkyū Hands

⏰ 10am-11pm; 🚇 JR Yamanote line to Shibuya (Hachikō exit)
Yep, it's a chain, but this Tower is Tokyo's largest music store. Despite its size, this place gets packed. Tower also carries a large selection of English-language books and an extensive array of magazines and newspapers from around the world. Magazines here are considerably cheaper than elsewhere around town.

🍴 EAT
🍴 DEN ROKUEN-TEI
デンロクエンテイ
Asian Fusion   ¥¥

☎ 6415 5489; 8F, Parco Part 1, 15-1 Udagawacho, Shibuya-ku; ⏰ 11am-

midnight; 🚇 JR Yamanote line to Shibuya (Hachikō exit)
Modern twists on seasonally changing Japanese *izakaya* dishes are matched with an array of wine, beer and sake cocktails. Private tatami (woven floor matting) rooms are available, but at this relaxed, stylish perch on the top of Parco 1, the lovely open-air terrace is the prime property.

🍴 KAIKAYA 開花屋
Izakaya   ¥¥

☎ 3770 0878; www.kaikaya.com; 23-7 Maruyamachō, Shibuya-ku; ⌚ 11.30am-3pm & 5-11pm Mon-Fri, 11.30am-11pm Sat; 🚇 Keiō Inokashira line to Shinsen (main exit) 🚇 JR Yamanote line to Shibuya (Hachikō exit)
This friendly *izakaya* is a little tricky to find, but once you're there you'll be rewarded by its friendly atmosphere and excellent, seasonal fish dishes that use fusion elements without losing too much of the food's essential Japanese strengths. Also, happily, this place has an English menu. Walking along Dōgenzaka away from Shibuya station, turn right at the police box and ask for directions.

🍴 NABEZO *Shabu-shabu*   ¥¥
☎ 3461-2941; http://nabezo.jp; Beams 6F 31-2 Udagawachō, Shibuya-ku; ⌚ dinner; 🚇 JR Yamanote line to Shibuya, Hachikō exit

The Shibuya branch of this all-you-can-eat chain is a great spot for first-timers to try *shabu-shabu*. Diners are given two hours to dunk as many slices of raw pork and beef as they can into the gurgling pot at the centre of the table.

🍴 SAKANA-TEI 酒菜亭
Izakaya   ¥¥

☎ 3780 1313; 4th fl, Koike Bldg, 2-23-15 Dōgenzaka, Shibuya-ku; ⌚ 5.30-11pm Mon-Sat; 🚇 JR Yamanote line to Shibuya (Hachikō exit)
This unpretentious but slightly posh *izakaya* is a sake specialist much sought after by connoisseurs, and is good value for the quality. Though there's no English menu, you can point to dishes displayed on the counter, and start with a sampler set of sake. Call ahead for reservations, but turn off your mobile phone once you're in – house rules.

🍴 TORIYOSHI 鳥良
Yakitori   ¥¥

☎ 5784 3373; B1F Sekaido Bldg, 2-10-10 Dōgenzaka, Shibuya-ku; ⌚ 5pm-midnight Mon-Thu, 5pm-4am Fri & Sat; 🚇 JR Yamanote line to Shibuya (Hachikō exit)
Toriyoshi does *yakitori* (skewers of grilled chicken) stepped up a notch in sophistication, pairing it with wine and cocktails without sacrificing its earthy, charcoal-grilled appeal. Set dinners are a good way to try a variety of *yakitori* and tofu.

NEIGHBOURHOODS

SHIBUYA

🍽 TSUKIJI HONTEN
築地本店 *Sushi & Sashimi*   ¥
24-8 Udagawacho, Shibuya-ku; ⏰ lunch
& dinner; 🚇 JR Yamanote line to
Shibuya (Hachikō exit)
When it comes to *kaiten* sushi
(conveyor-belt sushi), it's hard
to beat this local stalwart situ-
ated smack in the middle of the
Shibuya chaos. After a hearty
welcome yell, you'll be escorted
to the benches on the right while
waiting for a stool to open up.
There's a seven-plate minimum.

🍸 DRINK
🍸 BEAT CAFÉ *Bar*
33-13-3 Udagawachō, Shibuya-ku; 🚇 JR
Yamanote line to Shibuya (Hachikō exit)
It's all about the music at this
shabby bar in the centre of the
action. Join an eclectic mix of local
and international regulars who
swig beers and chat beats under
the watchful eyes of taxidermic elk.

🍸 CHESTNUT & SQUIRREL *Bar*
3F Ooishi Bldg 3-7 Shibuya, Shibuya-ku;
⏰ Wed; 🚇 JR Yamanote line to Shibuya
(East exit)
Hugely popular lesbian hang-out
with an international flavour and
English speaking mama-san. The
name is a tricky li'l play on words –
'Chestnut and Squirrel' is *kuri to
risu* in Japanese (say it a few times
fast with your best attempt at a
Japanese accent to recognise the
homophone).

🍸 NONBEI-YOKOCHŌ
Pubs, Lounges
Although Shibuya mainly caters
to teens and 20-somethings, you'll
find an eclectic assortment of pubs
and lounges scattered around,
particular along Nonbei-yokochō –
northeast of the Shibuya station
near the JR tracks. It's Shibuya's
version of Golden Gai (p14) with a
gaggle of cramped bars each seating but a handful of people.

🍸 PINK COW ピンクカウ
Bar
☎ 3406 5597; www.thepinkcow.com;
B1F, Villa Moderna, 1-3-18 Shibuya,
Shibuya-ku; ⏰ 5pm-late Tue-Sun; 🚇 JR
Yamanote line to Shibuya (Hachikō exit)
Pink Cow is a funky, sociable place
where something's always going
on – local artwork adorns the
walls, live music happens, and it
hosts gatherings of venture-capital
seekers and stitch-and-bitchers
(knitting groups) alike. There's
often a cover charge for a special
event. Come for the terrific all-you-
can-eat buffet (¥2800) every Friday
and Saturday evening, and mingle
with an international crowd.

⭐ PLAY
⭐ BUNKAMURA THEATRE COCOON
文化村シアターコクーン
Theatre
☎ 3477 9111; www.bunkamura.co.jp
/english; 2-24-1 Dōgenzaka, Shibuya-ku;

tickets from ¥4000; 🕙 10am-7pm Sun-Thu, 10am-9pm Fri & Sat; 🚊 JR Yamanote line to Shibuya (Hachikō exit); ♿ Bunkamura, a behemoth of an arts centre, houses a cinema, theatre, concert hall and art gallery. Theatre Cocoon provides an intimate space for musical and theatrical performances from a variety of backgrounds, from the innovative to the offbeat traditional. Check the website for info on current productions.

✴ CINE AMUSE EAST & WEST
シネアミューズ *Cinema*
☎ 3496 2888; 2-23-12 Dōgenzaka, Shibuya-ku; tickets ¥1800/1000, ¥1000 on 1st day of month (except Jan); 🕙 10am-11pm; 🚊 JR Yamanote line to Shibuya (Hachikō exit)
Equipped with two screens and an excellent sound system, Cine Amuse has regular screenings of Japanese movies subtitled in English, as well as international releases. It's a small but comfy space, and well placed for post-cinema amusement in Shibuya.

✴ CINEMA RISE
シネマライズ *Cinema*
☎ 3464 0051; 13-17 Udagawachō; tickets ¥1800/1000, ¥1000 on 1st day of month (except Jan); 🕙 10am-11pm; 🚊 JR Yamanote line to Shibuya (Hachikō exit)
Quality independent films are what you'll catch at Cinema Rise, another cinema in the heart of Shibuya.

✴ CLUB ASIA クラブアジア
Club
☎ 5458 2551; www.clubasia.co.jp in Japanese; 1-8 Maruyamachō, Shibuya-ku; cover around ¥2500; 🕙 5pm-5am; 🚊 JR Yamanote line to Shibuya (Hachikō exit)
This massive techno/soul club is worth a visit if you're on the younger end of 20-something. Events here are usually jam-packed every night. If you need some fuel to burn on the dance floor, they have a restaurant serving Southeast Asian food until 10pm.

✴ CLUB QUATTRO
クラブクアトロ *Live Music*
☎ 3477 8750; www.club-quattro.com /schedule_shib.php in Japanese; 4F & 5F, Parco Quattro Bldg, 32-13 Udagawachō, Shibuya-ku; cover varies; 🕙 6pm-late; 🚊 JR Yamanote line to Shibuya (Hachikō exit)
Club Quattro is an established showcase venue for local and international rockers. It's actually in one of the Parco department store buildings (Parco Quattro), which makes for a slightly odd entry. Be sure to buy tickets in advance.

✴ HARLEM *Club*
☎ 3461 8806; www.harlem.co.jp; 2F & 3F, Dr Jeekahn's Bldg, 2-4 Maruyamachō, Shibuya-ku; cover ¥2000-3000; 🕙 10pm-5am Tue-Sat; 🚊 JR Yamanote line to Shibuya (Hachikō exit)
On the 2nd and 3rd floors of the Dr Jeekahn's Building, this club is

where Tokyo B-boys and B-girls come for soul and hip-hop spun by international DJs. Harlem maintains a policy of not admitting groups of foreign males, so guys, come with a girlfriend.

⭐ JZ BRAT *Live Music*
☎ 5728 0168; www.jzbrat.com in Japanese; 2F, Cerulean Tower Tōkyū Hotel, 26-1 Sakuragaokachō, Shibuya-ku; cover varies; ⏱ from 6pm Mon-Sat; 🚉 JR Yamanote line to Shibuya (south exit)
This sleek jazz club is an intimate venue with a sophisticated vibe, hosting performances not limited solely to jazz, though even the jazz ranges from solo vocalists to improvisational trios. Touring performers of folk and electronica also pass through; check local listings to find out what's on.

⭐ KANZE NŌ-GAKUDŌ 観世能楽堂 *Theatre*
☎ 3469 5241; 1-16-4 Shōtō, Shibuya-ku; tickets from ¥3000; ⏱ times vary; 🚉 JR Yamanote line to Shibuya (Hachikō exit)
This theatre is associated with one of the oldest and most highly respected schools of *nō* (classical Japanese musical drama) in Tokyo. By far the most exciting performances are the occasional outdoor night ones of Takigi Nō, where the masked actors are illuminated by huge burning torches. It's a transporting experience, only a 15-minute walk from Shibuya station.

⭐ LA.MAMA ラママ *Live Music*
☎ 3464 0801; www.lamama.net, in Japanese; B1F, Primera Dogenzaka Bldg, 1-15-3 Dōgenzaka, Shibuya-ku; cover from ¥2000; ⏱ 6pm-late; 🚉 JR Yamanote line to Shibuya (Hachikō exit)
For a dose of current local-centric music, La.mama is a good bet for catching live, mainstream Japanese acts. The room is fairly spacious, but even when the place gets crowded you'll be close enough to get be-sweated by the next rising star out of Tokyo.

⭐ RUBY ROOM ルビルーム *Lounge*
☎ 3780 3022; www.rubyroomtokyo.com; 2F, Kasumi Bldg, 2-25-17 Dōgenzaka, Shibuya-ku; cover ¥2000; ⏱ 9pm-late; 🚉 JR Yamanote line to Shibuya (Hachikō exit)
This cool, sparkly gem of a cocktail lounge is on the hill behind the 109 Building. With both DJed and live music, the Ruby Room is an appealing spot for older kids hanging in Shibuya. The cover includes one drink, but if you dine downstairs at Sonoma, admission is free. There's a simple map with directions on their website.

⭐ SHIBUYA O-EAST 渋谷オーイースト *Live Music*
☎ 5458 4681; www.shibuya-o.com; 2-14-8 Dōgenzaka, Shibuya-ku; cover from ¥2500; ⏱ 7pm-late; 🚉 JR Yamanote line to Shibuya (Hachikō exit)
One of an empire of 'O' clubs on Love Hotel Hill, O-East is the most

massive, playing host to well-known Japanese and international performers. You'll need to book ahead, as this is a popular place that tends to sell out.

⭐ SHIBUYA O-WEST
渋谷オーウエスト *Live Music*

☎ 5784 7088; www.shibuya-o.com; 2-3 Maruyamachō, Shibuya-ku; cover from ¥2500; ⏰ 7pm-late; 🚇 JR Yamanote line to Shibuya (Hachikō exit)
Another outpost in the 'O' empire of Shibuya TV, O-West is just across the street from its eastern counterpart and tends more towards punk rock and J-pop. As with its sister club, reserve your tickets in advance.

⭐ TOKYO METROPOLITAN CHILDREN'S HALL
東京都児童会館
Amusement Park

☎ 3409 6361; www.fukushihoken .metro.tokyo.jp/jidou/English/index.html; 1-18-24 Shibuya, Shibuya-ku; admission free; ⏰ 9am-5pm; 🚇 JR Yamanote line to Shibuya (Hachikō exit)
This place has six floors of fun activities for children and, best of all, it's free! At weekends, the rooftop playground is open for romping around. But every day there are age-appropriate art projects, storytelling and music-making, and lots of creative indoor play areas.

⭐ WOMB ウーム *Club*

☎ 5459 0039; www.womb.co.jp, in Japanese; 2-16 Maruyama-chō, Shibuya-ku; cover ¥1500-4000; ⏰ 8pm-late; 🚇 JR Yamanote line to Shibuya (Hachikō exit)
'Oomu' (as pronounced by the Japanese) is all house, techno and drum 'n' bass. The four floors of this place get jammed at weekends. Check Shibuya record shops to pick up a flyer beforehand, or print one from the website, and they'll knock ¥500 to ¥1000 off the cover. Photo ID required at the door.

>HARAJUKU

Travelling from Harajuku to Aoyama takes you from pop culture consumption to upscale, grown-up refinement. From the Harajuku JR station, take the Takeshita exit to Takeshita-dōri, a treasure-trove of teenybopper accessories and hair salons that can kink straight hair into dreads and 'fros. Or exit to Omote-sandō, the boulevard lined with branches of Chanel, Prada and Tokyo's favourite: Louis Vuitton. You'll also come across the slanted walkways of the neighbourhood's newest shopping centre, Omotesandō Hills.

On either side of Omote-sandō, Ura-Hara (a nickname for the back alleys of Harajuku) hides tiny European-style cafes, innovative art galleries, restaurants and boutiques catering both to youth and to moneyed sophisticates. The further southeast you travel down Omote-sandō, the closer you'll get to Aoyama, where internationally recognised home-grown designers have based their flagships. And if your credit card has rolled over and is playing dead, you can at least window-shop and watch the live fashion walking the streets.

HARAJUKU

◉ SEE
Laforet Museum
   Harajuku .... (see 16)
Meiji-jingū 1 C2
Nezu Museum 2 G6
Omote-sandō-dōri 3 E5
Ōta Memorial Art
   Museum 4 D4
Prada Aoyama 5 F5
Spiral Building 6 E5
Watari Museum of
   Contemporary Art 7 F3
Yoyogi-kōen 8 B4

⬜ SHOP
Bapexclusive 9 F5
Chicago 10 D4
Commes des Garçons ..11 D5
Condomania 12 D4
Hysteric Glamour 13 C5

Issey Miyake 14 F5
Kiddyland 15 D5
Laforet 16 D4
On Sundays 17 D3
Oriental Bazaar 18 E4
Pass the Baton 19 E4
Sou-Sou ....(see 24)
Takeshita-dōri 20 D3
Tsukikageya 21 A4
Undercover 22 F6
WE GO 23 D4
Yohji Yamanoto 24 F6

⬛ EAT
A to Z Café 25 E6
Harajuku Gyoza Rō 26 D4
Honoji 27 D4
Kinokuniya 28 E5
Kyūsyū Jangara 29 D4
Le Bretagne 30 E4

Maisen 31 E4
Mominoki House 32 E3
Mother Kurkku 33 E3
Nid Café 34 E3
Ume-no-hana 35 F4

▼ DRINK
Den Aquaroom 36 F6
Tokyo Apartment
   Café ....(see 16)

★ PLAY
Jingū Stadium 37 G2
Le Baron 38 F4
National Stadium 39 F1
Tokyo Metropolitan
   Gymnasium 40 F1

Please see over for map

⊙ SEE
⊙ LAFORET MUSEUM HARAJUKU ラフォーレミュージアム原宿
☎ 6406 6378; www.lapnet.jp/index
.html in Japanese; 6F, Laforet Bldg, 1-11-6
Jingūmae, Shibuya-ku; admission varies;
⏱ 11am-8pm; ☒ JR Yamanote line to
Harajuku (Omote-sandō exit), ⊙ Chiyoda
line to Meiji-jingūmae (exit 5); ♿
This museum, on the 6th floor
of the teenybopper fashionista
mecca that is Laforet department
store, is gallery or performance
space depending on the event.
Small film festivals, art installations
and launch parties are held here
regularly – after browsing the art-
as-streetwear on the floors below,
check out art-as-art upstairs.

⊙ MEIJI-JINGŪ 明治神宮
☎ 3379 5511; www.meijijingu.or.jp;
1-1 Yoyogi Kamizonochō, Shibuya-ku;
admission free; ⏱ dawn-dusk;
☒ JR Yamanote line to Harajuku
(Omote-sandō exit)
In the grounds of Meiji-jingū,
Meiji-jingū-gyoen (admission ¥500/200;
⏱ 9am-4.30pm) is a beautiful garden
created by Emperor Meiji as a gift
for the Empress Shōken. There's
also a **Treasure Museum** (admission ¥300;
⏱ 9am-4pm Sat, Sun & public holidays) on
the grounds, displaying some imperial artefacts such as ceremonial
clothing worn by the emperor and
empress.

⊙ NEZU MUSEUM 根津美術館
☎ 3400 2536; www.nezu-muse.or.jp;
6-5-1 Minami-Aoyama, Minato-ku;
admission ¥1000/700; ⏱ 10am-5pm
Tue-Sun; ⊙ Chiyoda, Ginza, Hanzōmon
lines to Omote-sandō (exits A4 & A5)
Past the Prada Aoyama building
when walking from Omote-sandō,
the Nezu is a welcome refuge from
shopping scene outside. Slatted
planks of wood mark the demure
entrance and, once inside, visitors
will discover a gorgeous collection
of artefacts including a brilliant
gallery of Chinese bronze. The
biggest draw, however, is the lush
garden out back where over-
grown trees shelter four hidden
teahouses.

⊙ OMOTE-SANDŌ-DŌRI
Chiyoda, ⊙ Ginza & Hanzomon line to
Omote-sandō
The Champs-Elysées of Tokyo,
Omote-sandō-dōri is a regal boulevard lined with shade-bestowing
trees and a parade of upscale
fashion houses. As Christmas ap-
proaches, it's here that you'll find
city's most elaborate showcase of
festive lights and ornaments.

⊙ ŌTA MEMORIAL ART MUSEUM 太田記念美術館
☎ 3403 0880; www.ukiyoe-ota-muse.jp
/english.html; 1-10-10 Jingūmae, Shibuya-
ku; admission ¥1000/700 ⏱ 10.30am-
5.30pm Tue-Sun, closed from 27th to end

of each month; 🚆 JR Yamanote line to Harajuku (Omote-sandō exit), Ⓜ Chiyoda line to Meiji-jingūmae (exit 5)
Leave your shoes in the foyer and pad in slippers through this museum to view its stellar collection of ukiyo-e (wood-block prints), which includes works by masters including Hiroshige and Hokusai. There's an extra charge for special exhibits. The museum is up the hill on a narrow road behind Laforet; there's a clear map on the museum's website.

🅲 PRADA AOYAMA
プラダ青山
☎ 6418 0400; 5-2-6 Minami-Aoyama, Minato-ku; ⏰ 11am-8pm; Ⓜ Chiyoda,

Ginza & Hanzōmon lines to Omote-sandō (exits A4 & A5)
Of course you could shop here, but you can also ogle the gorgeous, convex glass bubbles of the exterior. Designed by Herzog & de Meuron, this is one of Aoyama's sexier organic-looking structures.

🅲 SPIRAL BUILDING
スパイラルビル
☎ 3498 1171; 5-6-23 Minami-Aoyama, Minato-ku; admission free; ⏰ 11am-8pm; Ⓜ Chiyoda, Ginza & Hanzōmon lines to Omote-sandō (exit B1); ♿
Its asymmetrical, geometric shape may not look very sinuous on the outside, but the Spiral Building's name will make more sense upon

The dazzling Prada Aoyama building

DESIGN FESTA

Nowadays the biannual Design Festa happens in May and December at the Tokyo International Exhibition Centre, more fondly known as Tokyo Big Sight (p157). Hundreds of young, undiscovered artists and designers, including budding fashion designers, performance artists, filmmakers and musicians, rent spaces in the massive West Hall to reveal the fruits of their creative genius. Design Festa is *the* place to get a good idea of what Tokyo's working artists are doing, and to get your paws on a one-off T-shirt or piece of jewellery. If you're not in town for Design Festa, check out the insanely embellished **Design Festa Gallery** (☎ 3479 1442; www.designfestagallery.com; 3-20-18 Jingūmae, Shibuya-ku; admission free; ⏱ 11am-8pm), which is open year-round except during Design Festa.

entry. The 1st-floor gallery features changing exhibits, shows, dining and a CD-listening station. Check out the shop on the 2nd floor for art books, jewellery, *washi* (handmade paper) and stylishly designed loot.

🄲 WATARI MUSEUM OF CONTEMPORARY ART
ワタリウム美術館

☎ 3402 3001; www.watarium.co.jp, in Japanese; 3-7-6 Jingūmae, Shibuya-ku; ¥1000/800; ⏱ 11am-7pm Tue-Sun; 🄼 Ginza line to Gaienmae (exit 3)
Known as the Watarium, this place showcases lots of brilliant conceptual and performance art, with visiting Scandinavians choreographing ballets involving vacuum-cleaners, and resident Japanese embalming themselves with glue. Ergo, lots of cutting-edge contemporary art can be found here, especially mixed-media art installations.

🄲 YOYOGI-KŌEN
代々木公園

☎ 3469 6081; 2-1 Yoyogi Kamizonochō, Shibuya-ku; admission free; ⏱ 24hr; 🚉 JR Yamanote line to Harajuku (Omote-sandō exit), 🄼 Chiyoda line to Yoyogi-kōen (exit 4); ♿

LINK UP: TOURING TOKYO FOR FREE

Although the language barrier is apparent upon arriving in Tokyo, you might be surprised to learn that there are many groups in the city that show visitors around. Best part? It's free! Advance booking is a must. Check out:
Edo Tokyo Guides (http://blog.goo.ne.jp/edo_tokyo_int)
Free Walking Tour (http://freewalkingtour.org)
Shinagawa SGG Club (www1.cts.ne.jp/~koasa/SGG)
Tokyo SGG Club (www2.ocn.ne.jp/~sgg/introduction.html)
Volunteer Walking Tour Blog (http://volunteerfreewalking.blogspot.com)

NEIGHBOURHOODS

HARAJUKU

The 54 hectares of Yoyogi Park were originally developed as part of the 1964 Olympic Village and was established as a city park in 1967. From the Harajuku JR station, exit right and turn right again, then follow the road along the edge of park until you reach an entry on your right. Across the road, look for the dramatic swooping lines of the National Yoyogi Gymnasium.

🛍 SHOP

🏠 BAPEXCLUSIVE
ベイプエクスクルーシヴ
Fashion

☎ 3407 2145; 5-5-8 Minami-Aoyama, Minato-ku; 🕐 11am-7pm; 🚇 Chiyoda, Ginza, Hanzōmon lines to Omote-sandō (exit A5)

BAPE (A Bathing Ape) is no longer the madly exclusive brand that made it so desirable – this shop is testament to how underground designer Nigo's brand *isn't*, but how wildly successful it's become. BAPE has a dozen or so 'secret', hard-to-find shops around Harajuku and Aoyama; this one's a good starting point for brand fans and architecture buffs.

🏠 CAT STREET *Fashion*
🚇 Chiyoda line to Meiji-jingūmae
A welcome alternative to Takeshita-dōri, this Omote-sandō backstreet is filled with an ever-changing assortment of designer boutiques, many with names that sound like Swedish swear words. The retail architecture is also quite a spectacle, as this is where smaller brands strike their monuments to consumerism if they can't afford to do so on the main drag.

🏠 CHICAGO *Vintage*
www.chicago.co.jp; 6-31-21 Jingūmae, Shibuya-ku; 🕐 11am-8pm; 🚇 Chiyoda line to Meiji-jingūmae (exit 1)
Classic American second-hand clobber never seems to go out of fashion in Tokyo, and Chicago has been the reseller of choice since belly shirts were in fashion. Dig through the racks to find everything from tweed coats to Harvard varsity jerseys.

🏠 COMME DES GARÇONS
コムデギャルソン *Fashion*
☎ 3406 3951; 5-2-1 Minami-Aoyama, Minato-ku; 🕐 11am-8pm; 🚇 Chiyoda, Ginza & Hanzōmon lines to Omote-sandō (exit A4)
When Rei Kawakubo hit international recognition status in the early '80s, it was with her revolutionary, minimalist, matte-black designs. Her lines have evolved from that simple chic, but even with asymmetrical cuts, illusions of torn fabric and sleeves gone missing, her style

Catch the hipsters and cutting-edge fashion of Laforet (p111)

MARTIN MOOS / LONELY PLANET IMAGES ©

is consistently a departure from the norm. This Aoyama architectural wonder is her flagship store.

🄰 CONDOMANIA
コンドマニア

Homewares & Novelties

☎ 3797 6131; 6-30-1 Jingūmae, Shibuya-ku; ⏰ 10.30am-11pm; 🚃 JR Yamanote line to Harajuku (Omote-sandō exit), Ⓜ Chiyoda line to Meiji-jingūmae (exit 4)

Inside this tiny shop you'll find more condoms than you can poke a… stick at. For your love-hotel expeditions or footloose friends back home, pick up enigmatic prophylactics such as the 'Masturbator's Condom' or the more conservative glow-in-the-dark variety.

🄰 HYSTERIC GLAMOUR
ヒステリックグラモー

Fashion

☎ 3409 7227; www.hystericglamour.jp, in Japanese; 6-23-2 Jingūmae, Shibuya-ku; ⏰ 11am-8pm; 🚃 JR Yamanote line to Harajuku (Omote-sandō exit), Ⓜ Chiyoda line to Meiji-jingūmae (exit 4)

It's more attitudinal tongue-in-cheek than hysterical or glamorous, but whatever you want to call it, it's fun stuff spiked generously with that Tokyo flavour. There's even a toddler line, the ultimate in designer punk for your little rocker. Design junkies will want to check out the curvy, futuristic branch at Roppongi Hills.

🏛 ISSEY MIYAKE 三宅一生
Fashion

☎ 3423 1407; 3-18-11 Minami-Aoyama, Minato-ku; ⏰ 10am-8pm; 🚇 Chiyoda, Ginza & Hanzōmon lines to Omote-sandō (exit A4)

Anarchic but wearable conceptual fashion continues to flow from Issey Miyake. At the cluster of Aoyama shops along the south end of Omote-sandō, eye his famous pleated designs, or the A-POC garments – each made from a single piece of fabric. The gallerylike window displays are worth a look, after checking out the many-faceted Prada spaceship down the street.

🏛 KIDDYLAND
キディランド *Toys*

☎ 3409 3431; www.kiddyland.co.jp; 6-14-2 Jingūmae, Shibuya-ku; ⏰ 10am-8pm, closed 3rd Tue of each month; 🚇 Chiyoda line to Meiji-jingūmae (exit 4)

Eep! Three floors of *kawaii* (cute) paraphernalia for your children – or, let's face it, you – to fall in love with. Stuffed with stuffed animals, a candy-store selection of hair baubles, 200-yen toy vending machines, an abundance of Hello Kitty products, plastic action

figures and noisy games, this store can be dangerously tempting (and *very* crowded at weekends). The flagship store along Omote-sandō-dōri is under construction until the end of 2012 – the address above is for the smaller location on Cat Street.

🏛 LAFORET ラフォーレ
Fashion

☎ 3475 0411; 1-11-6 Jingūmae, Shibuya-ku; ⏰ 11am-8pm; 🚉 JR Yamanote line to Harajuku (Omote-sandō exit)

Expressing identity and individuality is a function of fashion, and Tokyo youth are famous for taking this concept to the next level. Sample this in action at Laforet; surveying the shoppers is equal to the window-shopping, and once you've got the hang of the half-floor concept, you can count your way up to the 6th-floor museum (p103).

🏛 ON SUNDAYS *Books*

☎ 3470 1424; www.watarium.co.jp in Japanese; 3-7-6 Jingūmae, Shibuya-ku; ⏰ 11am-8pm Tue-Sun; 🚇 Ginza line to Gaienmae (exit 3)

Connected to Watari Museum of Contemporary Art (p107), On Sundays carries an eclectic collection of avant-garde art for sale. It has a humongous selection of funky to classic postcards, and a marvellous array of functional arthouse objects, such as purses in the shapes of origami balloons and Scandinavian-style office accoutrements. In the basement is a wonderful cafe and bookshop.

🏠 ORIENTAL BAZAAR
オリエンタルバザー
Handicrafts

☎ 3400 3933; 5-9-13 Jingūmae, Shibuya-ku; ⏱ 10am-7pm Thu-Tue; Ⓜ Chiyoda line to Meiji-jingūmae (exit 4)

Set right along the main thoroughfare and noticeably out of place with its gaudy Disney-meets-temple facade, Oriental Bazaar is a decent spot for one-stop shopping if you're looking to buy a variety of different souvenirs. Though the collection of fans, sake sets, *yukata* and pottery can feel a bit uninspired, the prices are surprisingly low considering the store's location.

🏠 PASS THE BATON *Accessories*

www.pass-the-baton.com; B2 Omote-sandō Hills 4-12-10 Jingūmae, Shibuya-ku; Ⓜ Ginza, Chiyoda & Hanzomon lines to Omote-sandō (exit A3)

Representing the new wave in secondhand shopping, Pass the Baton isn't just a shop, it's a museum. Self-described as the 'new recycle', this fascinating space is a veritable treasure trove of once-loved possessions rang-

ing from handmade T-shirts to ornate candelabras. Everything's been meticulously catalogued, so when you purchase your (rather overpriced) item, you'll also inherit its colourful history.

🏠 SOU-SOU そうそう
Fashion

☎ 3407 7877; 2F, from 1st Bldg, 5-3-10 Minami-Aoyama, Minato-ku; ⏱ 11am-8pm; Ⓜ Chiyoda, Ginza, Hanzōmon lines to Omote-sandō (exit A5)

Details matter to Japanese fashionistas – socks included. Contemporary *tabi* (split-toe socks) are sold all over Tokyo in endless patterns and colours. Sou-Sou designs its high-quality *tabi* with playful style, in addition to producing serious footwear like steel-toed, rubber-soled *tabi* worn by Japanese construction workers.

🏠 TAKESHITA-DŌRI *Fashion*
�? JR Yamanote line to Harajuku (Takeshita exit)

Nippon neophytes will chuckle at the name, but the local brigade of Harajuku girls strut down Takeshita-dōri with the utmost seriousness. The human gridlock is bewildering as eager youngsters bounce between boutiques while trying on the latest fashion trends. Crepe stalls, faux hip-hop hagglers, and tonnes of camera-clicking tourists come standard.

NEIGHBOURHOODS

HARAJUKU

⌂ TSUKIKAGEYA 月影屋
Fashion

☎ 3465 7111; www.tsukikageya
.com; 1-9-19 Tomigaya, Shibuya-ku;
🕐 noon-8pm Thu-Mon; Ⓜ Chiyoda line
to Yoyogi-kōen (exit 2)

So you want to go to a *matsuri*
(temple festival) all dolled up in
a traditional *yukata* (cotton kimono), but you're more punk rock
than Hello Kitty? No problem, just
head to Tsukikageya for black-
and-white *yukata*, along with
Swarovski-studded or snakeskin
accessories.

⌂ UNDERCOVER *Fashion*

☎ 3407 1232; 5-3-18 Minami-Aoyama,
Minato-ku; 🕐 11am-8pm; Ⓜ Chiyoda,
Ginza & Hanzōmon lines to Omote-sandō
(exit A5)

Former punk-band frontman Jun
Takahashi's take on youth-minded
streetwear is still pretty crazy after
all this time. His Undercover Lab,
designed by architect Astrid Klein,
is just up and across the street
from Tsumori Chisato.

⌂ WE GO *Clothing*

www.wego.jp; 1F & 2F Iberia Biru 6-5-3
Jingūmae, Shibuya-ku; Ⓜ Chiyoda line
to Meiji-jingūmae (exit 1)

A popular chain with a mixed bag
of new and vintage clothing. This
multistorey outpost features
everything from lens-less nerd
glasses to furry purses.

⌂ YOHJI YAMAMOTO
耀司山本 *Fashion*

☎ 3409 6006; 5-3-6 Minami-Aoyama,
Minato-ku; 🕐 11am-8pm; Ⓜ Chiyoda,
Ginza & Hanzōmon lines to Omote-sandō
(exit A4)

Yohji Yamamoto has maintained
some of the mystique of himself
and his aesthetic, flouting conven-
tion decade after decade in a
mischievous way that keeps his
style fresh – a feat when your
colour of choice is black. He is one
of the locals who has set up house
here in Aoyama.

🍴 EAT

🍴 A TO Z CAFÉ *Cafe* ¥

http://atozcafe.exblog.jp; 5F 5-8-3
Minami-aoyama, Minato-ku; 🕐 lunch &
dinner; Ⓜ Ginza, Chiyoda & Hanzomon
lines to Omote-sandō (exit B3)

A fortuitous partnership between
a local design agency and celebrity artist Yoshitomo Nara, A to
Z mixes country-style wooden
slatting (there's a freestanding
cottage within the cafe) with
white-washed industrial piping
overhead. Seemingly effortless yet
undeniably inviting, this is one of
Aoyama's best chill-out spots, and
the food is delicious too.

🍴 HARAJUKU GYOZA RŌ
原宿餃子楼 *Chinese* ¥

6-4-2 Jingumae, Shibuya-ku; 🕐 lunch &
dinner; Ⓜ Ginza, Chiyoda & Hanzomon
lines to Omote-sandō (exit A2)

This unassuming dumpling station is tucked behind regal Omote-sandō on a quiet backstreet that begins to bustle at mealtime when hoards of lip-lickers line up for the cheap and tasty grub. Look for the kanji on a glowing red sign if you don't see the dozens of people making the queue first.

🍴 HONOJI ほの字

Shokudō ¥¥

http://harajuku.honoji.com; 4F 5-10-1 Jingūmae, Shibuya-ku; ⏰ lunch & dinner; 🚇 Chiyoda line to Meiji-jingūmae (exit 4)

Sharing a building with the likes of Chanel and Bulgari hasn't given Honoji a big head. In fact, this was once an expensive *kaiseki* restaurant that has been transformed into a more modest place. Enjoy fish and croquettes for lunch and skewers for dinner while taking in the amazing views of the city from the floor-to-ceiling windows.

🍴 MOTHER KURKKU *Cafe*

¥

www.kurkku.jp; 2-18-15 Jingūmae, Shibuya-ku; ⏰ lunch & dinner; 🚉 JR Yamanote to Harajuku (Takeshita exit)

Our pick of the Kurkku restaurant trifecta, Mother Fucker – as it's affectionately known by repeat customers – is a sleek space with sky-high ceilings and giant windows. It's popular with the local design crowd who come to

scribble in their Moleskines and down glasses of house wine.

🍴 KINOKUNIYA 紀ノ国屋

International groceries

☎ 3409 1231; www.super-kinokuniya .jp; B1F, AO Bldg, 3-11-7 Kita-Aoyama, Minato-ku; ⏰ 9.30am-9pm; 🚇 Chiyoda, Ginza, Hanzōmon lines to Omote-sandō (exit B2)

Kinokuniya carries expat lifesavers such as Marmite and peanut butter, Belgian chocolate and herbal tea. Foreign imports including cheese, salami and Finnish bread generally fetch high prices, much like the flawless fruit in the produce section. It's moved back to its original location, now in the basement of the glitzy new AO Building.

🍴 KYŪSYŪ JANGARA 九州じゃんがら *Rāmen*

¥

☎ 3404-5572; 1-13-21 Jingūmae, Shibuya-ku; plates ¥600-1050; ⏰ 10.45am-2am Mon-Thu, 10.45am-3am Fri, 10am-3am Sat, 10am-2am Sun; 🚇 🚉 JR Yamanote Line to Harajuku (Omote-Sando exit), 🚇 Chiyoda or Fukutoshin Line to Meiji-jingūmae (exit 3)

There always seems to be a queue for seats outside this Kyūshū-style *rāmen* shop near Harajuku station, and with good reason: elegantly thin noodles, your choice of a half-dozen broths, silky *chashu* (roast pork) and energetic staff.

Shimizu Takashi
Highly acclaimed Japanese movie director, best known internationally for his work on The Grudge.

If there were a Tokyo version of *Paris, Je T'aime*, which neighbourhood would you choose for your chapter? I'd capture a lesser-known side of Tokyo by setting it in Nakano Broadway (p125) or Akihabara (p50) – the '*otaku* meccas', from which *anime* culture is transmitted worldwide. I'd make a bittersweet sci-fi comedy about characters coming of age while idolising superheroes. **What is your favourite film about Tokyo?** *The Demon (Kichiku)*, by Yoshitaro Nomura. I saw this as a child and was traumatised by the scene of a girl abandoned at Tokyo Tower by her father. Still today, passing the tower, I'm struck by this fear of abandonment. Most plotlines in Japanese horror films come from stories from the Edo era. **Which stories would you bring to the screen?** Since my debut with a horror film, I've found that people see me as a horror expert, when actually I was too scared to watch them as a kid! Given my track record, I'd make a version of *Yotsuya Kaidan*, the most famous Japanese ghost story.

🍴 LE BRETAGNE
ル ブ ル ターニュ *French* ¥¥

☎ 3478 7855; 3-5-4 Jingūmae, Shibuya-ku; ⏱ 11.30am-11pm Mon-Sat, 11.30am-10pm Sun; ⊖ Chiyoda, Ginza & Hanzōmon lines to Omote-sandō (exit A2); ♿ Ⓥ

Le Bretagne's wonderful set menus, with their buckwheat *galettes* as the centrepieces, are authentic and filling. The sweet or savoury Breton-style crêpes can also be ordered à la carte for mere pocket change – money well spent on these fresh and tasty creations.

🍴 MAISEN まい泉
Japanese ¥

☎ 3470-0071; 4-8-5 Jingūmae, Shibuya-ku; ⏱ 11am-10pm; ⊖ Chiyoda, Ginza, Hanzōmon lines to Omote-sandō (exit A2)

Maisen is famous for its crispy and tender *tonkatsu* (deep-fried pork cutlets) that draws a continuous crowd. Thankfully, the place occupies a converted bathhouse, so there's plenty of room for the many hungry souls craving Kagoshima *kurobuta* (black pig). If you're on the run, pick up a *bentō* (boxed meal) at the takeaway window.

🍴 MOMINOKI HOUSE
モミノキハウス
Organic Vegetarian ¥¥

☎ 3405 9144; www2.odn.ne.jp /mominoki_house; 1F, YOU Bldg, 2-18-5 Jingūmae, Shibuya-ku; ⏱ noon-10.30pm; ⊖ JR Yamanote line to Harajuku, Takeshita exit); Ⓥ

For herbivorous relief, stop into Mominoki House, where the largely macrobiotic menu covers the vegan to the vegetarian. There's also free-range organic chicken for the carnivorously inclined. The rambling space is cosily welcoming, as is the friendly chef-owner.

🍴 NID CAFÉ *French* ¥¥

☎ 5772-7639; www.ctn139.com; 3F 3-13-23 Minami-aoyama, Minato-ku; ⏱ lunch & dinner; ⊖ Ginza, Chiyoda & Hanzomon lines to Omote-sandō (exit A3)

With the quaintness of a charming Parisian brasserie, the 'nest' features mouthwatering French fare and perfect, unobstructed views of Tokyo Tower (at least until something's built in the lot across the street) – in the evening, after a glass of wine, you really could trick yourself into thinking that you were dining in the City of Lights.

🍴 UME-NO-HANA 梅の花
Traditional Japanese ¥¥¥

☎ 3475 8077; 6F, Aoyama Bell Commons, 2-14-6 Kita-aoyama, Minato-ku; ⏱ 11am-3pm & 5-9pm Mon-Sat, 5-10pm Sun; ⊖ Ginza & Hanzōmon lines (exit 2)

This traditional restaurant is rightfully well known for its *kaiseki* (elegant, multicourse Japanese meals) dishes that exquisitely showcase tofu and *yuba* (tofu 'skin') in

115

NEIGHBOURHOODS

HARAJUKU

beautifully presented small courses. Both *niku-nashi* (vegetarian) and meat-inclusive sets are available, but ordering will be problematic unless you have a Japanese speaker make the reservation for you and help you decide the best set for you and your party.

▼ DRINK

▼ DEN AQUAROOM
デンアクアルーム *Lounge*

☎ 5778 2090; B1F, 5-13-3 Minami-Aoyama, Minato-ku; cover ¥700; ⏱ 6pm-2am Mon-Sat, 6-11pm Sun; ⊕ Chiyoda, Ginza, Hanzōmon lines to Omote-sandō (exit B1)

Darting fish within the walls of backlit, blue aquariums make a visual counterpoint to the bop of jazz bass-lines. Even prettier than the dark décor is the chic clientele floating around in here.

▼ TOKYO APARTMENT CAFÉ
東京アパートメントカフェ *Lounge*

☎ 3401 4101; 1-11-11 Jingūmae, Shibuya-ku; ⏱ 11am-4am; ⊕ Chiyoda line to Meiji-jingūmae (exit 5); 🚃 JR Yamanote line to Harajuku (Omote-sandō exit)

The Apartment Café is a good afternoon refuge for snacks like pasta or spring rolls, but in the evenings it transforms into more of a cocktail lounge where you can spend a low-key evening among locals.

116

⭐ PLAY

⭐ JINGŪ STADIUM 神宮球場
Spectator Sports

☎ 3404 8999; 1-13 Kasumigaokamachi, Shinjuku-ku; tickets from ¥1500; ⊕ Ginza line to Gaienmae (north exit)

Jingū Baseball Stadium was originally built to host the 1964 Olympics and is where the Yakult Swallows are based. Baseball season runs from April through to the end of October; check the *Japan Times* to see who's playing.

⭐ LE BARON *Club*

www.lebaron.jp/; 3-8-40 Minami-aoyama, Minato-ku; ⏱ Wed-Sun; ⊕ Ginza, Chiyoda & Hanzomon lines to Omote-sandō (exit A4)

A swank import from Paris, Le Baron is Tokyo's new *it* venue for the partying jetset.

⭐ NATIONAL STADIUM
国立競技場 *Spectator Sports*

☎ 3403 1151; 1-15 Kasumigaokamachi, Shinjuku-ku; tickets from ¥2000; ⊕ Toei Ōedo line to Kokuritsu Kyōgijō (exit A2); 🚃 Chūō line to Sendagaya (east exit)

J-League soccer is booming in Japan, though nay-sayers had predicted its rapid decline with the departure of the 2002 World Cup (awarded to Japan, jointly with Korea). The increased interest in the game has remained, and the Japanese have embraced it

almost as enthusiastically
as baseball.

⭐ TOKYO METROPOLITAN GYMNASIUM 東京体育館
Sports & Recreation
☎ 5474 2111; www.tef.or.jp/tmg
/index.php; 1-17-1 Sendagaya,
Shibuya-ku; pool/gym for 2 hrs
¥600/450; ⏱ 9am-11pm Mon-Fri, 9am-
10pm Sat, 9am-9pm Sun;
🚃 Chūō & Sōbu lines to Sendagaya
(main exit), Ⓜ Toei Ōedo line to
Kokuritsu Kyōgijō (exits A4 & A5)
Easily accessed and with comprehensive facilities that include
two swimming pools, this space-
shiplike structure is just across
the street from Sendagaya
Station.

>SHINJUKU

Shinjuku immediately immerses you in the sheer scale and manic energy of Tokyo, and thus is the perfect introduction to the city. Shinjuku Station is Tokyo's largest hub, serving several major rail lines with an average of over 3.6 million commuters each day. Getting from A to B within the station can be akin to negotiating the levels of a chaotic videogame you've never played before – keep your eyes on the signs and you'll get where you need to go.

Above the station are the requisite gigantic department stores owned by major rail lines such as Odakyū and Keiō, and the Takashimaya Times Square complex to the south. Based in Nishi-Shinjuku (the west side) are the Tokyo Metropolitan Government Offices and a spate of luxury hotels catering to business folk, while Shinjuku's east side shows off a seedier angle in Tokyo's red-light district. The best known landmark on the east side is the Studio Alta building, an easy target for a meet-up in this lively quarter that many would consider downtown Tokyo.

SHINJUKU

⊙ SEE
Kabukichō 1 C2
Seiji Togo Memorial
  Sompo Japan Museum
  of Art 2 B3
Shinjuku-gyōen 3 D4
Tokyo Metropolitan
  Government Offices ...4 A4

🏠 SHOP
Beams 5 C3
Comme Ça 6 C3
Disk Union 7 C3
Don Quijote 8 C3
Isetan 9 C3
Journal Standard 10 C4
Kinokuniya 11 C4

Kinokuniya 12 C3
Marui Young 13 C3
Odakyū 14 B3
Sakuraya Camera 15 C3
Sekaido 16 D4
Tōkyū Hands 17 C4
Yodobashi Camera 18 B4

🍴 EAT
Chaya Macrobiotics ...(see 9)
Keika Kumamoto
  Rāmen 19 D3
Nakajima ....(see 5)
New York Grill 20 A4
Omoide-yokochō 21 B3
Tsunahachi 22 C3
Zauo 23 A4

🍸 DRINK
Advocates Bar 24 D3
Arty Farty 25 D3
Golden Gai 26 D3
New York Bar ....(see 20)
phonic:hoop 27 C3
Zoetrope 28 B2

⭐ PLAY
Loft 29 C2
National Nō Theatre
  (Kokuritsu Nō-
  Gakudō) 30 D6
Shinjuku Piccadilly 31 C3
Shinjuku Pit Inn 32 D3
Shinjuku Suehirotei 33 D3

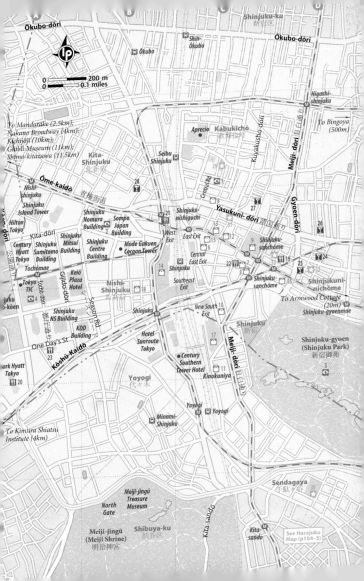

Ōkubo-dōri

Shinjuku-ku
新宿区

Ōkubo-dōri

■ Ōkubo

Shin-
Ōkubo

Higashi-
shinjuku

To Mandarake (2.5km);
Nakano Broadway (4km);
Kichijōji (10km);
Ghibli Museum (11km);
Shimo-kitazawa (11.5km)

Aprecio ● Kabukichō 歌舞伎町

To Bingoya
(500m)

Kita-
Shinjuku
北新宿

Seibu
Shinjuku

29

Kuyakusho-dōri

Meiji-dōri 明治通り

Gyoen-dōri

Ōme-kaidō 青梅街道

Nishi-
shinjuku

28

Central Rd

27

Nishi-
Shinjuku
Island Tower

Shinjuku
Nomura
Building

Sompo
Japan
Building

21

Shinjuku-
nishiguchi

Yasukuni-dōri 靖国通り

Hilton
Tokyo

2

West
Exit

East Exit

26

Century
Hyatt
Tokyo

Kita-dōri

Shinjuku
Sumitomo
Building

Shinjuku
Mitsui
Building

Shinjuku
Centre
Building

● Mode Gakuen
Cocoon Tower

4 12

15

9

Shinjuku-
sanchōme

Tochōmae

Keiō
Plaza
Hotel

14

Central
East Exit

22

7

5

19

25

24

Tokyo
TIC

Tōchō
bldg

Nishi-
Shinjuku
西新宿

18

Shinjuku

Southeast
Exit

5

Shinjuku-
sanchōme

16

Shinjukuni-
nichōme

-kōen

4

To Arnwood Cottage
(20m)
Shinjuku-gyoenmae

Shinjuku
NS Building

Shinjuku

New South
Exit

10

KDD
Building

Shinjuku
新宿

Shinjuku-gyoen
(Shinjuku Park)
新宿御苑

One Day's St

23

Kōshū-kaidō

Hotel
Sunroute
Tokyo

17

11

Meiji-dōri 明治通り

3

Park Hyatt
Tokyo

20

Yoyogi
代々木

● Century
Southern
Tower Hotel

Kinokuniya

To Kimura Shiatsu
Institute (4km)

Minami-
Shinjuku

Yoyogi

● Yoyogi

Sendagaya
千駄ヶ谷

30

Meiji-jingū
Treasure
Museum

North
Gate

Shibuya-ku
渋谷区

Kita-sandō

See Harajuku
Map (p104–5)

Meiji-jingū
(Meiji Shrine)
明治神宮

Kita-
sandō

NEIGHBOURHOODS

SHINJUKU

👁 SEE

👁 KABUKICHŌ 歌舞伎町

🚉 JR Yamanote line to Shinjuku (east exit)

Kabukichō is Tokyo's red-light district, and it wears its gaudy neon bling on its sleeve. It's home to host clubs and soaplands ('massage' parlours) that the authorities are attempting to clean up, and *yakuza* (mafia) and wannabes do maintain a visible presence in the area. However, while Japanese people may warn you that it's a dangerous neighbourhood, never fear, taking the usual precautions after dark should suffice.

👁 SEIJI TOGO MEMORIAL SOMPO JAPAN MUSEUM OF ART 東郷青児美術館

☎ 3349 3080; www.sompo-japan.co.jp/museum; 42F 1-26-1 Nishi-shinjuku, Shinjuku-ku; admission ¥1000; 🕙 10am-6pm Tue-Sun; 🚉 JR Yamanote line to Shinjuku, West exit)

Art buffs will appreciate this modest museum devoted to the works of Seiji Togo, a Japanese painter who was admired early on for his hypnotic depictions of the female figure. The views from the museum's vestibule are worth the admission alone.

The crowded Kabukichō entertainment district by night

JOSE FUSTE RAGA / CORBIS

SPIRITED AWAY TO MITAKA

Visiting *anime* master Hayao Miyazaki's wondrous, imaginative **Ghibli Museum** (☎ 0422-40-2233; www.ghibli-museum.jp; 1-1-83 Shimo-Renjaku, Mitaka-shi; adult ¥1000, child ¥100-700; ☒ 10am-6pm Wed-Mon; ◉ JR Chūō line to Mitaka, south exit) is most easily arranged by reserving an appointment in advance (up to three months prior to your visit). If you can't plan that far ahead, it's possible – though slightly more complicated – to purchase tickets once you arrive in Tokyo (see the website for detailed ticketing information). The museum maintains a daily visitor quota and staggers admittance over two-hour blocks throughout the day – all for the sake of providing the highest-quality, least crowded experience for everyone.

A cute shuttle bus (roundtrip/one-way ¥300/200) runs from Mitaka Station to the museum if you'd prefer not to walk. But it's a flat 15-minute stroll from Mitaka, or a pleasant 20-minute walk from Inokashira Park (p122) in Kichijōji.

◉ SHINJUKU-GYŌEN
新宿御苑
☎ 3350 0151; 11 Naitochō, Shinjuku-ku; admission ¥200/50/free; ☒ 9am-4pm Tue-Sun; ◉ Marunouchi line to Shinjuku-gyōenmae (exit 1)

Dating back to 1906, this downtown park provides the perfect escape from winter cold, as it boasts a hothouse full of exotic tropical plants, allegedly even including peyote! There's also a French garden and a pond full of giant carp. Keep this park in mind when you're exhausted by all that busy Shinjuku has to offer.

◉ TOKYO METROPOLITAN GOVERNMENT OFFICES
東京都庁
☎ 5321 1111; 2-8-1 Nishi-Shinjuku, Shinjuku-ku; admission free; ☒ observatories 9.30am-11.30pm, north tower closed 2nd & 4th Mon, south tower closed 1st & 3rd Tue; ◉ Toei Ōedo line to Tochōmae (exits A3 & A4); ♿

Known as Tokyo Tochō, these colossal towers designed by Kenzō Tange comprise Tokyo's

HANAMI REMIX

For cherry blossom viewing, everyone knows Ueno-kōen is the big cheese. These spots are known only to locals:
Meguro-gawa (Map p83, B5; ◉ JR Yamanote line to Meguro) The riverbank is lined with concrete, but the gnarled trunks above curl high over the stream, creating a gauntlet of colour.
Aoyama-reien (Map pp104-5, H5; ◉ Ginza line to Gaienmae) A stunning cemetery overflowing with radiant blooms. Superstitious locals daren't enter in the evening.
Seijo (◉ Odakyū line to Seijoenmae) A garden suburb in Setagaya-ku with awesome blossom viewing, especially near the river.

WORTH THE TRIP

On the western edge of Tokyo's 23 wards, **Kichijōji** is a short train ride from Shinjuku or Shibuya and makes an easy getaway for those suffering from urban overload. Kichijōji is one of Tokyo's most desirable neighbourhoods, with its university-town feel, understated hipness factor and high quality of living. Take a walk in the park, browse a few boutiques and finish off with a cocktail in one of the cool little local bars.

The centrepiece of Kichijōji is **Inokashira Park** (☎ 042-247 6900; Inokashira, Mitaka-shi; boat rentals ¥200; 24hr; JR Chūō & Sōbu lines to Kichijōji, Park exit; Keiō Inokashira line to Kichijōji, Park exit). The park is at its lively but low-key best on the weekends, when artists and musicians come out to play. Stroll the shaded edge of the small lake, visit the temple to Benzaiten (goddess of love and the arts), rent a paddle boat and feel the urban tension melt away. However, cherry-blossom season is the exception to the peaceful rule.

From Kichijōji Station, take the park exit and look for the Marui department store. Walk down the road to the right of the building, which will lead you down the gentle slope to the park. Take your time on the way down, and poke around the cafes, bohemian-style shops and ethnic restaurants lining the road.

If you have arranged an appointment at the Ghibli Museum (p121), an alternative way to get there is walking through the park from Kichijōji. Allow at least 20 minutes for the walk.

bureaucratic heartland. From the amphitheatrelike Citizen's Plaza below, check out the architecture and complex symmetry of the towers. Then whiz up to the twin observation decks, over 200m above urban Shinjuku, for a look at Tokyo below.

SHOP

BEAMS *Fashion*

☎ 5368 7300; www.beams.co.jp; 3-32-6 Shinjuku, Shinjuku-ku; 11am-8pm; JR Yamanote line to Shinjuku (south exit)

The Beams chain has spread across Japan and over to Hong Kong, but all the best of Beams – from basic to superstylish men's and women's clothes, accessories, cool housewares and a gallery – has been concentrated into the seven floors of this Shinjuku shop.

COMME ÇA *Fashion*

☎ 5367 5551; 3-26-6 Shinjuku, Shinjuku-ku; 11am-9pm Mon-Sat, 11am-8pm Sun; JR Yamanote line to Shinjuku (east exit)

Provided you fit into local sizes, this branch of the Japanese chain has six floors of quality basics and inexpensive accessories. Plus: cake!

🏠 DISK UNION
ディスクユニオン
Music

☎ 3352-2691; http://diskunion.net in Japanese; 3-31-4 Shinjuku, Shinjuku-ku; ⏰ 11am-9pm Mon-Sat, 11am-8pm Sun; 🚇 JR Yamanote line (east exit)

This seven-storey branch has an excellent selection of CDs, both new and used. It has another branch on Shibuya (p93).

🏠 DON QUIJOTE
ドンキホーテ
Homewares & Novelties

☎ 5291 9211; www.donki.com; 1-16-5 Kabukichō, Shinjuku-ku; ⏰ 24hr; 🚇 JR Yamanote line to Shinjuku (east exit)

Meet Don Quijote, Tōkyū Hands' trashy cousin. In Kabukichō, the fluorescent-lit corner shop is filled to the brink with weird loot. Chaotic piles of knockoff electronics and designer goods sit alongside sex toys, fetish costumes and packaged foods. They have quite a presence in Tokyo, though not all shops are open 24 hours.

🏠 ISETAN 伊勢丹
Department Store

☎ 3352 1111; 3-14-1 Shinjuku, Shinjuku-ku; ⏰ 10am-8pm 🚇 Marunouchi & Toei Shinjuku lines to Shinjuku-sanchōme (exit A1)

In addition to having a stunning food basement, Isetan offers a free service called I-club, matching English-speaking staff to visiting shoppers; the membership desk is on the 6th floor of the main Isetan building. While you're there take a peek at the current exhibition in the 5th-floor art gallery.

🏠 JOURNAL STANDARD
Fashion

☎ 5367 0175; www.journal-standard .jp; 4-1-7 Shinjuku,Shinjuku-ku; ⏰ 11.30am-8.30pm Mon-Fri, 11am-8pm Sat & Sun; 🚇 JR Yamanote line to Shinjuku (south exit)

Browsing the corners and surfaces of this hip shop turn up all sorts of items to add style to your wardrobe. Collections here are smart but bohemian, and sizes tend towards the Japanese figure (ie small). This is also a great place to end a shopping spree, as there's a lovely rooftop cafe on the 3rd floor.

🏠 KINOKUNIYA
紀伊國屋書店
Books

☎ 5361 3301; Annexe Bldg, Takashimaya Times Square, 5-24-5 Sendagaya, Shibuya-ku; ⏰ 10am-8pm Sun-Fri, 10am-8.30pm Sat; 🚇 JR Yamanote line to Shinjuku (new south exit)

Kinokuniya's large annexe store in the Takashimaya Times Square complex surpasses the main **Shinjuku store** (☎ 3354 0131; 3-17-7 Shinjuku, Shinjuku-ku; ⏰ 10am-9pm;

🚇 JR Yamanote line to Shinjuku, east exit), with its variety and depth of titles in English. Find foreign-language books on the 6th floor, and a rainy day's worth of art books, magazines and manga everywhere else.

🏬 MARUI YOUNG
マルイヤング
Department Store

☎ 3354 0101; 3-18-1 Shinjuku, Shinjuku-ku; ⏱ 11.30am-9pm Mon-Sat, 11.30am-8.30pm Sun; 🚇 JR Yamanote line to Shinjuku (east exit)

You can't swing a coat hanger in Shinjuku without hitting a speciality branch of Marui (look for the Marui logo: OIOI). Marui Young is the place to begin shopping if you want to buy Goth-Lolita garb with the local whitest-shade-of-pale girls.

🏬 ODAKYŪ
小田急百貨店
Department Store

☎ 3342 1111; 1-1-3 Nishi-Shinjuku, Shinjuku-ku; ⏱ shops 10am-8pm, restaurants 11am-10pm; 🚇 JR Yamanote line to Shinjuku (west exit)

The 16-floor behemoth of a department store that sits atop Shinjuku Station, Odakyū contains several restaurant floors, high-end boutiques and low-budget accessories shops, as well as just about anything you'd need to live inside the station for the next 10 years.

📷 SAKURAYA CAMERA
さくらやカメラ
Cameras & Electronics

☎ 3352 4711; 3-2-6 Shinjuku, Shinjuku-ku; ⏱ 10am-10pm; 🚇 JR Yamanote line to Shinjuku (east exit)

One of the big three camera emporiums, Sakuraya Camera offers many of the same inventory as the others, at similar prices. It has an incredible selection of long lenses and tiny digital cameras. You'll find some great deals here but, like anywhere, comparison shopping is essential.

🏬 SEKAIDO 世界堂
Stationery

☎ 5379 1111; 3-1-1 Shinjuku, Shinjuku-ku; ⏱ 9.30am-9pm; 🚇 Marunouchi & Toei Shinjuku lines to Shinjuku-sanchôme (exit C1)

Art-supply junkies should visit Sekaido only on a preset budget, as they're otherwise doomed to blow a fortune on the blindingly broad array of art supplies, exquisite *washi* (handmade paper) and vast selection of manga.

🏬 TŌKYŪ HANDS
東急ハンズ
Homewares & Novelties

☎ 5361 3111; Takashimaya Times Square, 5-24-2 Sendagaya, Shibuya-ku; ⏱ 10am-8.30pm; 🚇 JR Yamanote line to Shinjuku (new south exit)

Ostensibly a do-it-yourself store, Tōkyū Hands carries a compre-

WORTH THE TRIP

A retro shopping arcade on the outskirts of the city centre, **Nakano Broadway** (http://bwy.jp; 5-52-15 Nakano, Nakano-ku; ⊝ Tozai line to Nakano, north exit) is another place of pilgrimage for fanatical *otaku* who scour the land for obscure action figures and collectible comics. **Mandarake** (まんだらけ; 2F-4F Nakano Broadway), the manga and *anime* behemoth, has its flagship store here. Enjoy miles of endless reading, or splurge on a collectible action figure, but never take it out of the plastic!

hensive collection of everything you didn't know you needed, from blown-glass pens to chainsaws, tofu tongs to party supplies. The Takashimaya Times Square branch is probably the least maddening to shop in, but there are others in Shibuya (p96) and Ikebukuro (p136).

YODOBASHI CAMERA
ヨドバシカメラ
Cameras & Electronics
☎ 3346 1010; 1-11-1 Nishi-Shinjuku, Shinjuku-ku; ⊕ 9.30am-9.30pm; ⊝ Toei Shinjuku line to Shinjuku (exit 5), ⊠ JR Yamanote line to Shinjuku (west exit)
Yodobashi is Sakuraya's largest competitor and sits directly across the street. This store stocks

anything from digital camcorders to secondhand enlargers. Prices at Yodobashi are very competitive, and if you can't dig it up here then it probably can't be found in Japan.

🍴 EAT

🍴 ARMWOOD COTTAGE
Cafe ¥
☎ 5935-8897; www.atticroom.jp/arm; 2F 1-10-5 Shinjuku, Shinjuku-ku; ⊕ lunch & dinner; ⊝ Marunouchi line to Shinjuku-gyoenmae
Bright blue scaffolding holds this inviting wooden structure up over a two-car parking lot near Shinjuku-gyoen. Log beams and cosy furnishings welcome customers with a quaint, chalet-like atmosphere.

🍴 CHAYA MACROBIOTICS
チャヤマクロビオティックス
Macrobiotic ¥¥
☎ 3357 0014; 7F, Isetan Bldg, 3-14-1 Shinjuku, Shinjuku-ku; ⊕ 11am-10pm; ⊝ Marunouchi line to Shinjuku-sanchōme (exit A1); V
Marrying the concepts of Japanese macrobiotics and French cuisine, Chaya offers healthy whole foods alongside lists of organic tea, wine and French apple cider. Though the seasonal menu is anchored by mostly vegan offerings such as

NEIGHBOURHOODS

SHINJUKU

red rice risotto, seitan-and-millet burgers and seaweed side salads, fish also figures prominently. Desserts like the soy crème brûlée are a particular treat.

🍴 KEIKA KUMAMOTO RĀMEN
桂花熊本ラーメン

Rāmen ¥

☎ 3354 4591; 3-7-2 Shinjuku, Shinjuku-ku; ⏰ 11am-11pm; 🚇 Marunouchi & Toei Shinjuku lines to Shinjuku-sanchōme (exit C4); ♿ ⚥

The Kyūshū-style *tonkotsu rāmen* (pork broth–based noodles), is worth queuing for at this nationally famous *rāmen* shop. You order and pay as you enter; try the *chāshū-men* (*rāmen* with sliced pork). There's no English sign, so look for the large, multicoloured cartoon mural of a chef and pigs on its exterior.

🍴 NAKAJIMA 中嶋

Traditional Japanese ¥¥

☎ 3356 7962; http://shinjyuku-nakajima.com; 3-32-5 Shinjuku, Shinjuku-ku; ⏰ 11.30am-2.30pm & 5.30-10pm Mon-Sat; 🚇 Marunouchi line to Shinjuku-sanchōme (exit A1)

Having garnered one Michelin star in 2008, Nakajima hasn't let this honour change its delicious ways. The house speciality is the *iwashi* (sardine) – whether simmered in sweet broth with egg, served as sashimi, or delicately fried and laid

on a bed of rice, you can't go wrong. Down the alley next to the Beams building, look for a black building with an outside stairwell leading down to basement-level Nakajima.

🍴 NEW YORK GRILL
ニュヨークグリル

American ¥¥¥

☎ 5323 3458; 52F, Park Hyatt Tokyo, 3-7-1-2 Nishi-Shinjuku, Shinjuku-ku; ⏰ 11.30am-midnight; 🚇 Toei Ōedo line to Tochōmae (exit A4); ♿ Ⓥ ⚥

The drop-dead-delicious view notwithstanding, this sky-high spot continues to earn its reputation as one of Tokyo's top restaurants with its slabs of steak and racks of lamb. Worth waking for is the sumptuous daily brunch (¥6200; open 11.30am to 2.30pm), which on Sundays includes a glass of champagne. On the 1st floor, the New York Deli is lovely for a more casual lunch, with a delectable selection of fine cheeses, olives and cured meats.

🍴 OMOIDE-YOKOCHŌ
思い出横丁

Yakitori ¥

Memory Lane; 1 Nishi-shinjuku; skewers from ¥100; ⏰ dinner; 🚇 Toei Oedo line to Shinjuku Nishiguchi (exit D3)

Since the postwar days, smoke has been billowing nightly from the little shacks lining this alley by the train tracks, purveying *yakitori* and cold beers to long-time regulars. Literally translated as 'Memory Lane' (and less politely known as Shoben-yokochō, 'Piss Alley') Omoide-yokochō may actually be just a memory someday; there's been on-again, off-again talk of razing it to make way for new development. Stop by around 7pm to indulge in a few skewers and pre-emptive nostalgia.

🍴 TSUNAHACHI つな八

Tempura ¥¥

☎ 3352 1012; 3-31-8 Shinjuku, Shinjuku-ku; 🕙 11am-10pm; 🚆 JR Yamanote line to Shinjuku (east exit); ♿ 🚼

Sit at the counter for the pleasure of watching the efficient chefs fry each perfect tempura and plate them one by one. From Shinjuku-dōri as you face Mitsukoshi department store, go down the small street to its left; Tsunahachi will be on your left. There is another, airier branch located on the 13th floor at Takashimaya Times Square.

🍴 ZAUO ざうお *Seafood*

☎ 3343-6622; www.zauo.com; 1F Shinjuku Washington Hotel 3-2-9 Nishi-shinjuku, Shinjuku-ku; 🕙 dinner; 🚆 JR Yamanote line to Shinjuku (South exit)

The idea may sound gimmicky – a boat-shaped restaurant where guests fish from the aquarium

below – but Zauo is a riot for any age. Toss the line in from your table and wait for a tug. When you catch a critter you'll get praise from the waitstaff in the form of a chant, a cheer and a clap.

🍸 DRINK

Shinjuku is one Tokyo's best neighbourhoods for a night out on the town, featuring the most diverse array of drinking options. Tokyo's most notorious red-light district, Kabukichō, lies east of Seibu Shinjuku station. This is one of the world's more imaginative red-light districts, with 'soaplands' (massage parlours), love hotels, pink cabarets ('pink' is the Japanese equivalent of 'blue' in English) and strip shows. And, next door, you won't find another low-lying cluster of bars like the Golden Gai anywhere else in Tokyo.

🍸 ADVOCATES BAR

Gay & Lesbian Bar

☎ 3358 3988; 1F, Dai-7 Tenka Bldg, 2-18-1 Shinjuku, Shinjuku-ku; 🕙 8pm-5am Mon-Sat, 8pm-1am Sun; 🚇 Toei Shinjuku line to Shinjuku-sanchōme (exit C8)

Advocates Bar is just that – a bar, and a small one. As the crowd gets bigger over the course of the evening, it overflows onto the street and becomes more like a block party. The staff here speaks English,

Relaxing in the stratospheric New York Bar at Park Hyatt Tokyo

MARK HEMMINGS / LONELY PLANET IMAGES ©

and it's another good venue to start off a night in Nichōme.

▼ ARTY FARTY
アーティファーティ
Gay & Lesbian Bar
☎ 5362 9720; www.arty-farty.net; 2F, 2-11-7 Shinjuku, Shinjuku-ku; ⌚ 7pm-late Mon-Sat, 5pm-3am Sun; ⊚ Toei Shinjuku line to Shinjuku-sanchōme (exits C5 & C8)
Arty Farty is another stalwart of the queer scene, and has good all-you-can-drink specials. There's a reason it has been around for so long and it's a tried-and-true (although often incredibly crowded) place to start your evening and get the lowdown

on what else is happening in the neighbourhood.

▼ BON'S ボンズ *Bar*
☎ 3209 6334; 1-1-10 Kabukichō, Shinjuku-ku; cover ¥900; ⌚ 7pm-5am; ⊚ Marunouchi line to Shinjuku-sanchōme (exit B5)
Drinks start at ¥700 at this sure-fire spot in the Golden Gai. Look for its corner location with 'Old Fashioned American Style Pub' painted across its exterior wall.

▼ GOLDEN GAI *Bars*
(Kabukichō, Shinjuku-ku; ⊚ Marunouchi line to Shinjuku-sanchōme B5)
Golden Gai is a neighbourhood unlike anywhere else in Tokyo.

Over 300 bars – each one smaller than the next – are crammed into the miniature backstreets of this seemingly neglected district. Although there are myriad options to choose from, Golden Gai isn't the place for a pub-crawl. It's more about choosing a seat for the night, hunkering down and chatting with the other patrons until sunrise. In fact, many of these hovel-like bars have themes – not so much in the decor but more in coversation. You'll find dens dedicated to all stripes of people from tango fanatics to French film connoisseurs. This is why most places have a seating fee (anywhere from ¥300 to ¥2500) – you're essentially renting real estate for the night, especially since most joints only have six or eight stools. **Araku** (2F 1-1-9 G2) and **Albatross** (www.alba-s.com; 2F 5th Avenue) are among the dozen or so bars that accept foreigners.

NEW YORK BAR
ニューヨークバー *Bar*
☎ 5323 3458; www.parkhyatttokyo.com; 3-7-1-2 Nishi-Shinjuku, Shinjuku-ku; cover after 8pm ¥2000; ⏲ 5pm-midnight Sun-Wed, 5pm-1am Thu-Sat; ⊖ Toei Ōedo line to Tochōmae (exit A4)
Located in the stratosphere, both physically and socially, the New York Bar towers over the city on the 52nd floor of the Park Hyatt

Tokyo in west Shinjuku. With magnificent views, strong drinks and live jazz, this is a swank lounge for that special date.

PHONIC:HOOP *Bar*
www.ph-hp.jp; 5-10-1 Shinjuku, Shinjuku-ku; ⊖ Marunouchi line to Shinjuku-sanchōme (exit C7)
Effortlessly hip with too-cool-for-school surrounds including casually positioned potted plants and outmoded pieces of machinery.

ZOETROPE *Bar*
http://homepage2.nifty.com/zoetrope; 3F Gaia Bldg 7-10-14 Nishi-shinjuku, Shinjuku-ku; ⏲ Mon-Sat; ⊖ Toei Ōedo line to Shinjuku-nishiguchi (exit D5)
Spend a sociable, relaxed evening at this cosy spot, which boasts over 300 Japanese whiskies and screens silent films on the wall.

⭐ PLAY

⭐ LOFT ロフト *Live Music*
☎ 5272 0382; www.loft-prj.co.jp/LOFT/index.html; B2F, Tatehana Bldg, 1-12-9 Kabukichō, Shinjuku-ku; from ¥1000; ⏲ 5pm-late; ⊜ JR Yamanote line to Shinjuku (east exit)
This loud and smoky Shinjuku institution is a blast on a good night. Although a typically small venue, it draws both local and international acts ranging from punk to emo.

⭐ NATIONAL NŌ THEATRE
国立能楽堂
Theatre

☎ 3423 1331; 4-18-1 Sendagaya, Shibuya-ku; tickets ¥2800-5600; 🕐 reservations 10am-6pm; 🚇 Chūō & Sōbu lines to Sendagaya (west exit)

The National Nō Theatre stages its own *nō* (classical Japanese musical dramas) performances on week-ends only, for which it provides printed English synopses, but it also hosts privately sponsored performances. Exit Sendagaya Station in the direction of Shinjuku on the left and follow the road that hugs the railway tracks; the theatre will be on the left.

MANGA KISSA

Kissaten (coffee shops) have long been mainstays for socialising away from home, but the next-generation versions are serious escape hatches. *Manga kissa* (comic-book cafes) are a great place to get inexpensive internet access in a comfy private cubicle. You can also browse their manga library, get a bite to eat, watch DVDs or catch some Zs. *Manga kissa* are open 24 hours per day, and you can prepay for as little as 30 minutes or, if you get caught out after midnight when the trains stop running, overnight. Rates are typically around ¥2500 for eight hours. See p199 for listings.

⭐ SHINJUKU PICCADILLY
新宿ピカデリー
Cinema

☎ 5367-1144; www.shinjukupiccadilly .com in Japanese; 3-15-15 Shinjuku, Shinjuku-ku; tickets from ¥1300/800; 🚇 Marunouchi & Toei Shinjuku lines to Shinjuku-sanchōme (exits B7 & B8); ♿

One of Tokyo's great cinema experiences features a gleaming, translucent white exterior and interior. The theatre itself boasts over 600 seats, including sev-eral two-person private viewing booths outfitted with surround sound and leather sofas (¥30,000 per screening, or ¥3,000,000 per year for high rollers).

⭐ SHINJUKU PIT INN
新宿ピットイン
Live music

☎ 3354 2024; www.pit-inn.com/index _e.html; B1F, Accord Bldg, 2-12-14 Shinjuku, Shinjuku-ku; cover ¥1300-4000; 🕐 performances 2.30pm & 8pm; 🚇 Toei Shinjuku line to Shinjuku-sanchōme (exits C5 & C8)

Shinjuku Pit Inn is one of the bet-ter established jazz clubs in Tokyo, showcasing the talents of both foreign and local jazz musicians. The jazz could be generally cat-egorised as classically mainstream. Phone ahead for reservations. The cover includes one drink.

SENTŌ PRIMER

First you'll pay the *sentō* (public bath) fee to an attendant at the front desk, then head into the men's or women's changing room. In the changing room, place your clothes in one of the lockers and your toiletries in a *senmenki* (wash basin), and head into the bath area.

Before stepping into the bath, you'll need to wash at the banks of low showers and water spigots that line the walls. Grab a low stool and scrub thoroughly, making sure you remove all traces of soap so as not to cloud the water. Circulate between the hot tubs, cold pool, sauna and electric bath (which supposedly simulates the sensation of swimming with electric eels). If you soak everything just right, you'll float out in the desired state of *yude-dako* ('boiled octopus').

☆ SHINJUKU SUEHIROTEI

新宿末廣亭 *Rakugo*

www.suehirotei.com; 3-6-12 Shinjuku, Shinjuku-ku; ⏰ 12-4pm & 5-9pm, 🚇 Marunouchi line to Shinjuku-sanchōme

Popular shows include late-night *rakugō* (a type of comedic mono-logue by a kneeling performer), which are held at only five places in Japan. The casual atmosphere means that no advance booking is required and you can come and go as you please.

>IKEBUKURO

Ikebukuro's former claim to fame was having Japan's hugest department stores, Asia's tallest building and the world's longest escalator. While those days are well and truly behind it, Ikebukuro's very unpretentiousness gives it a humble appeal, and there are some fabulous places to take kids. East Ikebukuro has also become a haven for the quietly burgeoning fringe population of *otome* (literally 'maidens'; colloquially 'girl geeks'), the female counterparts of their more famous brethren, the *otaku* ('geek boys'). Although these fangirls themselves are not as colourful as the *cosplay-zoku* (costume-play gangs), this fascinating subculture exemplifies Ikebukuro's less obvious cultural appeal.

Most of the entertainment is on the east side, where the small alleys contain karaoke bars, *pachinko* (pinball) parlours, a few maid cafes and love hotels. Follow Sunshine 60-dōri to Sunshine City. On the west side, have a look at the folk arts on display at the Japan Traditional Crafts Center or grab some cheap eats at a local *kaitenzushi* (conveyor-belt sushi bar) or *rāmen* (egg noodles) shop.

IKEBUKURO

🜨 SEE
Sunshine International
    Aquarium .... (see 11)
Sunshine Starlight
    Dome .... (see 11)
Toyota Amlux 1 C3

🛍 SHOP
Animate 2 C3
Bic Camera 3 C3

Bic Camera (Main
    Store) 4 B3
Japan Traditional Crafts
    Center 5 B4
Sunshine City 6 C4
Tobu 7 B3
Tōykü Hands 8 C3

🍴 EAT
Akiyoshi 9 A3
Anpuku 10 B3
Namco Namjatown 11 D4

🍸 DRINK
Sasashū 12 A3

⭐ PLAY
Nekobukuro .... (see 8)

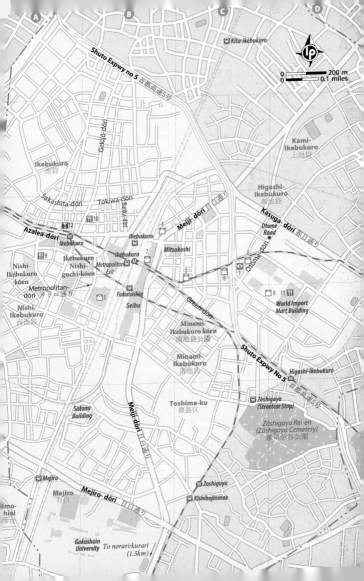

A

B

C

D

Kita-ikebukuro

Shuto Expwy no 5 首都高速5号

Gekijō-dōri

Ikebukuro
池袋

Kami-Ikebukuro
上池袋

Higashi-Ikebukuro
東池袋

Sakashita-dōri

Tokiwa-dōri

Bunka-dōri

Meiji-dōri 明治通

Kasuga-dōri 春日通り

Otome Road

Azalea-dōri

Ikebukuro

Ikebukuro
Nishi-guchi-kōen

Ikebukuro
Metropolitan
Exit

Mitsukoshi

Otome-dōri

Nishi-Ikebukuro
kōen

Metropolitan-
dōri

Nishi-Ikebukuro
西池袋

Fukutoshin
Seibu

Green-dōri

World Import
Mart Building

Minami-
Ikebukuro-kōen
南池袋公園

Shuto Expwy No 5

Higashi-ikebukuro

首都高速5号

Minami-
Ikebukuro
南池袋

Satomi
Building

Toshima-ku
豊島区

Zōshigaya
(Streetcar Stop)

Zōshigaya Rei-en
(Zōshigaya Cemetery)
雑司が谷公園

Mejiro

Mejiro-dōri 目白通り

Mejiro
目白

Zōshigaya

Kishibojinmae

imo-hiai

Gakushūin
University

To norarikurari
(1.5km)

200 m
0.1 miles

NEIGHBOURHOODS

IKEBUKURO

◎ SEE

◎ SUNSHINE INTERNATIONAL AQUARIUM
サンシャイン国際水族館

☎ 3989 3466; 10F, World Import Mart Bldg, 3-1-3 Higashi-Ikebukuro, Toshima-ku; admission ¥1800/900; ⏰ 10am-6pm; 🚇 JR Yamanote line to Ikebukuro (east exit); ♿ 🚻

Boasting the distinction of being the highest aquarium in the world, this high-rise water world has tanks full of electric eels, sharks and other intriguing sea life. Also living here are some incongruous land-lubbin' critters as well, like lemurs. The building is full of stimulating stuff for kids, such as a planetarium, shopping mall and food-themed amusement park.

◎ SUNSHINE STARLIGHT DOME サンシャインスターライトドーム

☎ 3989 3475; 10F, World Import Mart Bldg, 3-1-3 Higashi-Ikebukuro, Toshima-ku; admission ¥800/500; ⏰ noon-5.30pm Mon-Fri, 11am-6.30pm Sat & Sun; 🚇 JR Yamanote line to Ikebukuro (east exit); ♿ 🚻

We may be in down-to-earth Ike-bukuro but some of us are looking at the stars. Alas, the planetarium's show is narrated in Japanese, but the visuals are spectacular enough to lift you out of this earthly end of Tokyo.

◎ TOYOTA AMLUX
トヨタアムラックス

☎ 5391 5900; www.amlux.jp/about/ english.html; 3-3-5 Higashi-Ikebukuro,

You don't need a driver's licence to get behind the wheel in the Toyota Amlux showroom

IAIN MASTERTON / ALAMY

OTOME ROAD

'Maiden Road', as it's called, is like alternate-universe Akihabara for the *otome* (geek girls), the female equivalent of *otaku* (p132). Most *otome* – some of whom are actually grown women in their 40s – hang here at the local manga shops to browse 'boys' love' manga (exactly what it sounds like). They even have their own versions of role-play cafes featuring butlers instead of maids…with women in drag waiting tables as butlers.

Toshima-ku; admission free; ☽ 11am-7pm Tue-Sun; ☖ JR Yamanote line to Ikebukuro (east exit); &

Toyota's Auto Salon features concept cars and virtual-reality driving experiences, which are only two aspects of this fascinating showroom for the mechanically minded. It's a six-storey multi-media extravaganza, with short movies, aerodynamic architecture and visions of vehicular beauty everywhere. There's an English-language floor guide available.

SHOP

ANIMATE *Books*
www.animate.co.jp; 3-2-1 Higashi-Ikebukuro, Toshima-ku; ☖ JR Yamanote line to Ikebukuro (East exit)
Across from the western street-level entrance to Sunshine City, Animate marks the first stop for girl geeks and manga freaks when they reach Otome Rd.

BIC CAMERA
ビックカメラ
Cameras & Electronics
☎ 5396 1111; 1-41-5 Higashi-Ikebukuro, Toshima-ku; ☽ 10am-9pm; ☖ JR Yamanote line to Ikebukuro (east exit)
Bic Camera may or may not be, as it claims, the cheapest camera store in Japan, but its ubiquity cannot be contested. Bic has other branches in **Ikebukuro** (☎ 3590 1111; 1-11-7 Higashi-Ikebukuro, Toshima-ku; ☽ 10am-9pm; ☖ JR Yamanote line to Ikebukuro, east exit), as well as in Shibuya and Shinjuku. Deals are very competitive but, as always, shop around.

JAPAN TRADITIONAL CRAFTS CENTER
全国伝統的工芸品センター
Handicrafts
☎ 5954 6066; www.kougei.or.jp/english/center.html; 1F & 2F, Metropolitan Plaza Bldg, 1-11-1 Nishi-Ikebukuro, Toshima-ku; ☽ 11am-7pm; ☖ JR Yamanote line to Ikebukuro (Metropolitan exit)
Apart from being a wonderful place to find high-quality souvenirs such as weavings, regional ceramics, *washi* (handmade paper) and woodwork, this centre is a destination in its own right as a showcase for traditional crafts from all over Japan. Temporary exhibitions, demonstrations and classes are held on the 2nd floor.

NEIGHBOURHOODS

IKEBUKURO

🏢 SUNSHINE CITY
サンシャインシティ
Department Store

☎ 3989 3331; 3-1 Higashi-Ikebukuro, Toshima-ku; observation deck ¥620; 🕙 10am-10pm; 🚇 JR Yamanote line to Ikebukuro (east exit)

Billed as a 'city in a building', Sunshine City is another sprawling shopping centre, where for a small fee you can get catapulted in a speeding elevator to the 60th-floor observatory to peer out across the Tokyo skyline. If you're lucky, you might catch a glimpse of Mt Fuji beyond the haze.

🏢 TOBU *Department Store*
www.tobu-dept.jp; 1-1-25 Nishi-ikebukuro, Toshima-ku; 🚇 JR Yamanote line to Ikebukuro

Most of Tokyo's *depāto* are located in and around Ginza, but you'll find a few shopping behemoths in Ikebukuro, including Tobu. The prices here are noticeably less than in Ginza since the real estate is cheaper. Tobu's worth a visit for its vast basement *depachika* (see p57), boasting the cheapest sashimi in town (visit at 7pm when the prices are cut in half).

🏢 TŌKYŪ HANDS
東急ハンズ
Homewares & Novelties

☎ 3980 6111; 1-28-10 Higashi-Ikebukuro, Toshima-ku; 🕙 10am-9pm; 🚇 JR Yamanote line to Ikebukuro (east exit)

Not only does this branch of Tōkyū Hands sell all the fabulous booty for which it's famous, it also houses Nekobukuro (opposite). Other stores can be found in Shinjuku (p124) and Shibuya (p96).

🍴 EAT

🍴 AKIYOSHI 秋吉 *Yakitori* ¥¥
☎ 3982 0644; 3-30-4 Nishi-Ikebukuro, Toshima-ku; 🕙 5-11pm; 🚇 JR Yamanote line to Ikebukuro (west exit); 🚭

Akiyoshi is the place to try for tasty *yakitori* (skewers of grilled chicken) in approachable, noisy and laid-back surroundings. This *yakitori* specialist certainly knows its stuff, while the picture menu is also a boon for non-Japanese speakers.

🍴 ANPUKU あんぷく
Noodles ¥
☎ 6915-2646; 1-37-8 Nishi-Ikebukuro, Toshima-ku; 🕙 11am-3pm & 5pm-midnight Mon-Thu, 11am-5am Fri & Sat, 11am-midnight Sun; 🚇 JR Yamanote Line to Ikebukuro (west exit), Yurakucho, Fukutoshin or Marunouchi Line to Ikebukuro (exit C9)

Udon goes international at this new, spiffy little white-walled cafe. Creative young chefs make the noodles right there and put them in *so* not Japanese presentations: carbonara, chicken with mushrooms in cream sauce or spicy Sichuan eggplant. It's eaten with chopsticks, so staff supply you with a paper bib. There's also stellar traditional udon for purists, and side dishes including grills.

🍴 NAMCO NAMJATOWN
ナムコナンジャタウン
Food-themed Park ¥

☎ 5950 0765; 2F & 3F, World Import Mart Bldg, 3-1-3 Higashi-Ikebukuro, Toshima-ku; admission ¥300/200; ⏰ 10am-10pm; 🚃 JR Yamanote line to Ikebukuro (east exit)

Namco Namjatown houses three food-themed parks, specialising variously in *gyōza* (dumplings), cream puffs and ice cream. Is your mouth watering yet? Maybe it's just us. Admission fees only get you in; you pay for any goodies you eat.

🍸 DRINK
🍸 NORARI:KURARI *Cafe*
2F 14-6 Babashitachō; ⏰ 11am-midnight; Ⓜ Tozai line to Waseda)

Join the lounging Waseda students at this homely cafe decorated like a university dorm (ripped couches and amateur art on the walls). Tuck into a 'moffle' (*mochi*-waffle) and wash it down with an espresso.

🍸 SASASHŪ 笹周 *Izakaya*
☎ 3971 6796; 2-2-6; Ikebukuro, Toshima-ku; ⏰ 5-10pm Mon-Sat; Ⓜ Marunouchi line to Ikebukuro (exit C5); ♿

Serving delicacies such as *ka-monabe* (duck stew), Sasashū is a

---

DRINKING ETIQUETTE

When you're out for a few drinks, remember that you're expected to keep the drinks of your companions topped up. But don't fill your own glass, as this implies your guests aren't taking care of you; wait for someone to pour yours. It's polite to hold the glass with both hands while it's being filled. And most importantly, remember to say, *'Kampai!'* – cheers!

---

highly respected sake specialist maintaining a dignified old façade amid west Ikebukuro's strip joints. If you lack Japanese language ability, trust the master to guide your culinary experience by asking for *omakase* (chef's choice).

⭐ PLAY
🔲 NEKOBUKURO
ねこぶくろ *Petting Zoo*
☎ 3980 6111; 8F, Tōkyū Hands, 1-28-10 Higashi-Ikebukuro, Toshima-ku; admission ¥600; ⏰ 10am-8pm; 🚃 JR Yamanote line to Ikebukuro (east exit)

For Tokyoites who may not have the time or space to keep their own pets, Nekobukuro provides a venue for short-term cuddling with surrogate cats. Creep up to the 8th floor of the Ikebukuro branch of Tōkyū Hands (opposite) to get in on the kitten action.

>UENO

Ueno-kōen (Ueno Park), the preeminent attraction to this *shitamachi* neighbourhood, is a feast of culture with its numerous museums, temples and shrines. While most people enter the park at the museum plaza, another pleasant way to see the park before museum fatigue sets in is to start at the south end. From the Shinobazu exit of the Ueno JR station, cross the road and go up the stairs to the left of the Keisei Ueno station entrance, up to the small pavilion where the Takamori Saigō statue stands. From there, continue uphill to the temple complex before heading out, near the zoo, into the museum area.

Also near the south end of the park is Shinobazu-ike, a large pond where lotuses proliferate and where you can rent small **boats** (☎ 3828 9502; rowboats per hr ¥600, paddleboats 30min ¥600; ⏰ 9am-5pm Mar-Nov) for a serene stint on the water's surface. This pond also has its own temple, Benten-dō, on an island.

UENO

◉ SEE
Benten-dō (Ueno) 1 B4
Kiyōmizu Kannon-dō 2 C4
National Museum of
    Western Art 3 C4
National Science
    Museum 4 C4
Shitamachi History
    Museum 5 C5
Tokyo Metropolitan
    Museum of Art 6 C3
Tokyo National Museum
    (Tokyo Kokuritsu
    Hakubutsukan) 7 C3
Tōshōgū 8 B4
Ueno Zoo 9 B4
Yanaka-reien 10 B2

🛍 SHOP
Ameyoko Arcade 11 C5
Isetatsu 12 A2
Nippori Fabric Town 13 C1

🍴 EAT
Sasa-no-Yuki 14 D2
Ueno Yabu Soba 15 C5
Yanaka Ginza 16 B1

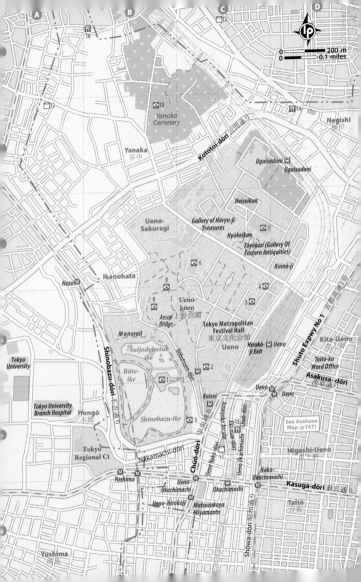

SEE

BENTEN-DŌ 弁天堂

☎ 3821 4638; 2-1 Ueno-kōen, Taitō-ku; admission free; ⏰ 9am-5pm; 🚉 JR Yamanote line to Ueno (Shinobazu exit)

Take a stroll down the causeway leading to the island on which Benten-dō stands. The temple is dedicated to Benzaiten, the Buddhist goddess of the arts, wisdom, the sea and the protector of children (she covers a lot of territory). More interesting than the temple itself is its location and the opportunity to see the birds and botany that thrive around the pond.

KIYOMIZU KANNON-DŌ 清水観音堂

1-4 Ueno-kōen, Taitō-ku; admission free; ⏰ 9am-5pm; 🚉 JR Yamanote line to Ueno (Shinobazu exit)

This red temple, up the path from the Takamori Saigō statue, was modelled after Kiyomizu-dera in Kyoto. During Ningyō-kuyō (p33), women wishing to conceive a child leave a doll here for Senjū Kannon (the 1000-armed goddess of mercy), and the accumulated dolls are ceremonially burnt each 25 September.

NATIONAL MUSEUM OF WESTERN ART 国立西洋美術館

☎ 5777 8600; 7-7 Ueno-koen, Taitō-ku, admission ¥420/130/free; ⏰ 9.30-5.30 Tue-Thu, Sat & Sun, 9.30am-8pm Fri; 🚉 JR Yamanote line to Ueno (Park exit); ♿

It may seem odd coming all this way just to check out Rodin sculptures and Le Corbusier architecture, but the Museum of Western Art can be well worth a stop during its frequent visiting exhibitions. Check local listings for what's on during your visit; there are often extra admission fees for special exhibitions.

NATIONAL SCIENCE MUSEUM 国立科学博物館

☎ 3822 0111; www.kahaku.go.jp/eng lish; 7-20 Ueno-kōen, Taitō-ku; admission ¥600/free, additional fee for special exhibitions; ⏰ 9am-5pm Tue-Thu, Sat & Sun, 9am-8pm Fri; 🚉 JR Yamanote line to Ueno (Park exit); ♿ 👶

Renovations in recent years have made this museum more user-friendly for foreigners, with interpretive English signage throughout. The interactive exhibits are great fun for kids, especially those that allow clambering. Between the dinosaur displays here and the animals at Ueno Zoo (p143), this is an excellent outing for children.

SHITAMACHI HISTORY MUSEUM 下町風俗資料館

☎ 3823 7451; 2-1 Ueno-kōen, Taitō-ku; admission ¥300/100; ⏰ 9.30am-4.30pm Tue-Sun; 🚉 JR Yamanote line to Ueno (Hirokōji exit); ♿ 👶

Learn some games and try on clothes in the style of Edo's *shitamachi*, the plebeian downtown quarter of old Tokyo. Hands-on or walk-in exhibits include a sweet shop, the home and business of a copper-boiler maker and a tenement house (don't forget to take off your shoes).

⊙ TOKYO METROPOLITAN MUSEUM OF ART
東京都美術館
☎ 3823 6921; www.tobikan.jp; 8-36 Ueno-kōen, Taitō-ku; admission varies; ⊙ 9am-5pm, closed 3rd Mon of each month; 🚇 JR Yamanote line to Ueno (Park exit); ♿
The Tokyo Met has several galleries that run temporary displays of contemporary Japanese art. Galleries feature all manner of Western-style art and Japanese-style works such as *sumi-e* (ink-brush painting) and ikebana. Apart from the main gallery, the rental galleries are curated by the artists and collectives who rent them, so exhibitions are a mixed bag.

⊙ TOKYO NATIONAL MUSEUM 東京国立博物館
☎ 3822 1111; www.tnm.jp; 13-9 Ueno-kōen, Taitō-ku; admission ¥600/400/free; ⊙ 9.30am-5pm Tue-Thu, Sat & Sun, 9.30am-8pm Fri; 🚇 JR Yamanote line to Ueno (Park exit); ♿

GREG ELMS / LONELY PLANET IMAGES ©
Armed to the teeth at Tokyo National Museum

This showcase of Japanese and Asian art and artefacts is the crown jewel of Ueno Park museums. Mull over your visit with a stroll in the peaceful Tokugawa Shōgun Cemetery, located just behind the museum.

⊙ TŌSHŌGŪ 東照宮
☎ 3822 3455; 1-9 Ueno-kōen, Taitō-ku; admission ¥200; ⊙ 9am-4.30pm; 🚇 JR Yamanote line to Ueno (Shinobazu exit)
Established in 1627, this shrine has the distinction of being one of the few extant early Edo

141

Terrie Lloyd
New Zealand–born entrepreneur and publisher of many of Japan's leading English-language magazines (including Metropolis*).*

What first brought you to Tokyo? I came on the first wave of Australia-Japan working holiday visas in 1983. I needed a change from my IT job in Sydney, and Japan was about as different a place as I could imagine. **What are the three most 'quintessentially Tokyo' things that everyone should experience?** First, Meiji Shrine (p20) just before sunset. Second, the bustling Takeshita-dōri – crammed to the brim with teenage girls trying to outdo each other's style. Third, anything related to food – eating out is the way of life. For sashimi, try one a small eatery near Tsukiji (p51). **What is the biggest misconception about Tokyo?** Before March 2011, it was that Tokyo is prohibitively expensive – but with 35 million people in the metropolis, there is plenty of variety. Beef bowls at ¥290! After the earthquake, the misconception is that it's unsafe. We take radiation measurements every day and there's been no significant exposure in the metropolis.

structures, having survived the Great Kantō Earthquake of 1923, WWII destruction and other historical disasters. The intricate decoration and the architecture of the shrine, typical to other Tōshōgū shrines throughout Japan, and the atypical copper lanterns lining the path, are well worth the price of admission.

🄲 UENO ZOO 上野動物園
☎ 3828 5171; 9-83 Ueno-kōen, Taitō-ku; admission ¥600/200/free; ⏲ 9.30am-5pm Tue-Sun; 🄼 Chiyoda line to Nezu (south exit), 🄬 JR Yamanote line to Ueno (Park exit); ♿ 🚻
Established in 1892, this is Japan's oldest zoo. It shouldn't feature on your Tokyo to-do list, but the little ones might enjoy cavorting with the veritable cast of the *Lion King*. Photographers will get a kick

out of shooting giraffes with a skyscraper backdrop.

🄲 YANAKA-REIEN 谷中霊園
7 Yanaka, Taito-ku; 🄬 JR Yamanote line to Nippori
One of Tokyo's largest graveyards, Yanaka-reien is the final resting place of over 7000 souls, many of whom were quite well known in their day, like Meiji-era novelist Soseki Natsume (you'll find his portrait on the ¥1000 bill). In spring, the cemetery comes alive with trillions of cherry blossoms that blanket the tombs and statues.

🄷 SHOP
🄷 AMEYOKO ARCADE
アメ横 *Market*
🄬 JR Yamanote line to Okachimachi (north exit) or Ueno (Hirokōji exit),
🄼 Ginza line to Ueno-Hirokōji (exit A5) or Hibiya line to Naka-Okachimachi (exit A5)
Ameya-yokochō, or Ameyoko for short, is one of the few old-fashioned outdoor markets in Tokyo. It was famous as a post-WWII black market, and even now it retains that throwback feel, with merchants calling out to attract customers and open-air stalls displaying dried seafood, herbs and mushrooms. The Ameyoko Center Building contains stalls that sell imported spices, produce and herbs from mainland Asia, and there are

GOT GRUTT?
Museum-crawlers planning on visiting several museums during a Tokyo visit should grab a Grutt Pass (¥2000) at the Tokyo Tourist Information Center (p202). The pass is a book of tickets entitling the bearer to free or discounted entry to nearly 50 Tokyo museums and zoos. It's valid for two months after the first visit and is a fabulous deal as it pays for itself in a few visits. The Grutt Pass is also available at participating museums.

143

Grilling yakitori at Ameyoko Arcade (p143)
MARK HEMMINGS / LONELY PLANET IMAGES ©

ing eyes, including that of van Gogh.

🏠 NIPPORI FABRIC TOWN
Handicrafts, Textiles
www.netlaputa.ne.jp/~nippori; 🚉 JR Yamanote line to Nippori (South exit)
After exiting the train station, pass the Mos Burger and you'll know you're heading in the right direction to uncover over 85 storefronts selling all sorts of textiles. The **Tomato** group of shops – there are five of 'em, most located about halfway across the area – have great deals on inexpensive fabric, weird cotton prints and end-of-spool cuts. Leather goods and strange ribbons can be scouted in the neighbourhood too.

a few clothing and shoe bargains around the market area.

🏠 ISETATSU いせ辰
Japanese Crafts
www.norenkai.net/shop/isetatsu; 2-18-9 Yanaka, Taito-ku; 🚉 JR Yamanote line to Nippori)
Tokyo's last maker of *chiyogami* (Edo-style woodblock-printed paper with bright colours; ¥2625), Isetatsu sells vibrant floral prints that have attracted many discern-

🍴 EAT
🍽 SASA-NO-YUKI 笹乃雪
Traditional Japanese   ¥¥
☎ 3873 1145; 2-15-10 Negishi, Taitō-ku; www.sasanoyuki.com; ⏰ 11am-8pm Tue-Sun; 🚉 JR Yamanote line to Uguisu-dani (north exit); Ⓥ ♿
Sasa-no-Yuki, or 'snow on bamboo', opened in Edo over 300 years ago. Staying true to its roots, this establishment continues to serve tofu in dozens of forms and in *tōfu-ryōri* (multicourse, tofu-based meals). Strict vegetarians should note that many dishes include chicken and fish stock; ask the friendly staff for advice if the

English menu doesn't provide you with enough information.

🍴 UENO YABU SOBA
上野やぶそば

Soba   ¥

☎ 3831 4728; 6-9-16 Ueno, Taitō-ku; ⏰ 11.30am-9pm Thu-Tue; 🚉 JR Yamanote line to Ueno (Hirokōji exit); ♿

Near the arcade, this busy, famous place rustles up top-class *soba,* from the simple *zaru soba* – plain, cold buckwheat noodles to dip in broth – to the richly filling *tenseiro* (noodles topped with shrimp and vegetable tempura). There's a picture menu to help you choose. Look for the black-granite sign in front that says in English 'Since 1892'.

🍴 YANAKA GINZA *Street*
                                              ¥

snacks from ¥60; 🚉 JR Yamanote line to Nippori (West exit)

Toto, I don't think we're in Tokyo any more. Like a yellow brick road unfurling down the hill, Yanaka Ginza's cluttered cluster of street stalls feels more like a bustling village thoroughfare than it does a Tokyo backstreet. Amblers will be treated to a variety of cheap eats from *yakitori* skewers to crunchy croquettes. Hunker down on a milk carton with the other locals and wash it all down with a beer.

>ASAKUSA

While Asakusa does draw significant tourist traffic, it carries on with the rough-around-the-edges Shitamachi spirit that powered the low city of old Edo. With its bustling centrepiece the temple Sensō-ji drawing devotees as well as photo-snapping visitors, the streets, temples and shrines of Asakusa imbue this area with a historical feel. So too do the neighbourhood's working artists busily keep customs alive by labouring over traditional handicrafts.

The neighbourhood, with kitchenware district Kappabashi-dōri to the west and the Sumida River to the east, is compact enough to take in with a walking tour. But near Kaminarimon you'll probably also be wooed by *jinrikisha* (people-powered rickshaw) drivers in traditional dress, who can cart you around on tours (from ¥2100 per person for 10 minutes), stopping at sights to provide insightful commentary in English, Japanese or other languages. Asakusa runs at a steady hum throughout the day, but tends to shut down after night falls.

ASAKUSA

◎ SEE
Asakusa-jinja 1 C2
Chingodō-ji (Chingodō
    Shrine) 2 B3
Dembō-in 3 B3
Edo Shitamachi
    Traditional Crafts
    Museum 4 B2
Sensō-ji 5 C2
Taiko-Kan
    (Drum Museum) 6 A3

🛍 SHOP
Kappabashi-Dōri 7 A3
Yoshitoku 8 A6

🍴 EAT
Daikokuya 9 B3
Ef 10 C3
Irokawa 11 B4
Komagata Dojō 12 B4
Vin Chou 13 A3

▼ DRINK
Asahi Sky Room 14 C4
Kamiya Bar 15 C4

⭐ PLAY
Asakusa Kannon
    Onsen 16 B2
Jakotsu-yu 17 B3

Imado

Kokusai-dōri

Kototoi-dōri

Taitō-ku

Asakusa

Kototoi-dōri

Sumida-kōen

Asakusa View Hotel

Hisago-dōri

Hanayashiki Amusement Park

Asakusa-kōen

Yoshino-dōri

Kototoibashi

Kappabashihon dōri

Asakusa

Hanamichi-dōri

Hanakawadokōen

Nishi-Asakusa

Asakusa Engei Hall

Dembō-in

Hōzō-mon

Asakusa Tourist Information Center

Hanakawado

Shuto Expwy No 6

Shin-Nakamise-dōri

Orange-dōri

Tōbu Asakusa

Tōbu Asakusa

Edo-dōri

Tokyo Hongan-ji

Kaminarimon-dōri

Empodo-dōri

Nakamise-dōri

Metro-dōri

Asakusa

Suijo Bus Pier

Kaminarimon

Asahi Super Dry Building

Tawaramachi

Azuma-bashi

Asakusa-dōri

Asakusa

Komagata-bash

Honjo-Azumabashi

Kokusai-dōri

Kotobuki

Shuto Expwy No 6

Sumida River (Sumida-gawa)

Misume-dōri

Kasuga-dōri

Kuramae

Kuramae

Asakusabashi

👁 SEE

👁 ASAKUSA-JINJA 浅草神社
2-3-1 Asakusa, Taitō-ku; admission free; 🚇 Ginza & Toei Asakusa lines to Asakusa (exits 1 & A5)

Buddhist Sensō-ji sits just in front of its Shintō neighbour, Asakusa-jinja, in silent architectural testament to the peaceful coexistence of these two religions in Japan. Also known as Sanja-sama, this shrine is the site of one of Tokyo's most important *matsuri*, the Sanja Matsuri (p31).

👁 CHINGODŌ-JI 鎮護寺
2-3-1 Asakusa, Taitō-ku; admission free; 🚇 Ginza & Toei Asakusa lines to Asakusa (exits 1 & A5)

This quiet, odd little shrine on the banks of Dembō-in (right) pays tribute to *tanuki* – the 'raccoon dog' tricksters who figure in Japanese mythology. Shape-shifting *tanuki* are normally depicted with enormous testicles on which they can fly.

👁 DEMBŌ-IN 伝法院
☎ 3842 0181; 2-3-1 Asakusa, Taitō-ku; admission free; 🕘 9am-4.30pm, closed for ceremonies; 🚇 Ginza & Toei Asakusa lines to Asakusa (exits 1 & A5)

Adjacent to the Sensō-ji precinct is Dembō-in, a temple with an attached garden. Inside this secret sanctuary there's a picturesque pond and a replica of a famous Kyoto teahouse. Although it's not open to the public, you can make an appointment to visit by calling a few days ahead to the temple office (inside the Five-Storeyed Pagoda).

👁 EDO SHITAMACHI TRADITIONAL CRAFTS MUSEUM 江戸下町伝統工芸館
☎ 3842 1990; 2-22-13 Asakusa, Taitō-ku; admission free; 🕘 10am-8pm; 🚇 Tsukuba Express to Asakusa (exit A1) or Ginza line to Tawaramachi (exit 3)

This hall is a wonderful place to view the handicrafts that continue

---

VISITING A SHRINE

Just past the *torii* (shrine gate) is a *chōzuya* (water trough), with long-handled ladles perched on a rack above. This is for purifying yourself before entering the sacred precincts of the shrine. If you choose to purify yourself, take a ladle, fill it with fresh water from the spigot, pour some over one hand, transfer the spoon and pour water over the other hand. Then pour a little water into a cupped hand and rinse your mouth, spitting the water onto the ground beside the trough.

Head to the *haiden* (hall of worship), which sits in front of the *honden* (main hall) enshrining the *kami* (shrine god). Toss a coin into the offerings box, ring the gong by pulling on the thick rope in order to summon the deity, pray, then clap your hands twice, bow and then back away from the shrine.

Sensō-ji Temple illuminates the sky at dusk

GREG ELMS / LONELY PLANET IMAGES ©

to flourish in Shitamachi. The gallery on the 2nd floor of this museum displays a rotating selection of works (such as fans, lanterns, knives, intricate woodcarvings and glass) by neighbourhood artists, and crafts demonstrations take place around noon on most weekends.

SENSŌ-JI 浅草寺

☎ 3842 0181; 2-3-1 Asakusa, Taitō-ku; admission free; Ⓜ Ginza & Toei Asakusa lines to Asakusa (exits 1 & A5)

With its pagoda and shrines nearby, Sensō-ji is one of Tokyo's most popular sights. It lies in the heart of Asakusa and serves as a community temple. As you reach

Hōzōmon, the second gate leading into the temple itself, have a look at the Five-Storeyed Pagoda to the left, the second tallest in Japan.

TAIKOKAN (DRUM MUSEUM) 太鼓館

☎ 3842 5622; 2-1-1 Nishi-Asakusa, Taitō-ku; admission ¥300/150; ☽ 10am-5pm Wed-Sun; Ⓜ Ginza line to Tarawachō (exit 3)

It's tellingly human that the vast majority of us can't resist the temptation to bang a gong, given half the chance. Luckily for our percussive tendencies, this drum museum makes its instruments fair game unless they're marked with a red dot. From *taiko*

149

(traditional Japanese drums) to African finger-harps, this museum displays examples of drums from around the world.

SHOP

Nakamise-dōri, the lively pedestrian street leading to Sensō-ji, is chock-a-block with shops selling tourist wares like *geta* (wooden sandals worn with kimonos), lacquer combs, purses and cigarette cases made from kimono fabric and Edo-style toys and trinkets. Look out for stalls selling *sembei* (savoury rice crackers), *anko* (azuki-bean paste) sweets and freshly made *mochi* (sticky-rice cakes). But don't just stick to the main drag; the alleys off to both sides of Nakamise-dōri and the streets around Sensō-ji are full of small shops selling *tenugui* (traditionally dyed hand towels) or accessories to be worn with kimonos and other fine handicrafts.

KAPPABASHI-DŌRI
かっぱ橋通り
Homewares & novelties
On the west side of Asakusa is this kitchenware shopping strip, which supplies restaurants and locals with items such as ceramic ware, woven bamboo trays, iron

GREG ELMS / LONELY PLANET IMAGES ©

These plastic food models go down a treat on Kappabashi-dōri, Asakusa's kitchenware shopping strip

teapots, *noren* (doorway curtains) and, best of all, those excellent plastic food models. They don't come cheap though – a couple of pieces of sushi will set you back about ¥2500.

🏠 **YOSHITOKU** 吉徳 *Dolls*
☎ 3863 4419; 1-9-14 Asakusabashi, Taitō-ku; ⏰ 9.30am-5.30pm Mon-Sat; 🚋 JR Sōbu line to Asakusabashi (main exit) 🚇 Toei Asakusa line to Asakusabashi (exit A2)
Dollmaker to the emperor, Yoshitoku has been in business since 1711. The dolls here are exquisitely crafted in silk and porcelain, dressed in sumptuous replicas of elaborate kimonos and accessories. Small pieces can sell for ¥2000, while more elaborate dolls can go for a hundred times as much.

🍴 EAT

🍴 **DAIKOKUYA** 大黒家
Tempura ¥¥
☎ 3844 1111; 1-38-10 Asakusa, Taitō-ku; ⏰ 11.30am-8.30pm Mon-Fri, 11.30am-9pm Sat; 🚇 Ginza & Toei Asakusa lines to Asakusa (exits 1 & A5); ♿
Near Nakamise-dōri, this famous place serves great, authentic tempura, a speciality in Asakusa. The queue out the door usually snakes around the corner at lunchtime, but if it looks unbearably long,

try your luck at the branch on the next block.

🍴 **EF** *Cafe* ¥¥
www.gallery-ef.com; 2-19-18 Kaminarimon, Taitō-ku; ⏰ lunch & dinner; 🚇 Ginza & Asakusa lines to Asakusa (exit 2)
Set in a wobbly wooden house that beat the 1923 earthquake and WWII, this wonderfully unpretentious space serves simple bites and doubles as a small gallery showcasing local artists.

🍴 **IROKAWA** 色川 *Unagi* ¥¥
☎ 3844 1187; 2-6-11 Kaminarimon, Taitō-ku; ⏰ 11.20am-1.30pm & 5-8.30pm Mon-Sat; 🚇 Ginza & Toei Asakusa lines to Asakusa (exits 2 and A1)
Irokawa serves some of the best, most beautifully grilled *unagi* (eel) around. Try the *unaju* (broiled eel on rice). It has a humble, traditional-looking exterior, with plants flanking the entrance, and is a friendly neighbourhood spot to try *unagi* with the locals.

🍴 **KOMAGATA DOJŌ** 駒形　どぜう
Dojō ¥¥
☎ 3842 4001; 1-7-12 Komagata, Taitō-ku; ⏰ 11am-9pm; 🚇 Ginza & Toei Asakusa lines to Asakusa (exits 2 & A5); ♿
The 6th-generation chef at the helm of this marvellous restaurant

continues the tradition of elevating the simple *dojō* (a small, eel-like river fish) to a thing of delicious wonder. You can try it 10 different ways, and there's an English menu. Floor seating at the shared, low wooden plank tables heightens the traditional flavour, but ladies: don't wear a skirt for this dining expedition.

🍴 VIN CHOU 萬鳥
Yakitori ¥¥
☎ 3845 4430; 2-2-13 Nishi-Asakusa, Taitō-ku; ⏱ 5pm-11pm Thu-Sat, Mon & Tue, 4-10pm Sun; 🚇 Ginza & Toei Asakusa lines to Asakusa (exits 1 & A5)
Tucked away in this corner of Asakusa, Vin Chou is an odd bird: a French-style *yakitori* joint, offering foie gras with your *tori negi* (chicken and spring onion). With cheeses and fowl imported from Europe, it's chic and unique. It's just round the corner one block west of the Taikokan (p149).

🍸 DRINK

Asakusa is another of those neighbourhoods without a compelling nightlife, but you can certainly throw back a few at these local bars.

🍸 ASAHI SKY ROOM
アサヒスカイルーム *Bar*
☎ 5608 5277; 22F, Asahi Super Dry Bldg, 1-23-1 Azumabashi, Sumida-ku;

⏱ 10am-10pm; 🚇 Ginza & Toei Asakusa lines to Asakusa (exits 4 & A5)
Spend the day at religious sites and end at the Asahi altar, on the 22nd floor of the golden-tinged Asahi Super Dry Building. Directly adjacent to the infamous *Flamme d'Or* sculpture (aka the 'Golden Turd') on the east bank of the Sumida River, the venue itself isn't noteworthy, but serves up Asahi brews and a spectacular view, especially at sunset.

🍸 KAMIYA BAR 神谷バー
Bar
☎ 3841 5400; 1-1-1 Asakusa, Taitō-ku; ⏱ 11.30am-10pm Wed-Mon; 🚇 Ginza & Toei Asakusa lines to Asakusa (exits 3 & A5)
Once popular with the Tokyo literati, this smoky old place hasn't changed much since it was founded in 1880. The 1st floor is a beer hall where you pay for drinks as you enter. Its best-known offering is the brandy-based cocktail *denki-bran*. The restaurants upstairs serve Japanese and Western food, but that's not the reason to come here.

⭐ PLAY

ASAKUSA KANNON ONSEN
浅草観音温泉 *Hot Spring*
☎ 3844 4141; 2-7-26 Asakusa, Taitō-ku; admission ¥700; ⏱ 6.30am-6pm Thu-Tue;

Ginza & Toei Asakusa lines to Asakusa
(exits 1 & A5)

Look for the ivy-covered exterior of this large, traditional bath-house. The water here is a steamy 40°C, and Asakusa's historic ambi-ence makes this a great place for a soul-soothing soak.

⭐ JAKOTSU-YU 蛇骨湯
Hot Spring

☎ 3841 8645; www.jakotsuyu.co.jp, in Japanese; 1-11-11 Asakusa, Taitō-ku; admission ¥450; ☼ 1pm-midnight Wed-Mon; Ⓢ Ginza line to Tawaramachi (exit 3)

Jakotsu-yu is a wonderful little neighbourhood *onsen* (hot spring) with mineral-rich dark water at a hot-hot-hot 45°C. This *onsen* has a small *rotemburo* (outdoor bath) with a garden

> ### TATTOO BLUES
> Long the mark of the *yakuza* (mafia), *irezumi* (tattoos) are still largely taboo in Japan. Although body art is becoming more popular with younger people, tattoos are still not as commonplace as in the West. If your skin bears a tattoo or a few, be discreet when visiting a *sentō* (public bath) or *onsen* (hot spring). They usually post signs prohibiting entry to tattooed individuals, ostensibly to keep out the *yakuza*. In reality, if the *yakuza* want in, they'll get in – and in all likeli-hood you won't be mistaken for one. Keep in mind, however, that your ink may get you ejected.

setting. From Kokusai-dōri, turn into the second alley north of Kaminarimon-dōri, then slip into the first narrow alley on the right and you're there.

>ODAIBA

Odaiba, an artificial island built on landfill in Tokyo Bay, is a great way to escape from Tokyo without leaving the city. Most people will arrive here via the driverless monorail from Shimbashi station, and will be treated to superb views of Tokyo and the bay. But this isn't all. Odaiba is an entertainment district, a setting for unconventional architecture and a showcase for futuristic innovations, displayed in museums and showrooms around town. Kids couldn't get bored here, between the Tokyo Joypolis (an indoor, high-tech amusement park), the world's biggest Ferris wheel and excellent museums whose exhibits include remote-controlled boats. Lovers of kitsch will be equally delighted to come across the replica of the Statue of Liberty and the theme parks made in the images of old Edo, Hong Kong and even 17th-century Italy (a bathhouse, restaurant row and shopping mall, respectively). If there's a comprehensive theme to the architecture of Odaiba, you could call it 'experimental', but mostly it stands as a record of the 'bubble era' and the futuristic aesthetics and intentions of that period.

ODAIBA

⊙ SEE
Fuji TV 1 A3
Museum of Maritime
    Science 2 A4
National Museum of
    Emerging Science &
    Innovation (Miraikan) .. 3 A4
Tokyo Big Sight (East
    Exhibition Hall) 4 D2
Tokyo Big Sight (West
    Exhibition Hall) 5 D3

🏠 SHOP
Decks Tokyo Beach 6 A3
Venus Fort 7 B4

🍴 EAT
Daiba Little
    Hong Kong .... (see 6)
Khazana .... (see 6)
Tsukiji Tama Sushi .... (see 6)

▾ DRINK
Hanashibe .... (see 8)
Sunset Beach
    Brewing Company .... (see 6)

★ PLAY
Cinema Mediage 8 A3
Muscle Park .... (see 6)
Ôedo Onsen
    Monogatari 9 B5
Tokyo Joypolis .... (see 6)

Tokyo Bay
東京湾

Kōtō-ku
江東区

Ariake
Tennis-
no-mori

Ariake
Colosseum

Shuto Expwy No.11
首都高速11号

Ariake
Tennis
Park

Ariake
有明

Ariake

Kokusai
Tenjijō

Daiba-
kōen

Shuto Expwy Wangan Line
首都高速湾岸線

Odaiba
Kaihin-
kōen

Kokusai-
tenjijō-
Seimon

To Narita
International
Airport
(65 km)

Odaiba
Marine
Park

Aqua
City

Dream Bridge
夢の大橋

Center Promenade

Tokyo
Teleport

Neo Geo
World

Toyota
Mega Web

Daiba

Aomi
青海

Palette
Town

Aomi

Tokyo
International
Pier

West Promenade

Fune-no
Kagakukan

Shiokaze-kōen
潮風公園

Telecom
Center

Telecom
Center

Jugochi
Wharf
West

Tokyo
International
Pier

Akatsuki
Futō-
kōen

Tokyo Bay
東京湾

Tokyo Bay
東京湾

👁 SEE

Because Odaiba doesn't have the typical glut of traffic that mainland Tokyo has, the island is quite pleasant to traverse on foot. But if you're covering a lot of ground between museums and malls and *onsen* (hot springs), you might opt to take the free shuttle bus that makes a circuit around Odaiba between 11am and 8pm. The red buses come around every 15 minutes or so and stop at a dozen locations on the island, including Aqua City and Fuji TV. Bus stops are not signposted in English but have red markers with bus symbols on them.

🅲 FUJI TV フジテレビ

☎ 5500 8888; 2-4-8 Daiba, Minato-ku; observation deck ¥500/300; ⏰ 10am-8pm Tue-Sun; 🚉 Rinkai line to Tokyo Teleport or Yurikamome line to Odaiba Kaihin-kōen

Designed by the late, great Kenzō Tange, the Fuji TV headquarters building is recognisable by the 90-degree angles of its scaffold-inglike structure, topped with a 1200-tonne ball. You can actually go into the ball, which is a terrific observation deck. Pick up an English guide at the information desk out front, and take a self-guided tour.

🅲 MUSEUM OF MARITIME SCIENCE 船の科学館

☎ 5500 1111; www.funenokagakukan.or.jp; 3-1 Higashi-Yashio, Shinagawa-ku; admission ¥700/400; ⏰ 10am-5pm Tue-Sun; 🚉 Yurikamome line to Fune-no-Kagakukan; ♿ 👶

This is one of Tokyo's better museums, containing four floors of excellent displays with loads of detailed models, lots of hands-on exhibits that kids will love, and a pool on the roof where, for ¥100, they can wreak havoc with radio-controlled boats and submarines.

🅲 NATIONAL MUSEUM OF EMERGING SCIENCE & INNOVATION (MIRAIKAN) 日本科学未来館

☎ 3570 9151; www.miraikan.jst.go.jp; 2-3-6 Aomi, Kōtō-ku; admission ¥600/200, kids free on Sat; ⏰ 10am-5pm Wed-Mon; 🚉 Yurikamome line to Fune-no-Kagakukan or Telecom Center; ♿ 👶

Kids will love the engaging exhibits at this science museum, where most displays have excellent explanations in English and English-speaking guides fill in the blanks. There's the spectacular planetarium (buy tickets for a show as soon as you arrive), demonstrations of robots and opportunities to interact with them, and tons of exhibits about space, medicine and the environment.

TOKYO BIG SIGHT
東京ビッグサイト

☎ 5530 1111; www.bigsight.jp/english;
3-21-1 Ariake, Kōtō-ku; ⊖ Rinkai line
to Kokusai-Tenjijō or Yurikamome line
to Kokusai-Tenjijō-Seimon; ⑤

Odaiba is full of oddball architecture and Tokyo Big Sight (officially known as Tokyo International Exhibition Hall) is certainly no exception – appropriate, since it is the semi-annual venue for Tokyo's coolest design festival, Design Festa (p107). Keep a look out for the upside-down pyramids of the conference tower rising above the exhibition complex.

🛍 SHOP
DECKS TOKYO BEACH
デックス東京ビーチ

Department Store

☎ 3599 6500; www.odaiba-decks.com;
1-6-1 Daiba, Minato-ku; ⏰ 11am-9pm;
🚃 Yurikamome line to Odaiba
Kaihin-kōen; ⑤ ⑤

Fashioned after a beachside boardwalk, Decks Tokyo Beach is split into two sides: the Seaside Mall and Island Mall. Both house shopping and dining, and this is also the place you'll find the indoor amusement park, Tokyo Joypolis (p159).

VENUS FORT
ヴィーナスフォート

Department Store

☎ 3599 0700; www.venusfort.co.jp;
Palette Town, Aomi 1-chōme, Kōtō-ku;
⏰ 11am-9pm, restaurants 11am-11pm;
🚃 Yurikamome line to Aomi or Rinkai
line to Tokyo Teleport; ⑤

Venus Fort embodies a Japanese vision of a young woman's shopping paradise, in a building that mimics 17th-century Rome where the ceilings simulate the sky turning from day to night. With around 170 boutiques and restaurants all aimed at young women, this kitsch shopping centre also boasts the distinction of having Japan's biggest lavatory (64 stalls).

RICHARD T NOWITZ / CORBIS
Open skies inside the Romanesque Venus Fort

157

NEIGHBOURHOODS

ODAIBA

🍴 EAT
🍴 DAIBA LITTLE HONG KONG
Food-themed Park ¥¥

☎ 3599 6500; 6F & 7F, Decks Tokyo Beach, 1-6-1 Daiba, Minato-ku; ⏰ 11am-10pm; 🚉 Yurikamome line to Ōdaiba Kaihin-Kōen; ♿ 🚻

Among the quirky attractions of Odaiba is this kooky replica of Hong Kong's streets, complete with a recorded soundtrack of simulated street noise, neon signs, souvenir shops and restaurants slinging *gyōza* (dumplings) and *yum cha*.

🍴 KHAZANA カザーナ
Indian ¥

☎ 3599 6551; 5F, Decks Tokyo Beach, 1-6-1 Daiba, Minato-ku; ⏰ 11am-10pm; 🚉 Yurikamome line to Ōdaiba Kaihin-Kōen; ♿ V

Come early to snag one of the coveted tables out on the deck for maximum sensory pleasure. This Indian restaurant serves a good all-you-can-eat buffet lunch and has a fair number of vegetarian options on the menu.

🍴 TSUKIJI TAMA SUSHI
築地玉寿司
Sushi & Sashimi ¥¥

☎ 3599 6556; 5F, Decks Tokyo Beach, 1-6-1 Daiba, Minato-ku; ⏰ 11am-11pm; 🚉 Yurikamome line to Odaiba Kaihin-kōen

Seat yourself near the windows and sip from a huge cup of green tea while you wait for your sushi – it will come immaculately presented and perfectly fresh. The menu also includes set meals and *udon*.

🍸 DRINK
HANASHIBE はなしべ
Izakaya

☎ 3599 5575; 3F, Aqua City, 1-7-1 Daiba, Minato-ku; ⏰ 11am-11pm; 🚉 Yurikamome line to Daiba; ♿ 🚻

For Kyoto specialities and house-brewed sake, check out Hanashibe in the Mediage entertainment complex in Aqua City. You can try three types of sake in a tasting set (¥700), which you can match with small dishes typical of an *izakaya* (pub eatery).

🍸 SUNSET BEACH BREWING COMPANY サンセットビーチブルーイングカンパニー
Brewery

☎ 3599 6655; 5F, Decks Tokyo Beach, 1-6-1 Daiba, Minato-ku; ⏰ 11am-11pm; 🚉 Yurikamome line to Ōdaiba Kaihin-Kōen; 🚻

After roaming around Odaiba put your feet up and enjoy expansive views with an island-brewed beer. There are reasonably priced lunch and dinner buffets, but the house Italian food isn't worth the trip.

⭐ PLAY

CINEMA MEDIAGE
シネマメディアージュ
Cinema

☎ 5531 7878; 1F & 2F, Mediage, Aqua City, 1-7-1 Daiba, Minato-ku; tickets ¥1800/1500/1000, women ¥1000 on Wed; 🕐 ticket sales 11am-11pm; 🚃 Yurikamome line to Daiba; ♿

This enormous 3000-seat multiplex shows Japanese and foreign films, many of which are subtitled and some of which are dubbed into Japanese. Check the *Japan Times* or *Metropolis* for current listings. Mediage is located inside the Aqua City shopping centre.

⭐ MUSCLE PARK マッスル
パーク *Amusement Park*

☎ 6821 0091; www.musclepark.jp; 5F, Island Mall, Decks Tokyo Beach, 1-6-1 Daiba, Minato-ku; admission ¥1000-3900/600-1000; 🕐 11am-9pm Sun-Fri, 11am-10pm Sat; 🚃 Yurikamome line to Ōdaiba Kaihin-Kōen; ♿

A rarity in Tokyo, where much of the high-tech entertainment is of the sedentary variety, this amusement space features physical challenges and games from popular TV shows and even includes a kids park.

⭐ ŌEDO ONSEN MONOGATARI
大江戸温泉物語 *Hot Spring*

☎ 5500 1126; www.ooedoonsen.jp /english; 2-57 Aomi, Kōtō-ku; admission ¥2900/1600; 🕐 11am-9am, last entry at 7am; 🚃 Yurikamome line to Telecom Center

This *onsen* is set up like an Edo-era town and pipes in natural mineral water from 1400m beneath Tokyo Bay. Although the set-up might seem cheesy, the *onsen* is attractively designed, with old-fashioned restaurants and souvenir shops for a postbath bite and browse. Admission fees cover the rental of *yukata* (cotton kimonos) and towels. Fees vary between morning and night, so check the website for full details.

⭐ TOKYO JOYPOLIS
東京ジョイポリス
Amusement Park

☎ 5500 1801; 3F-5F, Decks Tokyo Beach, 1-6-1 Daiba, Minato-ku; passport ¥3500/3100, after 5pm ¥2500/2100; 🕐 10am-11pm; 🚃 Yurikamome line to Ōdaiba Kaihin-Kōen; ♿ 🚻

Joypolis is Sega's high-tech playland for overstimulating your kids, or yourself. Your visit here will be full of nonstop action, with crazy indoor roller coasters, video games and virtual-reality rides.

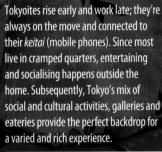

Tokyoites rise early and work late; they're always on the move and connected to their *keitai* (mobile phones). Since most live in cramped quarters, entertaining and socialising happens outside the home. Subsequently, Tokyo's mix of social and cultural activities, galleries and eateries provide the perfect backdrop for a varied and rich experience.

> Accommodation	162
> Anime & Manga	164
> Architecture	165
> Food	166
> Galleries	168
> Gay & Lesbian	169
> Kids	170
> Live Music	171
> Markets	172
> Museums	173
> Nightlife	174
> Parks & Gardens	175
> Sentō & Onsen	176
> Shrines & Temples	177
> Shopping	178
> Spectator Sports	180

The essence of spring is captured in the fabric and design of the kimono

> ACCOMMODATION

Staying anywhere along the Yamanote loop (p194) gives you easy access to nearly every corner of the city. If it's not on the loop, some subway line will quickly connect you. Central Tokyo hotels put you within strolling distance of Ginza shopping and myriad dining options, while Shinjuku has a slew of solid hotels catering to business travellers. Ebisu doesn't have many places to stay, but is a quieter, stylish part of the city that's also connected to the Yamanote loop. For those who want nothing to do with quiet nights in, staying around Roppongi means being able to stumble into bed at any hour without worrying about the trains shutting down at midnight. Additionally, despite its reputation as an exorbitantly expensive city to visit, Tokyo does have pleasant budget options, including capsule hotels, generic but reasonably priced 'business hotels' and some excellent ryokan (Japanese-style inns).

Ryokan in Tokyo don't fit the traditional definition in the strictest sense – in this city, they typically won't include meals, and on the budget end you may even have to bring (or buy) your own towel. Most have tatami (woven matting) floors; you should always remove your shoes or slippers before entering a tatami room. At a typical Japanese ryokan, a futon is usually laid out and made up in the evenings, then folded and put away in the mornings; however, in budget ryokan you'll do this yourself or simply leave the futon out all day. Be sure to also take advantage of at least one soak in the *sentō* (public baths; see p176) available here, an experience most modern hotels don't offer. You'll find most of Tokyo's ryokan in Asakusa and Ueno.

Seekers of Japanese kitsch will want to stay in one of the famed love hotels (p93). These days they're more politely referred to as 'boutique' or 'fashion' hotels, and there's one for every taste, from miniature Gothic

Need a place to stay? Find and book it at lonelyplanet. com. Over 120 properties are featured for Tokyo – each personally visited, thoroughly reviewed and happily recommended by a Lonely Planet author. From hostels to high-end hotels, we've hunted out the places that will bring you unique and special experiences. Read independent reviews by authors and other travellers, and get practical information including amenities, maps and photos. Then reserve your room simply and securely via Hotels & Hostels – our online booking service. It's all at lonelyplanet.com/hotels.

castles to Middle Eastern temples – and these are just the buildings. Some rooms even have bath grottoes or ceiling swings. Love hotels are most highly concentrated on Love Hotel Hill (p92).

Solo travellers could also check into that uniquely Japanese invention: the capsule hotel. Making the most of limited space, these individual capsules are not as cheap as you might imagine (around ¥4000), but they are tall enough for lounging and come outfitted with personal TVs. Personal storage space is limited to lockers, so don't bring a ton of baggage; personal space is obviously at a premium, so do bring earplugs.

To search for and book Tokyo accommodations, check out www.jpinn .com for ryokan, and www.japanhotelfinder.com or Lonely Planet's own online booking service (see the boxed text opposite).

BEST RYOKAN
> Ginza Yoshimizu (www.yoshimizu .com/en/ginza/index.html)
> Hōmeikan (www.homeikan.com)
> Kimi Ryokan (www.kimi-ryokan.jp)
> Sawanoya Ryokan (www.sawanoya .com)
> Sukeroku no Yado Sadachiyo (www .sadachiyo.co.jp)

BEST LUXURY HOTELS
> Conrad Hotel (www.conradtokyo.co.jp)
> ANA Intercontinental (www.anainter continental-tokyo.jp)
> Grand Hyatt (www.tokyo.grand.hyatt. com)
> Peninsula Tokyo (www.peninsula.com/ Tokyo/en/default.aspx)
> Park Hyatt (www.tokyo.park.hyatt.com)

BEST BUSINESS BETS
> Tokyu Hotels (www.tokyuhotels.co.jp)
> Villa Fontaine (www.hvf.jp/eng)
> Ishin Hotels Group (www.ishinhotels)

BEST HOTEL WEBSITES
> Tocoo! (www.tocoo.jp)
> Welcome Inn Reservation Center (www .itcj.jp/eng/tokyo_met)
> Sakura House (www.sakurahouse.com)
> Duplex (www.duplexcs.jp)

> ANIME & MANGA

Akihabara is *the* manga Mecca for Tokyoites and visitors alike, and is even becoming an attraction for those seeking a glimpse of the distinctly Japanese *otaku* (geek) subculture. It's the best place to start a quest for manga. The burly Mandarake chain, whose exhaustive flagship is located in Nakano, has a large outpost here, filled with all manner of manga from the kid-friendly *Doraemon* (a blue robotic cat from the future) to *dōjinshi* (self-published, fan-drawn spin-offs and parodies) to *hentai* (perverse) manga, DVDs, games and figurines.

One of the richest treasure troves in the city is the chain bookshop Book Off, which buys and sells used manga and has an entire section of paperbacks for only ¥100 apiece. You could easily collect an entire series for what amounts to lunch money. There's also a burgeoning female *otaku* culture (see the boxed text, p135) and its own geek haven in Ikebukuro, a hotbed of the 'boys' love' manga genre.

JOHN ASHBURNE / LONELY PLANET IMAGES ©

BEST PLACES TO PERUSE
> Mandarake (p94)
> Tora no Ana (p58)

BEST MUSEUMS TO VISIT
> Ghibli Museum (p15)

BEST OTAKU HANGOUTS
> Akihabara (p50)
> Otome Rd (p135)

> ARCHITECTURE

After WWII incendiary bombing flattened much of Tokyo, the city collected itself and began the long decades of reconstruction. Tokyo hit a boom period in the '50s, during which the subway system started to take shape. And when the city won the privilege of hosting the 1964 summer Olympics, buildings seemed to sprout like mushrooms after a long rain. One of the structures built for the Olympics was the National Yoyogi Stadium, a structure of curves sloping down from a suspension roof. The building was designed by Kenzō Tange, an Osaka-born architect who taught at Tokyo University and died in 2005. During his long career he influenced the reshaping of the cityscape, and his designs stand out all over Tokyo.

But diversity reigns in the vibrant architectural face of the city. Although it is not the most sustainable strategy, aging buildings are demolished to make way for bigger, newer and more innovative structures that astound and inspire. Because real estate is at a premium in this denser-than-dense megalopolis, the only way to go is up.

MICHAEL TAYLOR / LONELY PLANET IMAGES ©

BEST STRUCTURAL STATEMENTS
> Roppongi Hills (p72)
> Tokyo International Forum (p51)
> Tokyo Metropolitan Government Offices (p121)
> Tokyo Sky Tree (p16)

BEST COPYCATS
> Statue of Liberty (p154; pictured)
> Tokyo Tower (p72)

MOST FASHIONABLE & FUNCTIONAL
> BAPExclusive (p108)
> Prada Aoyama (p106)

SNAPSHOTS

> FOOD

Epicureans will find no shortage of new tastes to sample in the city, where renowned chefs from around the world set up shop, balancing Tokyo's wasabi and soy sauce with balsamic vinegar and olive oil. A taste of the traditional can be sampled in venues as humble as the local *rāmen* shop or in the refined, minimalist tatami room of a *kaiseki* (elegant, multicourse Japanese meals) restaurant, while there's also an incredible diversity of international cuisine, representing culinary traditions from Sweden to Senegal. And of course comfort foods like burgers or pasta – though usually Japanese renditions of those dishes – are easily found across the city.

Japanese food runs the gamut between the raw fish of your sushi or sashimi platter and the deep-fried *panko* (Japanese breadcrumb) crust of a crispy, tender pork cutlet *(tonkatsu)* on a bed of shredded cabbage. In addition to *tonkatsu*, there's tempura and *kushi-katsu* (deep-fried skewers of meat and vegetables), both of which are often served in small courses, as they are cooked so that everything comes to the table piping hot. If on an oppressively humid day the last thing you want to eat is fried food, do as the Tokyoites do and have an *unagi* (barbecued eel) lunch to keep up your stamina. *Unagi* is especially tasty when it's grilled perfectly in its sweet soy marinade and served in a *bentō* (boxed meal) over rice. An

ANTHONY PLUMMER / LONELY PLANET IMAGES ©

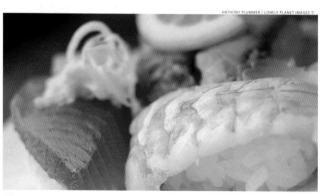

even cooler (temperature-wise) option is cold *soba* (buckwheat noodles) that you dip in cold broth and slurp noisily. *Soba* can also be served hot, as are *udon* (thick wheat noodles) and *rāmen*.

Cook-it-yourself affairs such as sukiyaki or *shabu-shabu* are the most fun with a few people, where the morsels of simmered meat and vegetables are meant to be shared and the communal pot is tended by all. You can do the DIY experience alone, cooking up *okonomiyaki* or *monjayaki* – egg-batter pancakes full of cabbage, vegetables, seafood and meat – at your own table.

Adventurous eaters can also have a festive meal of *fugu* (puffer fish), that famously poisonous *poisson* that is safely prepared by trained experts. *Fugu* restaurants usually offer multicourse dinners featuring *fugu* sashimi, *shabu-shabu* and *fugu* cooked a dozen ways. While the taste and texture of *fugu* may not wow you like the transcendent tuna of your sushi lunch, eating tuna doesn't come with the same satisfaction of having cheated death at the dinner table.

In general, most restaurants, whatever the type, often serve tasty *teishoku* (lunch sets) that are more reasonably priced than their dinner courses; keep this in mind if you wish to dine somewhere at the higher end of the spectrum, as lunch will often fit into your budget even if supper won't. Lunch sets at department store *resutoran-gai* ('restaurant towns') are very economical and tend to be of good quality. Browse the plastic food models and choose the shops specialising in one thing: *unagi*, tempura, *kushi-katsu*, sushi or *soba*. And if you just need something to tide you over for the next museum stop, convenience-store *onigiri* (rice ball; around ¥125) and iced tea is always just around the corner.

BEST UPMARKET JAPANESE
> Inakaya (p74)
> Kikunoi (p74)
> Ukai Tofu-ya (p76)
> Sushi Kanesaka (p61)
> Ninja Akasaka (p75)

BEST FUSION
> Beige (p58)
> Kaikaya (p97)

BEST BITES ON A BUDGET
> Omoide-yokochō (p126)
> Kiji (p60)
> Tsukiji Honten (p98)

BEST CHAIN RESTAURANTS
> Ippūdō (p86; www.ippudo.com)
> Goemon (www.yomeya-goemon.com)
> Sukiya (www.sukiya.jp)
> Mos Burger (www.mos.co.jp)

SNAPSHOTS

> GALLERIES

You can't really turn anywhere in Tokyo without seeing evidence of its thriving, dynamic visual arts scene. No self-respecting commercial district in Tokyo goes without its major department stores, and no department store worth its grand façade would dream of not installing an art gallery on one of its upper floors. Ginza is good place to start a gallery hop. Between its department store *grandes dames* and its well-established art galleries, there's a hefty concentration of classy exhibition spaces. For more experimental fare, you might also venture into Ura-Hara (p12), the back alleys off of Omote-sandō, and then still further west into Aoyama.

Japanese art has historically blurred the lines between art and craft, high and low, and this is reflected in many of the works you'll find in Tokyo's galleries. Graphic-style art is ubiquitous, but installation, sculpture, electronic media, painting and photography are well represented – sometimes all in one bright package.

JOHN ASHBURNE / LONELY PLANET IMAGES ©

BEST MIXED BAG
> Design Festa Gallery (p107; pictured)
> Japan Traditional Crafts Center (p135)
> Watari Museum of Contemporary Art (p107)

BEST NEIGHBOURHOODS FOR GALLERY CRAWLS
> Aoyama (p103)
> Ginza (p44)
> Marunouchi (p44)

> GAY & LESBIAN

Tokyo is more tolerant than most of its Asian counterparts in regard to homosexuality and alternative lifestyles, as long as public displays of affection are kept low key. The active international scene encompasses a healthy club and bar life, newsletters and support groups. Intriguing cultural phenomena include the relatively mainstream theatre of the all-women Tokyo Takarazuka Gekijō (p65), which attracts all manner of housewives and young women with crushes on the drag-king actors. Meanwhile, the defining feature of *otome* (p135) – the female version of *otaku* (p164) – is a shared obsession with 'boys' love' manga that depicts the romantic relationships between gay males. While on the ground level Tokyo society does not actively acknowledge the non-heterosexual population, its existence is normalised in a rich array of art forms and as a fact of fantasy life dissociated from quotidian concerns. So while the societal sanctions may be don't ask, don't tell, the social scene is alive and kicking.

For more information on the GLBT scene in Tokyo, check out the city guides on www.fridae.com and www.utopia-asia.com. Also look for the current issue of *Tokyo Journal* (p171), online and in print, for local listings on gay events and venues.

HARUYOSHI YAMAGUCHI / CORBIS

BEST BARS
> Advocates Bar (p127)
> Arty Farty (p128)
> Chestnut & Squirrel (p98)

TOP EVENTS
> Tokyo Pride Parade
  (p33; pictured)
> Tokyo International Lesbian & Gay Film
  Festival (p32)

> KIDS

Tokyo is a child-friendly, attention-deficit paradise, and foreign kids will find distractions aplenty in the cute toys, electronic gadgetry, weird candy, high-tech toilets and noisy *pachinko* games. All those novel things you'll pass on the streets will catch their interest, like *fugu* (poisonous puffer fish) jetting around the tanks in front of restaurants, or the flashing neon in Shinjuku and Shibuya. On weekends the parks are full of weird and wonderful culture that both adults and kids will get a kick out of – the rockabilly dancers of Yoyogi Park (p107) and the *cosplay-zoku* at Takeshita-dori and, on Sunday, Tokyo Dome (p28), for starters. But for specifically child-centric entertainments, Tokyo has many pleasure districts. Amusement parks, fun museums and tantalising toy stores abound in this, the world capital of *kawaii* (cute). The Ghibli Museum (p15) is a must, but absolutely sure to book your appointment well in advance.

Restaurants often provide children's menus or special set meals, and even picky eaters who might turn their noses up at sashimi will love tender, crunchy *tonkatsu* (deep-fried pork cutlets) or *yakitori* (grilled chicken on a stick) and noodles. And if you're desperate, convenience stores and fast-food chains exist everywhere for the little ones who subsist solely on burgers and pizza.

BEST PLACES TO WIND 'EM UP & RUN 'EM DOWN
> Muscle Park (p159)
> Namco Namjatown (p137)
> Paddleboating (p138)
> Tokyo Disneyland (p52)
> Tokyo Joypolis (p159)
> Tokyo Metropolitan Children's Hall (p101)

BEST SPOTS FOR YOUR KIDS TO EMPTY YOUR POCKETS
> Hakuhinkan Toy Park (p54)
> Kiddyland (p110)
> Tōkyū Hands (p124)
> Loft (p94)

BEST KID-FRIENDLY INTERACTIVE MUSEUMS
> Museum of Maritime Science (p156)
> National Museum of Emerging Science & Innovation (p156)
> National Science Museum (p140)
> Shitamachi History Museum (p140)
> Taikokan (p149)

BEST PLACES TO OGLE ANIMALS (LIVING & DEAD)
> Meguro Parasitological Museum (p84)
> Sunshine International Aquarium (p134)
> Tsukiji Market (p51)
> Ueno Zoo (p143)

> LIVE MUSIC

Aficionados of all genres will find kindred spirits in Tokyo, whether your aural medication of choice is jazz, electronica, Motown, punk, classical, *reggaetón* or hip-hop. Big international acts like U2 regularly play Tokyo, as do popular home-grown musicians such as J-pop songstress Hikaru Utada and jazz instrumentalists P'ez. Smaller venues often book more underground bands, which you might not see in such intimate environs abroad. Check *Metropolis* (www.metropolis.co.jp) or *Tokyo Journal* (http://tokyo.to) for current listings.

While 'live houses' are scattered all over the city, the best are naturally centred in active, hip neighbourhoods such as Shibuya, Ebisu and Roppongi. Live shows tend to keep school-night hours so that music fans can hop their trains before midnight, and it's best to purchase tickets beforehand from the venue itself, or using **Ticket Pia** (☎ 0570-029 999; http://t.pia.co.jp, in Japanese) with the help of a Japanese-speaking friend.

ANTHONY PLUMMER / LONELY PLANET IMAGES ©

BEST LIVE HOUSES
> Club Quattro (p99)
> Liquid Room (p88)
> Loft (p129)
> Shibuya O-West (p101)
> Abbey Road (p78)

BEST JAZZ JOINTS
> Blue Note (p78)
> JZ Brat (p100)
> Shinjuku Pit Inn (p130)
> STB 139 (p80)

BEST BEATLES ACTS
> Abbey Road (p78)
> Cavern Club (p79)

> MARKETS

Street markets are not such a large part of Tokyo's urban landscape as they are in other cities, as stratospheric real estate costs make open spaces prohibitively expensive. That said, one of Tokyo's highlights happens to be one of the few markets in town. Tsukiji Market, which moves more than 2000 tonnes of seafood every day, is slated to move to new digs sometime around 2012, so catch it here while you can. Blueprints for the new market plan for a larger, more modern space that visitors won't be able to get into as down and dirty as they can now.

The open spaces of some temple grounds become commercial squares on various Sundays. While it's unlikely that you'll find truly rare antiques at these flea markets, there's usually some decent vintage kimonos, metalwork, lacquerware and interesting odds and ends to browse. Most markets close down by around 3pm. Also operating outdoors is the unusual Ameyoko Arcade in Ueno, where you can wander among the stalls of dried squid and discount sneakers. And of course, Tokyo's take on the traditional market is the bountiful, beautiful *depachika*.

RACHEL LEWIS / LONELY PLANET IMAGES ©

BEST DEPACHIKA
> Takashimaya (p56)
> Mitsukoshi (p56)
> Matsuya (p55)

BEST MARKET HIGHLIGHTS
> Ameyoko Arcade (p143; pictured)
> Tsukiji Market (p51)

> MUSEUMS

The cup runneth over for museum-lovers in this city. There are not only art museums displaying archaeological artefacts from a couple of thousand years ago and contemporary works in all manner of media but also tiny one-room shacks showcasing only buttons or *byōbu* (folding screens). Some of Tokyo's top museums have been around for only a few years, like the wonderfully multifaceted experience of the Edo-Tokyo Museum (p17) and the sky-high singularity of the Mori Art Museum (p67) at Roppongi Hills.

If you'll be in town for an extended period of time or expect to hit several museums during your visit, consider picking up a Grutt Pass (p143) to save a significant amount on what can add up to hefty admission fees.

NOBORU KOMINE / LONELY PLANET IMAGES ©

BEST TOKYO MUSEUMS
> Edo-Tokyo Museum (p17)
> National Museum of Modern Art (p50)
> Ōta Memorial Art Museum (p103)
> Tokyo Metropolitan Museum of Photography (p84)
> Tokyo National Museum (p141)

QUIRKIEST SHOWCASES
> Yebisu Beer Museum (p85; pictured)
> Kite Museum (p48)
> Meguro Parasitological Museum (p84)

BEST FOR CONTEMPORARY ART
> Hara Museum of Contemporary Art (p92)
> Mori Art Museum (p67)
> National Art Center Tokyo (p70)
> Watari Museum of Contemporary Art (p107)

> NIGHTLIFE

Tokyo's thriving nightlife means no shortage of bars, karaoke lounges, dance clubs and *izakaya* (pub-eatery) populating every corner of the city. But for choice, some neighbourhoods are better than others. Roppongi has historically been the centre of rowdy all-night ragers, where military goons and newly arrived expats collide with hard-partying locals looking for foreign action. But it's not all downscale pick-up joints, and the diversity of clubs and bars all located in one area make it the obvious destination for a night out. Still, it's not the last word in nightlife – Love Hotel Hill on Shibuya's Dōgenzaka is packed with clubs, large live-music venues, and bars and *izakaya*. These clubs attract those in their 20s, and the music tends to be mainstream (ie hip-hop, marquee Japanese pop and flavour-of-the-month). For the slightly older and more indie-inclined, there are the hip clubs and bars of Ebisu and Daikanyama. East Shinjuku is probably the least pretentious of these hotspots.

Clubs typically charge a cover from ¥1500 to ¥3000, usually including a drink or two. Weekend covers tend to be higher than on weeknights, and at some venues men and women are charged differently. Some clubs give discounts if you bring in a flyer (check their websites or the record stores around Shibuya), and it's often a good idea to bring a photo ID.

BEST TOP-VIEW BARS
> Asahi Sky Room (p152)
> Mado Lounge (p77)
> New York Bar (p129)

BEST UNPRETENTIOUS CLUBS
> Club 328 (p79)
> Muse (p80)
> New Lex-Edo (p80)
> Unit (p88)

BEST BARS FOR LOOKING & LOUNGING
> Aux Amis des Vins (p62)
> Den Aquaroom (p116)
> Maduro (p78)

BEST SAKE IZAKAYA
> Sakana-tei (p97)
> Sasashū (p137)

> PARKS & GARDENS

Apartment-dwellers of Tokyo may not have the luxury of gardens, but they have hectares of open space in the city's large parks. All parks in Tokyo are free with the notable exception of Shinjuku-gyoen, and they provide respite and refuge from the rhythms of urban life. On weekdays you're likely to get a laid-back experience at the city's parks and gardens, but weekends see them at their best, when families and couples turn out for strolls and picnics.

During *hanami* (cherry-blossom viewing; see also p31) season, blue tarps are spread on the grass and the sake flows at *hanami* parties crowding popular parks such as Shinjuku-gyoen and Ueno-kōen. From around mid-October to early November, *kōyō* (autumn foliage season) brings its spectacular palette of golds, yellows, oranges and fiery scarlet hues to parks including Yoyogi-kōen (p107) and Koishikawa-Kōrakuen (p49).

The beautifully landscaped gardens of Tokyo make even better escapes. Gardens usually charge a small admission fee, and on weekdays you're likely to have the carp ponds and well-groomed paths practically to yourself.

GREG ELMS / LONELY PLANET IMAGES ©

BEST PARKS
> Shinjuku-gyoen (p121)
> Ueno-kōen (p22)
> Yoyogi-kōen (p107)

MOST GORGEOUS GARDENS
> Dembō-in (p148)
> Hama-rikyū-teien (p48)
> Imperial Palace East Garden (p48; pictured right)
> Meiji-jingū-gyoen (p103)
> National Institute for Nature Study (p84)

BEST PLACES FOR HANAMI
> Hama-rikyū-teien (p48)
> Shinjuku-gyoen (p121)
> Ueno-kōen (p22)

> SENTŌ & ONSEN

As much for gossip as for hygiene, *sentō* (public baths) and *onsen* (hot springs) are pulse points for strengthening social bonds in Japan. Although modern dwellings have bath facilities, many Tokyoites bathe regularly at *sentō* and often go with friends or family members. The metropolitan government generously subsidises the city's *sentō* and *onsen*, making them inexpensive (admission around ¥500) and easily accessible to everyone.

In Tokyo, where both institutions do business in modern buildings, the difference between *sentō* and *onsen* may not seem clear. The essential distinction is that *sentō* can heat up their own tap water, but water at an *onsen* must come from a natural hot spring. The concept of such a bubbling spring existing in this paved urban wilderness might sound laughable, but natural sources underneath Tokyo Bay actually do supply the city's *onsen* with mineral-rich, dark water.

Bathing communally in traditional Japanese baths is an excellent balm for the stresses of the streets and a transcendent experience even if the backdrop isn't the rushing waterfall of a mountain resort. In them you'll encounter people of all ages and walks of life, and catch a glimpse of city folk at their most relaxed. For more information see p131.

ANTHONY PLUMMER / LONELY PLANET IMAGES ©

BEST KITSCHY ONSEN EXPERIENCE
> Ōedo Onsen Monogatari (p159; pictured)

BEST OLD-SCHOOL NEIGHBOURHOOD ONSEN
> Jakotsu-yu (p153)
> Asakusa Kannon Onsen (p152)

> SHRINES & TEMPLES

Japan's two major religions, Shintōism and Buddhism, have coexisted peacefully and influenced each other for more than a thousand years. Shintō's animistic tradition, which views the environment as one inhabited with *kami* (gods or spirits), is Japan's native religion. Buddhism, and its belief in the cycle of reincarnation, was an import from India by way of China and Korea.

In day-to-day life most Tokyoites do not consider themselves religious, conducting and participating in religious ceremonies only at those defining moments of birth, marriage and death. But while Shintōism may not play an overt role in people's lives, its basic tenets have seeped so deeply into the Japanese culture that they are inseparable from what are considered quotidian matters. For example, the Shintō practice of purification isn't limited to the rinsing of mouths and hands at the entrance of shrines, but also led to the lasting tradition of the thorough, ritualistic cleansing at *sentō*.

Shintō shrines honour *kami*, which also reside in natural features such as waterfalls and mountains. Once a person dies, they too become a *kami*, but upon death Buddhism defines the funereal rituals. Keep this in mind when you notice that Buddhist temples often house cemeteries while Shintō shrines do not. Shintō shrines range in size from tiny *inari* (fox deity) shrines occupying narrow spaces between buildings to the grand Meiji-jingū (p103), and are scattered far and wide across Tokyo. Long-established Buddhist temples also dot the cityscape in every neighbourhood and make up an integral part of the community.

ANTHONY PLUMMER / LONELY PLANET IMAGES ©

BEST SHRINES
- > Asakusa-jinja (p148)
- > Chingodō-ji (p148)
- > Hie-jinja (p67)
- > Tōshōgū (p141)
- > Yasukuni-jinja (p52)

BEST TEMPLES
- > Benten-dō (p140)
- > Kiyomizu Kannon-dō (p140)
- > Meiji-jingū (p103; pictured)
- > Sensō-ji (p149)

SNAPSHOTS

> SHOPPING

Shopping is a serious endeavour in this city: it's the number-one recreational activity. It's therapy, investment and a way to socialise and show off status. It's also intertwined with ritual and expectation – on Valentine's Day, women are expected to give *giri* (obligation) chocolate to all the men in their lives, and it ain't for love. Shopping is part of the Tokyo lifestyle, and gift-giving is a tradition that has evolved into an art. It's no wonder, then, that this city is a candy store for the consumer with cash. And you don't need a lot of it for inexpensive treats like delicate *washi* (handmade paper), kitchen tools and stationery at ¥100 shops and small Japanese toys.

Stores are generally open daily but closed on one Monday or Wednesday of each month. Keep in mind that Japan may very well be the only Asian country where bargaining, unless you're at a flea market (p172), is simply not done. While plastic is being accepted at more shops nowadays, it's a good idea to come armed with cold, hard cash. On luxury items like pricey electronics, the 5% VAT can be waived for foreigners, but you'll have to have your passport on you to take advantage of it.

Upscale shopping districts such as Ginza (p52) and Aoyama (p102) are good places to start for luxury items at fashion houses of international re-

GREG ELMS / LONELY PLANET IMAGES ©

pute, including Chanel, Gucci or Mikimoto Pearl. If your stay is particularly short, hit Aoyama first – there's a good mix of international and Japanese heavyweights who've set up shop along Omote-sandō, and some of the architecture itself is as beautifully designed as the wares. Plus, the Harajuku backstreets (p108) adjacent to Aoyama complement the couture with Tokyo's famous street fashion. Takeshita-dōri is the best place to plunge in for an exploration of teenybopper culture. Ginza, on the other hand, has Tokyo's oldest, grand department stores, some of which have rooftop gardens and restaurant towns above and *depachika* (p57) below.

Other shopping districts around Central Tokyo include Jimbōchō, where bookshops trade in antique and rare books, as well as used books and manga. But a bigger scene for manga lies to the east of here in Akihabara, once famed (and still nicknamed for) its discount electronics.

Sprawling shopping malls that could each swallow several Southeast Asian villages whole include the older Sunshine City (p136) in Ikebukuro and the newer Roppongi Hills (p72). More intimate, human-scale shopping experiences can be sought in Daikanyama (p85) or Kichijōji (p122), where the smaller shops have their unique styles and sensibilities.

Even if shopping isn't your bag, any visitor to Tokyo should at least pop into Tōkyū Hands (p124), the 'Creative Life Store', which is sure to offer some captivating bauble to even the most consumption-averse. Shopping is leisure in this city, so come out to play and gain a little insight into the societal psyche in the bargain.

BEST SHOPS FOR OFFBEAT SOUVENIRS
> Don Quijote (p123)
> Kiddyland (p110)
> Kite Museum (p48)
> Meguro Parasitological Museum (p84)
> Tōkyū Hands (p124)

BEST TRADITIONAL HANDICRAFTS
> Hashi Ginza Natsuno (p54)
> Japan Traditional Crafts Center (p135)
> Kamawanu (p86)
> Takumi Handicrafts (p57)

BEST PLACES TO FIND WASHI
> Haibara (p54)
> Itōya (p54)
> Sekaido (p124)

> SPECTATOR SPORTS

No sport in Japan is more popular than baseball, and the Tokyo area is home to no fewer than six of the country's 12 professional teams. The most popular team in Japan, the Yomiuri Giants, is based at Tokyo Dome (also known as the 'Big Egg'). Tokyo Dome is probably the best place in town to catch a game, where fan clubs cheerleaders dressed in *happi* (half-coats) lead thousands of fans in synchronised cheers and singing. Beer girls with minikegs strapped to their backs run up and down the steep aisles pouring brews to customers while a small dirigible floats around the inside of the dome filming the action. In fair weather, however, it's equally enjoyable to take in a game at the outdoor Jingū Stadium, home of the Yakult Swallows. Baseball season begins at the end of March or the first week of April and runs until October.

Of course, besides the big two of baseball and sumō (p10), martial-arts events and smaller-scale sports competitions occur year-round. Check **Metropolis** (www.metropolis.co.jp) for extensive listings on current events.

LOU JONES / LONELY PLANET IMAGES ©

BEST (ONLY) PLACE TO WATCH SUMŌ
> Ryōgoku Kokugikan (p64)

BEST STADIUM FOR J-LEAGUE SOCCER
> National Stadium (p116)

BEST BASEBALL STADIUM
> Tokyo Dome (p28)
> Jingū Stadium (p116)

Get on board during rush hour at Ueno Station

>BACKGROUND

HISTORY

THE EARLY YEARS

Around the mid-15th century, a poet named Dōkan Ōta constructed Edo's first castle on the site of an old fortress. When Portuguese traders first set eyes on 16th-century Edo, it was little more than an outpost for aristocrats and monks who had fled a civil war in Kyoto. Within three centuries Edo would oust Kyoto as Japan's traditional seat of imperial power – and Tokyo would be born.

TOKUGAWA EDO

The father to this upstart child was the wily, madly ambitious shōgun, Ieyasu Tokugawa. His appointment by the emperor in 1603 was to change the fate of Tokyo (and Japan) forever.

A political survivor, Tokugawa knew he must divide and conquer his political foes. In a masterstroke, he forced all *daimyō* (feudal lords) throughout Japan to spend at least one year of every two in Edo. This policy of dislocation made it difficult for ambitious *daimyō* to usurp the Tokugawas.

Tokugawa systematically created a rigidly hierarchical society, comprising, in descending order: nobility; *daimyō* and their samurai; farmers; and finally artisans and merchants. Class dress, living quarters and even manner of speech were strictly codified. Class advancement was prohibited, though one could always, terrifyingly, descend to the underclasses, to the 'nonhuman' *hinin* and to *eta,* the untouchable class.

ISOLATION

After Ieyasu Tokugawa's death in 1616, his grandson Iemitsu Tokugawa, fearing Christian power, closed the country's borders in 1638. Japan was effectively removed from the world stage for nearly 300 years.

By the early 17th century, Edo (with a population of more than a million) was the largest city on earth. Its castelike society divided Edo into the *daimyō* high city (Yamanote) and a low working-class city (Shitamachi). Destructive fires often swept through its shantytowns. The locals christened these fires 'Edo-no-hana' ('flowers of Edo'). The cocky bravura of the expression sums up the tough Shitamachi spirit, still to be found in the backstreets of Ueno and Asakusa.

TOKYO RISING

When US Commodore Matthew Perry's armada of 'black ships' entered Edo (Tokyo) Bay demanding 'free trade' in 1853, despite spirited resistance from 2000 Tokugawa loyalists at the brief Battle of Ueno, the shōgunate fell apart and power reverted to Tokyo.

The Meiji Restoration refers to this consequent return of power to the emperor; however, Emperor Meiji's rule was more revolution than restoration. A crash course in industrialisation and militarisation began and by 1889 Japan had adopted a Western-style constitution – and Western-style empire-building.

Nowhere was revolutionary change more evident than on the streets of the country's new capital city. Job-seekers flocked from the country and Tokyo boomed.

CATASTROPHE & WAR

The Great Kantō Earthquake struck the boom town at noon on 1 September 1923. The subsequent fires, lasting some 40 hours, laid waste to the city. Although 142,000 lost their lives, worse was to come.

From the accession of Emperor Hirohito in 1926, nationalist fervour gripped the government. In 1931 the Japanese army invaded Manchuria, then China. By 1940 a pact with Germany and Italy had been signed and 'Greater Asia Co-Prosperity Sphere' was touted as the new order. On 7 December 1941 the Japanese attacked Pearl Harbor.

WWII was catastrophic for Tokyo. Incendiary bombing of the mostly wooden city commenced in March 1944. On the nights of 9 and 10 March 1945, 40% of the city was engulfed in a terrible firestorm and between 70,000 and 80,000 people perished. By the time Emperor Hirohito made his famous address to the Japanese people on 15 August 1945, much of Tokyo was a wasteland.

BUBBLE & BUST

Tokyo rose phoenixlike from the ashes of WWII, and the economy flourished as almost no other in history. Ironically, it was sparked by US involvement in the neighbouring Korean War. The 1960s, '70s and early '80s saw unprecedented growth. Japan was suddenly an economic superpower – incredibly wealthy, globally powerful and omnipotent.

And then, suddenly, it wasn't. Japan's `bubble economy' of the '80s floated ever higher on the strength of its technology and automobile exports. Emboldened by the belief that the bullish stock market and climbing property values would continue to rise, investors financed all manner of huge developments and projects. But this growth was unsustainable, and the burst of the bubble threw Japan into a recession from which it is still recovering.

But the cracks ran deeper than the fiscal fault lines. The Kōbe earthquake of January 1995 shook not only that city but also the nation's confidence in the government's ability to respond quickly and effectively to such a monumental disaster. In March 1995, when members of the Aum Shinrikyō cult released sarin nerve gas on a crowded Tokyo commuter train, killing 12 and injuring 5000, Japan's self-belief took a severe blow.

TOKYO TODAY

Despite an enduring entrepreneurial spirit and constant craving for all things new, Tokyo has taken its place among the pantheon of leading Asian metropolises rather than kept its title as the front-runner – a position it is none too happy about. Northern Honshū's earthquake in 2011 shook the capital's confidence, and although visitor numbers have gone down since, Tokyo will no doubt continue to reinvent itself until it's back on top.

LIFE AS A TOKYOITE

The life of the average Japanese citizen is bound by a massive network of obligation and counter-obligation to family, colleagues, the people next door, ancestors who passed away generations ago – the list is endless. Those individuals who just can't stand it flee to Tokyo. The anonymity of the megalopolis is a magnet for misfits, rebels, artists and all the famous 'nails that stand out' (and duly get bashed down) in mainstream Japanese society. Thus it is, in many senses, the most liberated of Japanese cities. People scarcely know their neighbours, or care to.

With the disintegration of the family and continuing economic lethargy, the times they are a-changing. The generation gap between conventional, self-sacrificing parent and pierced, part-time-employee child has never been greater. Younger people who were born after the bubble era are not hampered so much by the conventions of that time, and are more open to creativity and experimentation. Career adjustments – like bouncing back from losing a job – come more naturally to the younger generation. Old systems and cultural attitudes are slow to change, but the societal flux is probably most apparent and dynamic in Tokyo.

ETIQUETTE

Given Tokyo's distinctly different place in Japanese society, it's difficult to offend. Moreover, Japanese people are highly forgiving of foreign visitors' minor social gaffes. But there are a few rules of etiquette that must always be followed. When entering a house or any tatami (woven matting) room, always take off your shoes. If in doubt, do as everyone else does. It's considered rude (and disgusting) to blow your nose in public – maintain a stoic and noisy sniffle until you find a private place. Except for ice cream, eating while walking down the street is also just not done.

For those in Tokyo on business, *meishi* (business cards) carry a lot of weight in society and are ritually exchanged at first meetings. Politely accept – or offer – a card with both hands and examine it before putting it away, and don't write on a card that someone has given you.

And when invited to someone's home, bring a small gift that's presented attractively – an occasion for requesting the elaborate wrapping available when you make your purchase. As with *meishi,* offer the gift with both hands and a slight bow, and expect it to be politely refused a few times before you insist they accept it.

GOVERNMENT & POLITICS
THE CHRYSANTHEMUM THRONE

In September 2006 Princess Kiko (wife of Prince Akishino, second in line to the throne after Crown Prince Naruhito) gave birth to the first male heir to the Japanese throne in over 40 years. Man-on-the-street TV interviews showed the emotional reactions of Tokyoites to this momentous news. Although Emperor Akihito and Empress Michiko are but figureheads, the imperial family is still very much revered and deeply respected in Japan. This outpouring of happiness also coincided with a sudden – though not unexpected – tapering-off of the controversy that marked the years before the new prince was born.

Increasingly intense debate had been growing about changing the Japanese constitution to allow a female heir to ascend the Chrysanthemum Throne. Crown Prince Naruhito and Crown Princess Masako have only a daughter. And while recent polls showed that 76% of the general population supported the idea of female ascendancy, conservative elements in branches of the imperial family and Japan's governing body, the Diet, staunchly oppose it on the grounds that a female heir would break the traditional male lineage. The debate remains open, but for the moment Prince Hisahito's birth has significantly lessened its urgency.

Unfortunately, the pressure to have a son – coupled with the isolated life inside the Imperial Palace – has had a deleterious effect on Crown Princess Masako, once a promising young diplomat. Two years after the birth of her daughter, Princess Aiko, in 2001, she largely withdrew from public life, though of late she has begun making more frequent public appearances. It remains to be seen what the future will hold for young Princess Aiko, as times change and traditional restrictions do not.

THE RULING DIET

The governing body, known as the Diet, is based here in the capital and is made up of two houses. The party controlling the majority of seats in the Diet is the ruling party and has the right to appoint the prime minister. Since its inception in 1955, the conservative Liberal Democratic Party (LDP) has controlled the Diet, barring a few years during the mid-'90s.

In theory, Japan is a democratic country, with members of the Diet elected by popular vote. However, in practice, real power is held by powerful political cliques descended from generations of the nation's elite, who are allied with Japan's dominant *keiretsu* (business cartels). Until relatively recently, this seemed to suit Japanese voters just fine, but a recession plus structural reforms by former prime minister Junichirō Koizumi stoked more political fire among the populace.

Since Koizumi's resignation in 2006, the office of the PM has had a revolving door, with Shinzo Abe succeeding him for one year and Yasuo Fukuda following suit for another. In autumn 2008, Taro Aso was appointed by the LDP but lost the confidence of the nation with gaffes such as misreading kanji in speeches and offending the elderly population with insensitive comments about their value to society, all while a recession took hold. The LDP's grip on the Diet may be weakening; watch this space.

ECONOMY

With the world's second-largest GDP, Japan's economy is just behind that of the USA – though that hasn't meant easy street for Japan these past two decades. The country is still feeling, though no longer reeling from, the effects of the 'bubble economy' bursting in the early '80s. The

---

WORKING STIFFS

The Japanese love incorporating foreign words into their vocabulary; here are a few examples of local lingo for naming that employee.

> Salarymen – These are the guys in suits of sombre colours, often with a matching dour demeanour. But, after staying late at work to keep up appearances, they're often found red-faced and slap-happy at their favourite *izakaya* (pub-eatery) as they booze with their colleagues.

> OLs – Short for 'office ladies' – they may do the same work as salarymen but receive appallingly less pay. Others might be secretaries biding their time before they can marry a salaryman, quit the office job and take up recreational shopping. OLs often travel in packs, dressed in matching corporate vest-and-skirt combos.

> Freeters – A combination of 'freelance' and '*arbeiter*' ('worker' in German), these are the young people handing out advert-emblazoned packs of tissues on the streets or working that convenience-store register. They pick up work when they need it, and drop it when they don't.

Asiawide financial collapse, ineffectual government response and tough competition from the USA were all key contributing factors, and the resulting recession lasted well into the '90s and early 2000s.

However, the bright side of those darker financial days is that the economic slump inspired – or forced – businesspeople to reassess the traditional career arc that meant a lifetime allegiance to one's company. The concept of a job for life is no longer taken for granted, nor necessarily desired, by the younger generation. Part-time and casual employment are on the rise, with younger people working merely to make a living, and living more alternatively than their elders. Occasionally 'parasite singles' are blamed for the sluggish economy, with economic experts claiming that they should be buying property instead of living with (and mooching off) their parents. But unemployment hovered at a respectable 4.5% during 2011.

For visitors, the levelling-off of Japan's economy means a more even playing field for travellers to stretch their yen a little further.

ENVIRONMENT

On a fundamental geographical level, Japan is part of the Pacific 'Ring of Fire', the tectonic activity of which created the majestic conical shape of Mt Fuji and rocked northern Japan in March 2011. Although minor earthquakes occur all the time, there's no telling when the next big one

> **BAG IT**
>
> The straightforward request that your purchase not be bagged may be met with some confusion, but environmental awareness is growing in Tokyo. The tradition of wrapping every single solitary purchase is an art bordering on obsession in Japan, where even the humblest of items – a pastry, for example – is wrapped in plastic before being wrapped in paper before then being placed reverentially into a bag with handles (prominently displaying a status-bearing logo, for luxury items).
>
> You can cut down on the plague of bags by saying, *'Fukuro wa iranai desu'* ('I don't need a bag').

will strike. There's little point in paranoia, but it pays to note where exits are located.

On a more human level, Japan's limited land mass plus its dense population equals an environmental quandary. Consequently, Tokyo's garbage collection services are quite strict about adhering to their own stringent regulations, which require the separation of burnable, non-burnable and recyclable refuse. If it's not properly separated before being left out for pickup, it's simply not picked up. There's still too much plastic packaging in use in the first place, but you can do your small part by cutting back on plastic-bag consumption (see above).

Vending machines, convenience stores and some train stations usually have recycling receptacles clearly marked, but there's a distinct lack of rubbish receptacles around Tokyo in general.

THE ARTS

FILM

Akira Kurosawa, the most famous director of Japanese cinema's golden era, brought Japanese film into the spotlight when his *Rashōmon* (1950) took top prize at the Venice Film Festival. Illustrious filmmakers who followed include Shohei Imamura, who examines human behaviour with a piercing eye in such works as *The Profound Desire of the Gods* (1968) and Oshima Nagisa's *Ai no Corrida* (In the Realm of the Senses), a tale of an obsessive love that was banned in many countries when it was released in 1976.

More contemporary films include Jūzō Itami's *Tampopo* (1985), a characteristically quirky comedy about sex and food, and the award-winning *Zatoichi* (2003), featuring actor-director Takeshi 'Beat' Kitano as a blind swordsman. Japan's gorgeous *anime* gems, such as Hayao Miyazaki's *Spir-*

ited Away (2001), continue to issue from Tokyo onto international screens. More recent works include the brilliant but a tad depressing *Dare mo Shiranai* (2004) by Hirokazu Koreeda, based on a true story about a wayward mother who abandoned her four children in an apartment in Tokyo.

LITERATURE

Often with a surrealist edge or a dose of magical realism, Japanese contemporary literature – much of which is written by authors who've spent most of their lives in Tokyo – provides a perspective on the more elusive emotional side of life in the city. Nobel Laureate Kenzaburo Ōe's clear-eyed *A Personal Matter* tells the story of a man faced with a conflict of freedom and responsibility that transcends Japanese social mores. A departure from his more surrealist work, Haruki Murakami's celebrated *Norwegian Wood* chronicles the coming of age of a university student in late-1960s Japan. And for lighter but surprisingly solid fare, pick up *Kitchen* (1998) by Banana Yoshimoto; seemingly superficial themes of food, pop culture and unconventional sexuality speak to an immediate sort of urban existentialism.

MUSIC

Live gigs rock the 'live houses' every night of the week in Tokyo's basement bars, mostly on the city's west side. You name it, someone makes or hosts it – from Japanese hip-hop and punk rock to acid jazz.

Japan has an enormous domestic record market, and Tokyo is very much a part of the international live-music circuit. Many top performers, from every genre of contemporary and classical music, book shows here. Along with Tokyo's better-known exports, such as composer Ryūichi Sakamoto and food-fetish rockers Shonen Knife, are musical collage artists Buffalo Daughter and postmodern mixmaster Cornelius, who overlays samples of birdsong with harmonic vocal tracks, guitar and synthesized beats. Veteran DJ Takkyu Ishino packs 'em in, while bands like Dragon Ash and Kreva bring a Japanese flavour to hip-hop and reggae.

Tokyo mainstream consists significantly of *aidoru* (idol singers) and girl- or boy-bands, manufactured J-pop confections sweetened to perfection for mass marketing. Don't overindulge, or you'll get a toothache.

PERFORMANCE ARTS

Kabuki, *nō* (classical Japanese drama) and bunraku (puppet theatre) are well represented throughout the city, with several theatres featuring regular performances. *Taiko* (traditional Japanese drumming) is where music meets martial art and mysticism.

Tokyo is also a centre for Japan's enigmatic, challenging modern dance form, *butō*. Its bizarre movements, weird lighting and long periods of inaction are not everyone's cup of *o-cha* (green tea) but are most certainly memorable. Check with a tourist information centre (p202) or local listings for current performances. Seek out Dairakudakan (www.dairakudakan.com), Sankaijuku (www.sankaijuku.com) or, most powerful of all, Taihen (www.ne.jp/asahi/imaju/taihen), whose members are all severely physically disabled.

VISUAL ART

Tokyo's contemporary-art scene is thriving. Its galleries possess a lack of pretension that is startlingly refreshing – it's easy to walk into a show and start a conversation with the artists themselves. Progressive spaces all over town give space to exciting work, much of it by the talented young artists of the city's prestigious art colleges.

Bigger museums tend to go for heavy-hitting names: Rodin, Renoir, Da Vinci, Degas. The superstars of Western art are most-oft found at the National Museum of Western Art (p140). But don't be surprised if they pop up, along with their Japanese counterparts, in the department-store galleries dotted around town. The greatest concentration of small galleries – with roughly 400 exhibition spaces – clusters in Ginza (p45).

>DIRECTORY
TRANSPORT
ARRIVAL & DEPARTURE
AIR

Tokyo has two major airports **Narita Airport** (www.narita-airport.jp.en) and **Haneda Airport** (www.tokyo-airport-bldg.co.jp/en). Traditionally, most international flights operate through the former while domestic travel is usually funnelled through latter. However, Haneda opened an international wing in 2010, offering an assortment of late-night flights to many international destinations. In general, flights to Narita are cheaper; however, Narita is considerably further from the city centre than Haneda.

It is important to note that there are two distinct terminals at Narita, separated by a five-minute train ride. Airport officials recommend setting out four hours before your flight.

To/from Narita Airport

Narita airport is 66km from central Tokyo, and is used by most international airlines.

Depending on where you're headed, it's cheaper and faster to travel into Tokyo by train than by limousine bus. However, rail users will probably need to change trains, and this can be frustrating for a first visit. Bus services provide direct routes to a number of hotels, and you don't have to be a guest to use them. We don't recommend taking a taxi to Narita – it'll cost ¥30,000.

Count on one to two hours to get to/from Narita.

Narita Express (N'EX; www.jreast.co.jp/e/nex/index.html) Links the airport to Tokyo Station (¥2940, 53 minutes), Shinjuku Station (¥3110, 1½ hours), Ikebukuro Station (¥3110, one hour and 40 minutes; limited service) and Yokohama Station (¥4180, 1½ hours). N'EX runs half-hourly

---

CLIMATE CHANGE & TRAVEL

Travel – especially air travel – is a significant contributor to global climate change. At Lonely Planet, we believe that all who travel have a responsibility to limit their personal impact. As a result, we have teamed with Rough Guides and other concerned industry partners to support Climate Care, which allows people to offset the greenhouse gases they are responsible for with contributions to energy-saving projects and other climate-friendly initiatives in the developing world. Lonely Planet offsets all staff and author travel.

For more information, turn to the responsible travel pages on www.lonelyplanet.com. For details on offsetting your carbon emissions and a carbon calculator, go to www.climatecare.org.

STAY AWHILE

Short city breaks make great getaways, but air travel is a becoming a devastating contributor to global warming. What can you do to lessen the impact? Why not take a longer holiday? If a few days in Tokyo has given you a taste of the city in all its beautifully bizarre and uniquely Japanese glory, consider making your next trip a longer one: take a day trip out to the lovely mountain resort town of Hakone near Mt Fuji, or to the temples, shrines and Great Buddha statue in Kamakura. Or go even further and travel across Japan using its world-class rail system.

from 7am to 10pm. Seats are reserved only, but can be bought immediately before departure. The local 'Airport Narita' trains cost ¥1280 and take 1½ hours to/from Tokyo.

Keisei Skyliner (www.keisei.co.jp) The Sky Access express train (¥2400, 45 minutes) zips you to the airport in comfort. The Keisei Main Line (¥1000, 1½ hours) is its local (slow) counterpart. If you're transferring to/from the JR Yamanote line, access the train from Nippori station; metro passengers should use Ueno Station.

Limousine Bus (www.limousinebus.co.jp/en) Convenient airport shuttle buses connects Narita to an array of major hotels and metro stations (¥3000, 1½ to two hours). Service is hourly.

Keikyu line Runs between Narita and Haneda airports (¥1560; two hours), though you'll have to transfer to/from the Keisei line at Aoto Station.

Cab-Station Co (www.cab-station.co.jp) This company has announced plans to offer discounted bus rides between Narita and Asakusa – the ¥1000 fare is for backpackers.

To/from Haneda Airport

From the city centre, it takes far less time to reach Haneda than Narita. There's a transfer bus service between the two airports (¥3000, 1¼ hours). Taxis cost ¥6000.

Tokyo Monorail A direct link to Haneda from Hamamatsuchō Station on the JR Yamanote line (¥470, 25 minutes).

Keikyu Line Departs from Shinagawa Station. Alight at Keikyu Haneda Station (¥400, 16 minutes).

Limousine Bus (www.limousinebus.co.jp/en) More of a coach bus than a limousine; service connects major centres like Tokyo Station (¥900) to the airport.

TRAIN

Japan Railways' (JR) famed *shinkansen* (bullet trains) serve northern Honshū, central and western Japan and Kyūshū. The slower, less expensive *tokkyū* (limited express), *kyūko* (express) and *futsū* (ordinary) are options on every route between cities; however, not many people use them for long-distance travel. One-way, reserved-seat *shinkansen* fares for *nozomi* trains (which make the fewest stops) are ¥13,520 from Kyoto to Tokyo, ¥17,170 from Fukuoka to Tokyo, and ¥14,050 from Osaka to Tokyo. The main terminals are Tokyo (Map pp46–7, E5) and Ueno (Map p139, C4) stations.

Private lines running from stations on the Yamanote line are the quickest, cheapest bet to Kamakura, Mt Fuji, Hakone and Yokohama. They connect to Shinjuku (Map p119, B4) and Shibuya (Map p91, C4) stations. The Tōbu line for Nikkō runs from Asakusa Station (Map p147, C3).

BUS
Domestic long-distance buses mainly arrive at Tokyo Station's Highway Bus Terminal (Map pp46–7, E5) near the Yaesu south exit. Highway buses also depart from the west side of Shinjuku Station (Map p119, B4). Services to both Osaka and Kyoto are operated by JR (☎ 3844 1950); you can buy tickets from a Green Window office at most larger JR train stations.

VISA
Citizens of 61 countries, including Singapore, Hong Kong, Korea, Canada, USA, Australia, New Zealand, UK, France, Germany, the Netherlands and Sweden, do not require visas to enter Japan for stays of 90 days or fewer. Consult www.mofa.go.jp/j_info/visit/visa/short/novisa.html for a complete list of visa-exempt countries.

GETTING AROUND
Short-term visitors and long-term residents alike mainly use the city's excellent subway system and the JR train lines, especially the JR Yamanote line. It rings the inner city, making almost everywhere accessible in under an hour. All stations have signposts and maps in English. The Tokyo Metro (www.tokyometro.jp) subway lines are colour coded, and regular English signposting makes the system easy to use. The train and subway services in Tokyo are famed for their punctuality, and trains are frequent. Nearest stations are

---

ELUSIVE ADDRESSES
In Tokyo, finding a place by address alone is challenging at best, even for locals. Apart from *dōri* (main roads), very few streets have names – addresses indicate their locations in relation to their larger contexts. So, for example, an address listed as 1-11-2 Ginza, Chūō-ku in this book means that the place is in Tokyo's Chūō ward, in Ginza's 1-*chōme* (an area consisting of several blocks), in block 11, in building 2 of that block.

Chōme, blocks and building numbers aren't necessarily located in a logical order, so it's best to use a map (the bilingual *Tokyo City Atlas,* published by Kodansha, is invaluable if you'll be spending much time in Tokyo). Most establishments print simple maps on their business cards. Another effective way to find your way is to stop at a *kōban* (police box) in the area, where the friendly neighbourhood police spend much of their time giving directions.

listed after the 🚃 (for the Yamanote and above-ground lines) and 🚇 (for subway lines) in listings.

TRAVEL PASSES

The Tokyo Combination Ticket day pass can be used on all JR, subway and bus lines within the Tokyo metropolitan area. It costs ¥1580 (¥790 for children aged six to 11) and is available from station offices in most JR stations and major subway hubs like Ginza, Nihombashi and Shinjuku.

Longer-stay visitors should consider purchasing a Pasmo or Suica card, both of which can be used on both JR, Tokyo Metro subway lines, and several other rail lines in Tokyo. Both cards circumvent the hassle of puzzling over transfers, as they automatically calculate your fare each time you pass through a station wicket.

Pasmo cards are sold at ticket-vending machines in most subway stations in denominations of ¥1000, ¥3000 and ¥5000. Suica cards can be purchased at JR ticket windows with a ¥500 deposit. Suica cards can be topped up at JR ticket-vending machines.

TRAIN

Tokyo is serviced by a combination of JR, private inner-city subway lines and private suburban lines. Trains run from around 5am to midnight. The JR Yamanote line is augmented by the Chūo and Sōbu lines. Fares begin at ¥130, and the green maps above ticket-vending machines have fares clearly marked. If maps do not include English, simply buy the minimum fare and pay the balance at a fare-adjustment machine at your destination. For train information, call the **JR English information line** (☎ 050-2016 1603; 🕙 10am-6pm Mon-Fri).

SUBWAY

There are 13 subway lines zigzagging through Tokyo. Four are operated by TOEI; nine belong to Tokyo Metro. Ticket prices on the Tokyo Metro start at ¥160; it's ¥170 to ride TOEI. Tickets are priced according to distance, so if you ride the subway for around eight stops or more, the fare goes up to ¥190 (¥210 for TOEI).

Ticket-vending machines that operate in English are available at every station. If you can't work out how much your fare will be, buy the cheapest ticket and pay the difference at a fare-adjustment machine at your destination. Services run from around 5.30am to midnight.

TAXI

Rates start at ¥710 per 2km, then the meter rises by ¥90 every 300m or so. There's a 20% late-night sur-

RECOMMENDED SUBWAY ROUTES

	To Ginza	To Shinjuku	To Shibuya	To Roppongi	To Asakusa
From Ginza	n/a	Marunouchi line (16min)	Ginza line (15min)	Hibiya line (10min)	Ginza line (17min)
From Shinjuku	Marunouchi line (16min)	n/a	JR Yamanote line (7min)	Toei Ōedo line (9min)	Marunouchi line to Akasaka-mitsuke, transfer to Ginza line (34min)
From Shibuya	Ginza line (15min)	JR Yamanote line (7min)	n/a	Hanzōmon line to Aoyama-itchōme, transfer to Toei Ōedo line (12min)	Ginza line (32min)
From Roppongi	Hibiya line (10min)	Toei Ōedo line (9min)	Toei Ōedo line to Aoyama-itchōme, transfer to Hanzōmon line (12min)	n/a	Toei Ōedo line to Daimon, transfer to Toei Asakusa line (28min)
From Asakusa	Ginza line (17min)	Ginza line to Akasaka-mitsuke, transfer to Marunouchi line (36min)	Ginza line (32min)	Toei Asakusa line to Daimon, transfer to Toei Ōedo line (28min)	n/a

charge applied to fares between 10pm and 5am. You'll also rack up about ¥100 every two minutes you spend in a typical Tokyo traffic jam.

Taxi vacancy is indicated by a red light; a green light means there's a night-time surcharge and a yellow light means that the cab is on call. Watch out for the automatic doors on taxis; they'll magically close themselves when you get in or out. Taxi drivers can plug a venue's telephone number into their GPS system to find its location.

CAR & MOTORCYCLE

On a short trip to Tokyo you're unlikely to need or want your own wheels, what with Tokyo's outstanding rail system and miserable traffic congestion. However, if you do need to hire a vehicle, be sure to obtain an International Driving Permit before you arrive in Japan as well as bringing a driver's licence from your own country.

Typical rates for small cars are ¥8000 or ¥9000 for the first day and ¥5500 to ¥7000 each day thereafter. On top of this there is a ¥1000-per-day insurance fee. Mileage is usually unlimited.

We recommend the following:

Mazda Rent-a-Lease (☎ 5286 0740)
Nippon Rent-a-Car (☎ 3485 7196)
Toyota Rent-a-Lease (☎ 3264 0100)

BOAT

Water buses are a great way to see a different slice of Tokyo, either as a short tour or as a relaxing means of getting around. **Suijo Bus** (Map p147, C4; ☎ 3841 9178; www.suijobus .co.jp/english/index.html; Azumabashi-mae, Asakusa, Taitō-ku; from ¥720; ☯ 9.55am-7.10pm, hours vary seasonally; ☯ Ginza & Toei Asakusa lines to Asakusa, exits 4 & A5) lines can shuttle you from Asakusa to Central Tokyo and on again to Odaiba.

PRACTICALITIES

BUSINESS HOURS

Banks 9am-3pm Mon-Fri, 8am-noon Sat, closed public holidays
Bars 6pm-midnight or later, closed one day per week
Department stores 10am-7pm, closed one or two days per month
Museums 9.30am-4.30pm
Offices 9am-5pm or 6pm Mon-Fri
Post offices 9am-5pm Mon-Fri (major post offices 9am-7pm Mon-Fri & 9am-3pm Sat)
Public offices 9am-noon & 1-5pm Mon-Fri
Restaurants 11.30am-2.30pm & 6-10.30pm (family-run restaurants 11.30am-11.30pm)

CLIMATE & WHEN TO GO

Spring (March to May) and autumn (September to November) are the most balmy seasons. Typhoons usually occur in September and October. Summers are hot and humid, with temperatures getting into the

---

GOOD THINGS TO KNOW

> Electricity – 100V 50Hz AC, two-pronged flat-pin plugs.
> Metric System – Japan uses the international metric system.
> Newspapers & Magazines – The *Japan Times, Daily Yomiuri* and *Asahi/International Herald Tribune* are English-language newspapers available at newsstands in or near train stations. The free *Metropolis* is an excellent, intelligent weekly magazine available every Friday at cafes and bookstores around Tokyo.
> Radio – InterFM on 76.1FM broadcasts news and daily-life information mainly in English, and in seven other languages, including Spanish and Chinese.
> Time – Japan is nine hours ahead of Greenwich Mean Time (GMT). Daylight-saving time is not used in Japan.
> TV – NHK is the government-run TV station; its 7pm and 9pm reports are bilingual. CNN and BBC World Service are available in all major hotels.

high 30s. The *tsuyu* (rainy season), in June, means several weeks of torrential rain can wreak havoc with a tight travel itinerary. In winter the weather is good with mainly clear, sunny skies and the occasional snowfall. Avoid major holidays such as Golden Week (29 April to 5 May) and the mid-August O-bon festival. The city tends to close down over New Year (around 29 December to 6 January).

DISCOUNTS

In general, not many discounts are offered to sights in Tokyo. Most major sights offer discounts for children, and very young children may get in free. An international student card will earn discounts on entry fees to many museums and prices on long-distance train travel. Seniors can get discounts to some major sights, and Japanese domestic airlines (JAS, JAL and ANA) offer senior discounts of about 25% on some flights. However, that's about the extent of it.

Prices are listed in this book in the following order: adult/student/child six to 12/child under six; typically, a listing like $ ¥1000/500 refers to adult/child prices.

One excellent investment, if you'll be in Tokyo for a while and plan to visit several museums, is the Grutt Pass (p143). The pass grants discounted or free entry to nearly 50 museums and zoos around Tokyo.

EMERGENCIES

Violent crime and theft, though they exist, are rare in Tokyo; that said, you should exercise the same awareness of your surroundings as you would anywhere else. Women should be aware of *chikan* (gropers) working crowded trains. Yelling '*Chikan!*' will often shame the offender into stopping, but look before you let loose – sometimes a crowded train is just a crowded train.

Although most emergency operators in Tokyo don't speak English, they will immediately refer you to someone who does. For free English assistance or advice, you can also call the **Japan Helpline** (☎ 0120-461 997; 24hr) or the **Tokyo English Life Line** (☎ 5774 0992; www.telljp.com; 9am-11pm).

Other useful numbers:
Ambulance ☎ 119
Fire ☎ 119
Police ☎ 110

HEALTH

All hospitals listed here have English-speaking staff and 24-hour accident and emergency departments. Travel insurance is advisable to cover any medical treatment you may need while in Tokyo. Medical treatment is among the best in the world, but also the most expensive. Note also that you will be expected to pay in full for treatment or provide sufficient proof that your insurance company will cover the payment.

We recommend the following:
Japanese Red Cross Medical Center (Nihon Sekijūjisha Iryō Sentā; Map pp68-9, B6; ☎ 3400 1311; www.med.jrc.or.jp, in Japanese; 4-1-22 Hiro-o, Shibuya-ku; 🚇 Hibiya line to Hiro-o, exits 1 & 2)
St Luke's International Hospital (Seiroka Byōin; Map pp46-7, F7; ☎ 3541 5151; www.luke.or.jp; 9-1 Akashichō, Chūō-ku; 🚇 Hibiya line to Tsukiji, exits 3 & 4)
Tokyo Medical & Surgical Clinic (Map pp68-9, G6; ☎ 3436 3028; www.tmsc.jp; 2F, 32 Shiba-kōen Bldg, 3-4-30 Shiba-kōen, Minato-ku; 🚇 Toei Mita line to Onarimon, exit A1)

PHARMACIES

Pharmacies are easy to find and some have Japanese-English symptom charts. Staff speaks English at the listed pharmacies:
American Pharmacy (Map pp46-7, D5; ☎ 5220-7716; B1F, Marunouchi Bldg, 2-4-1 Marunouchi, Chiyoda-ku; 🕑 9am-9pm Mon-Fri, 10am-9pm Sat, 10am-8pm Sun; 🚇 Marunouchi line to Tokyo, exit 4)
National Azabu Supermarket (Map pp68-9; ☎ 3442 3181; 4-5-2 Minami-Azabu, Minato-ku; 🕑 9.30am-7pm; 🚇 Hibiya line to Hiro-o, exits 1 & 2).

HOLIDAYS

When a public holiday falls on a Sunday, the following Monday is taken as a holiday. If a business remains open on a holiday, it will usually be closed the following day.
New Year's Day 1 January
Coming-of-Age Day 2nd Monday in January
National Foundation Day 11 February
Spring Equinox Day 21 March
Green Day 29 April
Constitution Day 3 May
Children's Day 5 May
Marine Day 3rd Monday in July
Respect-for-the-Aged Day 3rd Monday in September
Autumn Equinox Day 23 September
Sports Day 2nd Monday in October
Culture Day 3 November
Labour Thanksgiving Day 23 November
Emperor's Birthday 23 December

INFORMATION & ORGANISATIONS

Contact the **Japanese Red Cross Language Service Volunteers** (Map pp68-9, H5; ☎ 3438 1311; http://accessible.jp.org /tokyo/en; 1-1-3 Shiba Daimon, Minato-ku) to get a copy of its indispensable *Accessible Tokyo* guide, or peruse the website for the same detailed, current information on getting around Tokyo.

INTERNET
ACCESS

Internet access is rapidly improving. Some bars and cafes offer net access and/or wi-fi for free – check out **Freespot** (www.freespot.com /users/map_e .html) for locations near you. Many midrange hotels and most top-end hotels offer in-room LAN access, though you may be charged a usage fee.

Alternatively, you could do as the Tokyoites do and head to one of the *manga kissa* (p130) around town.

Recommended internet cafes:

Aprecio (Map p119, C2; ☎ 3205 7336; www .aprecio.co.jp in Japanese; B1F, Hygeia Plaza, 2-44-1 Kabukichō, Shinjuku-ku; 1st 30min ¥300, 10min thereafter ¥100; 🕐 24hr; 🚇 JR Yamanote line to Shinjuku, east exit) This clean, comfortable spot in Kabukichō offers all the usuals in smoking and nonsmoking wings, and has massage and beauty services, billiards and darts.

Bagus Gran Cyber Cafe (Map p91, B3; ☎ 5428 3676; www.bagus-99.com/netcafe in Japanese; 6F, 28-6 Udagawachō, Shibuya-ku; 8 hours ¥1500; 🕐 24hr; 🚇 JR Yamanote line to Shibuya, Hachikō exit) This popular chain has branches all over Tokyo.

USEFUL WEBSITES

The LP website (www.lonelyplanet.com) offers a speedy link to many of Tokyo's websites. Other excellent sites include the following:

Hyperdia (www.hyperdia.com)
Metropolis (www.metropolis.co.jp)
Tabelog (http://r.tabelog.com/tokyo) In Japanese
Tokyo Art Beat (www.tokyoartbeat.com)
Tokyo Food Page (www.bento.com/ tokyofood.html)

LANGUAGE

Note: Letters in square brackets are not pronounced.

BASICS

Hello.	*konnichiwa.*
Goodbye.	*sayonara.*
How are you?	*o-genki des[u]. ka?*
I'm fine.	*genki des[u].*
Excuse me.	*sumimasen.*
Yes.	*hai.*
No.	*iie.*
Thanks.	*dōmo (arigatō).*
You're welcome.	*dō itashimashite.*
Do you speak English?	*eigo ga hanase mas[u] ka?*
I don't understand.	*wakarimasen.*

EATING & DRINKING

That was delicious!	*oishikatta.*
I'm a vegetarian.	*watashi wa bejitarian des[u].*
Please bring the bill.	*(o-kanjō/o-aiso) o onegai shimas[u].*

Local dishes

kabayaki	skewers of grilled eel
katsu-don	fried pork cutlet with rice
okonomiyaki	Japanese-style pancake
tempura moriawase	a selection of tempura
zaru soba	cold buckwheat noodles with seaweed strips

SHOPPING

How much is it?	*ikura des[u] ka?*
That's too expensive.	*taka-sugi mas[u].*

199

EMERGENCIES

I'm sick.	*kibun ga warui des[u].*
Help!	*tas[u]kete!*
Call the police.	*keisatsu o yonde kudasai!*
Call an ambulance.	*kyūkyūsha o yonde.*

DAYS & NUMBERS

today	*kyō*
tomorrow	*ash[i]ta*
yesterday	*kinō*
0	*zero/rei*
1	*ichi*
2	*ni*
3	*san*
4	*yon/shi*
5	*go*
6	*roku*
7	*nana/shichi*
8	*hachi*
9	*kyū/ku*
10	*jū*
11	*jūichi*
12	*jūni*
13	*jūsan*
14	*jūyon/jūshi*
20	*nijū*
21	*nijūichi*
30	*sanjū*
100	*hyaku*
1000	*sen*
10,000	*man*

MONEY

Despite its status as a top-tier, modern city, Tokyo still largely runs on a cash economy. Hotels and high-end restaurants will accept credit cards, but many less exclusive shops and services do not. Since it's generally safe to carry around large amounts of cash in Tokyo, line your pockets with some money just for walking around. You'll burn through yen quickly in Tokyo; if you're not on a tight budget, plan on spending a daily average of around ¥5000 to ¥8000 for meals, train fares and admission costs.

CURRENCY

The currency in Japan is the yen (¥). Coins come in denominations of ¥1, ¥5, ¥10, ¥50, ¥100 and ¥500; notes in denominations of ¥1000, ¥2000, ¥5000 and ¥10,000. Newer-issue ¥500 coins aren't accepted by some vending machines.

TRAVELLERS CHEQUES

There's little difference in commission charged by banks and big hotels. All major brands are acceptable, but cheques in yen or US dollars are preferred over other currencies.

CREDIT CARDS

Visa, MasterCard, Amex and Diners Club are widely accepted…where credit cards are accepted. For 24-hour card cancellations or assistance, call these numbers:

Amex ☎ 0120-020 120
Diners Club ☎ 0120-074 024

JCB (☎ 0120-500 544
MasterCard (☎ 0053-111 3886
Visa (☎ 0053-111 1555)

ATMS

Tokyo post offices have ATMs that accept foreign-issued cards, 9am to 5pm Monday to Friday. If you're caught without cash after-hours, most 7-11 convenience stores have international ATMs. Citibank is your best bet for 24-hour ATMs that accept international cards; some Citibank ATM locations include Shinjuku, Ginza and Roppongi.

TELEPHONE

Local telephone calls cost ¥10 for the first three minutes, and then ¥10 for each minute thereafter. Phonecards are available from both newsstands and convenience stores starting in denominations of ¥500 and ¥1000 and are the most convenient way to call either locally or internationally.

Japan's mobile-phone network runs on the CDMA standard – incompatible with the widespread GSM system used in Europe, Australia and the rest of Asia (South Korea being the exception). **Softbank** (www.softbank.jp) offers pre-paid SIM card plans, but you must acquire a Softbank phone for the SIM. You can shop for a used phone or purchase one at the Softbank shop for a reasonable price. Pre-paid cards comes

in denominations of ¥3000 and ¥5000. The Softbank retail shop at Roppongi Crossing has several fluent English speakers on staff.
DoCoMo (☎ 0120-680 100; www.mobile rental.jp/english/index.html)
GoMobile (☎ 5405 2298; www.gomobile .co.jp)
Pupuru (☎ 052-957 1801; www.pupuru.com)
Rentafone (☎ 0120-746 487; www.renta fonejapan.com)
Softbank (☎ 3560 7730; www.softbank -rental.jp)

COUNTRY & CITY CODES
Japan ☎ 81
Tokyo ☎ 03

USEFUL PHONE NUMBERS
International directory assistance ☎ 0057
International operator ☎ 0051
Local directory assistance ☎ 104
Reverse-charge (collect) ☎ 0051

TIPPING
Tipping is not standard practice in Japan. Expect to pay a service charge (10% to 20%) at upper-end restaurants and hotels.

TOILETS
Public toilets can be found everywhere. They also tend to be high tech, outfitted with bidet, dryer and rushing-water sound effects to mask unseemly noise. Japanese-style squat toilets are also still an option at most public toilets.

DIRECTORY

TOURIST INFORMATION

JNTO Tourist Information Center (TIC; Map pp46-7, E6; www.jnto.go.jp; 10F Kōtsu Kaikan Bldg 2-10-1 Yūrakuchō, Chiyoda-ku; ☼ 9am-5pm; ⓡ JR Yamanote line to Yūrakuchō) The main JNTO-operated TIC is just outside Yūrakuchō station. It has the most comprehensive information on travel in Tokyo and Japan, and is an essential port of call. The Kōtsu Kaikan Building is just opposite the station as you exit to the right.

Tokyo Tourist Information Center (Map p119, A3; www.tourism.metor.tokyo.jp; 1F, Tokyo Metropolitan Government Bldg 1 2-8-1 Nishi-Shinjuku, Shinjuku-ku; ☼ 9.30am-6.30pm; ⓞ Toei Ōedo line to Tochōmae, exit A4) Run by the municipal government, this is a handy stop for visitors looking for local info only. The staff isn't too helpful, but there are enough brochures to wallpaper your house. Internet access is available. There's also a branch at the entrance to the Keisei tracks in Ueno Station.

Asakusa Tourist Information Center (Map p147, C3; 2-18-9 Kaminarimon, Taitō-ku; ☼ 9.30am-8pm; ⓞ Ginza & Asakusa lines to Asakusa, exit 2) Free neighbourhood tours can be arranged here. English-speaking staff works from 10am to 5pm. At the time of research, the centre was under construction – the temporary location is 50m up the street closer to the river.

TRAVELLERS WITH DISABILITIES

Tokyo's size and complexity make it challenging for the mobility impaired, as well as the visually and hearing impaired. The upside is that attitudes to people with disabilities have vastly improved in the last two decades, and newer buildings tend to have excellent facilities. Advance planning is the key to a successful trip.

The ⓖ icon throughout this guidebook denotes listings that are wheelchair-accessible, have toilets accommodating wheelchairs and are otherwise navigable for those with ambulatory challenges.

>INDEX

See also separate subindexes for See (p213), Shop (p215), Eat (p212), Drink (p211) and Play (p213).

A

accommodation 162-3
action figures 125
addresses 193
airports
    Haneda Airport 191, 192
    Narita Airport 191-2
Akasaka, *see* Roppongi
Akiba 50, 81
Akihabara 50, 81
ambulance 197
amusement parks 52, 63, 101, 159
anime 30, 125, 164
    museums 15, 121
Aoyama, *see* Harajuku
Aoyama-reien 121
aquariums 134
Arashio 64
architecture 165
art 190
Art Fair Tokyo 31
Asakusa 146-53, **147**
Asakusa Samba Festival 33
Asakusa-jinja 148
ATMs 201

B

baseball 64, 180,
beer 85
Beer Museum Yebisu 85
Benten-dō 140
boat travel 138, 196

000 map pages

Bocuse, Paul 87
books 189
bubble economy 183-4
bunraku 63, 189-90
bus travel 193
business hours 196

C

car travel 195-6
cell phones 201
cemetaries 121, 143
central Tokyo 44-65, **46-7**
cherry-blossom viewing,
    see hanami
children, attractions for 170
Chingodō-ji 148
chopsticks 55
Christmas 103
cinema 33, 188-9, *see*
    also Play *subindex*
climate 196-7
clubbing 174
    Ebisu 88-9
    Roppongi 79, 80
    Shibuya 99, 101
comics, *see* anime
cosplay 28, 38, 62, 94, 132, 170
costs, *see* inside front cover
credit cards 200-1
culture 184-5

D

Daikanyama 85-6
dance 189-90
Dembō-in 148
depachika 57
Design Festa 31, 34, 107

Diet, the 186
disabilities, travellers with 202
drinking 137, *see also* Drink
    subindex
    Asakusa 152
    Ginza 62
    Harajuku 116
    Ikebukuro 137
    Odaiba 158
    Roppongi 76-8
    Shibuya 98
    Shinjuku 127-9

E

earthquakes 17, 142, 143, 183, 184, 187-8
Ebisu 82-9, **83**
economy 186-7
Edo Shitamachi Traditional
    Crafts Museum 148-9
Edo-Tokyo Museum 17, 64
electricity 196
electronics, *see* Shop *subindex*
emergencies 197
Emperor's Birthday 34
entertainment 174, *see also*
    Play *subindex*
environmental issues 187-8
etiquette 185
events, *see* festivals & events
exchange rates, *see* inside
    front cover

F

festivals & events 29-34
    anime 30
    art & design 31, 34, 107

film 33
  gay 32, 33
  lesbian 32, 33
  matsuri 30
  music 32
film 33, 188-9
food 166-7, *see also* Eat
  subindex
    Akasaka 75
    Asakusa 151-2
    central Tokyo 59-61
    depachika 57
    Ebisu 86-7
    fugu 167
    Ginza 58-9, 60, 61
    Harajuku 112-13, 115-16
    Ikebukuro 136-7
    kaiseki 75
    Meguro 87
    Odaiba 158
    Roppongi 73-6
    shabu-shabu 167
    Shibuya 97-8
    Shinjuku 125-7
    sukiyaki 167
    Ueno 144-5
    unagi 166
Fuji Rock Festival 32
Fuji TV 156

G
galleries 168, *see also* See
  subindex
gardens, *see* parks & gardens
gay travellers 169
  bars 127, 128
  festivals 32, 33
Ghibli Museum 15, 121
Ginza 18, 44-65
Ginza Graphic Gallery 45, 48
Golden Gai 14, 128-9
government 185-6
Grutto Pass 143, 197

H
Hachikō statue 92
Hama-rikyū-teien 48
hanami 31, 121, 175, *see
  also kōyō*
handicrafts 179
Hara Museum of
  Contemporary Art 92
Harajuku 12, 102-17, **104-5**
health 197-8
Hie-jinja 67
Hina Matsuri (Girls' Day) 30
history 182-90
holidays 198
hot springs 19, 152-3, 159,
  176

I
Idemitsu Art Museum 48
ikebana 71, 141
Ikebukuro 132-7, **133**
Imperial Palace 48
Imperial Palace East Garden 48
internet access 198-9
internet resources 199
iris viewing 32
itineraries 37-9
izakaya 174, *see also* Eat
  subindex, *see also* Drink
  subindex

J
jazz 78
Jinbōchō 54-5
Jingū-gaien 103

K
kabuki 17, 49, 63-4, 65,
  189-90
Kabukichō 120
Kagurazaka 45
kaiseki 75
karaoke 79-80, 88
Kichijōji 122

Kikuchi Rinko 53
Kite Museum 48-9
Kiyomizu Kannon-dō 140
Koishikawa Kōrakuen 49
kōyō 33, 175

L
Laforet Museum Harajuku
  103
languages 199-200
lesbian travellers 169
  bars 98, 127, 128
  festivals 32, 33
live music 171, *see also* Play
  subindex
Lloyd, Terrie 142
Love Hotel Hill 92, 93

M
maid cafes 62
magazines 196
manga 7, 125, 164
manga kissa 130
markets 13, 51-2, 143-4
Marunouchi 44-65, **46-7**
Meguro 82-9, **83**
Meguro Parasitological
  Museum 84
Meguro-gawa 121
Meiji-jingū 20, 32, 103
  festivals 30
Miyazaki Hayao 15, 121
mobile phones 201
money 197, 200
Mori Art Museum 67, 70
motorcycle travel 195-6
Museum of Maritime Science
  156
museums 22, 173,
  see also See subindex
    Akasaka 67, 70-1, 72
    Aoyama 103, 104
    Asakusa 148-50
    central Tokyo 48, 49, 50

museums continued
  Ebisu 84-5
  Harajuku 103, 106, 107
  Meguro 84
  Mitaka 121
  Odaiba 156
  Roppongi 67, 70, 71, 72
  Shibuya 93
  Shinagawa 92
  Shinjuku 120
  Ueno 140-1
music 189, see also Play
  subindex
music venues
  Akihabara 62-3
  Ebisu 88
  Meguro 88
  Roppongi 78, 79, 80
  Shibuya 99, 100, 101
  Shinjuku 129, 130

N
Nakame 84
Naka-meguro 84
National Diet Building 70-1
National Institute for Nature
  Study 84
National Museum of
  Emerging Science and
  Innovation (Miraikan) 156
National Museum of Modern
  Art 50
National Museum of Western
  Art 140
National Science Museum 140
newspapers 196
nightlife 174, see also Play
  subindex
Ningyō-kujō 33
nō 100, 130, 189-90

000 map pages

O
Odaiba 154-9, **155**
Ōedo Onsen Monogatari
  19, 159
Ōkura Shūkokan 71
Omote-sandō 12
onsen 19, 152-3, 159, 176
organised tours 107
Ōta Memorial Art Museum
  103-4
otaku 62, 125, 135, 164
Otoko-no-Hi (Boys' Day) 31
otome 132, 135

P
parks & gardens 22, 175,
  see also See subindex
    central Tokyo 48, 49
    Ebisu 84
    Harajuku 107-8
    Kichijōji 122
    Shinjuku 121
    Ueno 22, 138, 140-1,
      143, 175
pharmacies 198
planning 39, 197
police 197
politics 185-6
Prada Aoyama 106
public baths 19, 131, 176
puppets 63

R
radio 196
rakugō 131
responsible travel 191, 192
Roppongi 66-81, **68-9**
Roppongi Hills 72, 73
Ryōgoku Kokugikan 64
ryokan 162, 163

S
Sanja Matsuri 31
Seijin-no-Hi (Coming-of-Age
  Day) 30

Seijo 121
senior travellers 197
Sensō-ji 26, 30, 149
sentō 19, 131, 176
Setsubun 30
Shibuya 24, 90-101, **91**
Shichi-Go-San (Seven-Five-
  Three Festival) 34
Shimizu Takashi 114
Shimo-Kitazawa 21, 95
Shinjuku 118-31, **119**
Shinjuku-gyōen 121
Shiodome 50
Shitamachi History Museum
  140-1
Shōgatsu 30
shopping 172, 178, see
  also Shop subindex
    Akihabara 50, 52, 53,
      55, 58
    Asakusa 150-1
    central Tokyo 52-8
    Ebisu 85-6
    Ginza 18, 54, 55-7, 58
    Harajuku 103, 106-7,
      108-12
    Ikebukuro 135-6
    Marunouchi 55
    Meguro 86
    Odaiba 157
    Roppongi 72-3
    Shibuya 24, 93-6
    Shinjuku 122-5
    Ueno 143-4
shrines, see temples & shrines
Sky Tree 16
soccer 116-7, 180
Sōgetsu Kaikan 71
Sony Building 51
Spiral Building 106-7
sport 180, see also Play
  subindex
Statue of Liberty 154, 165

subway travel 194, 195
Sumida-Gawa 25, 32
Sumida River Fireworks 32
sumō 10-11, 64
Sunshine International
    Aquarium 134
Sunshine Starlight Dome 134
Suntory Museum of Art 71-2

T
Taikokan (Drum Museum)
    149-50
Tange Kenzō 165
tattoos 153
taxis 194-5
telephone services 201
temples & shrines 148, 177,
    see also See *subindex*
    Asakusa 148, 149
    central Tokyo 52
    Harajuku 103
    Roppongi 67, 71
    Ueno 140, 141-3
Tepco Electric Energy
    Museum 93
theatre 189-90, *see also* Play
    subindex
    central Tokyo 63-4, 65
    Shibuya 98-9, 100
    Shinjuku 130
time 196
tipping 201
Togo Seiji 120
toilets 201
Tokugawa Ieyasu 182
Tokyo Big Sight 157
Tokyo Disneyland 52
Tokyo International Anime
    Fair 30
Tokyo International Film
    Festival 33
Tokyo International Forum 51

Tokyo International Lesbian &
    Gay Film Festival 32
Tokyo Metropolitan
    Government Offices 121-2
Tokyo Metropolitan Museum
    of Art 141
Tokyo Metropolitan Museum
    of Photography 84-5
Tokyo National Museum
    22, 141
Tokyo Pride Parade 33
Tokyo Sky Tree 16
Tokyo Tower 72
Tōshōgū 141, 143
tourist information 198, 202
tours 107
toylets 81
Toyota Amlux 134-5
train travel 192-3, 194
travel passes 194
travellers with disabilities 202
Tsukiji Market 13, 51-2
TV 196

U
Ueno 138-45, **139**
Ueno Zoo 143
Ueno-kōen 22, 138, 140-1,
    143, 175

V
vacations 198
visas 193

W
washi 179
Watari Museum of
    Contemporary Art 107
weather 196-7
WWII 183

Y
yakuza 153
Yanaka-reien 143

Yasukuni-jinja 52
Yoyogi-kōen 107-8

Z
zoos 137, 143

🍸 DRINK

Bars
    300 Bar 62
    Advocates Bar 127-8
    Agave 77
    Arty Farty 128
    Asahi Sky Room 152
    Aux Amis des Vins 62
    Beat Café 98
    Bernd's Bar 77
    Bon's 128
    Chestnut & Squirrel 98
    Geronimo 77
    Ginza Lion 62-4
    Golden Gai 14, 128-9
    Heartland 77
    Kamiya Bar 152
    New York Bar 129
    Pink Cow 98
    Tableaux Lounge 87

Breweries
    Sunset Beach Brewing
        Company 158

Cafes
    norari:kurari 137

Gay Bars
    Advocates Bar 127-8
    Arty Farty 128

Izakaya
    Hanashibe 158
    Tonerian 137

Lesbian Bars
    Chestnut & Squirrel 98

Lounges
Den Aquaroom 116
Mado Lounge 77-8
Maduro 78
Nonbei-yokochō 98
Tokyo Apartment Café 116

Pubs
Nonbei-yokochō 98
What the Dickens 87-8

🍴 EAT

American
New York Grill 126

Asian Fusion
Daidaiya 125
Den Rokuen-tei 96-7

Brazilian
Barbacoa Steakhouse 158

Cafes
A to Z Café 112
Armwood Cottage 125
Ef 151
Meal Muji 60
Mikimoto Lounge 60
mother kurkku 113

Chinese
Harajuku Gyoza Rō 112-13

Food-Themed Parks
Daiba Little Hong Kong 158
Namco Namjatown 137

French
L'Atelier de Joël Robuchon 74-5
Le Bretagne 115
Lugdunum Bouchon Lyonnais 60-2

Maison Paul Bocuse 87
Nid Café 115

Fusion
Beige 58-9
Ninja Akasaka 75

Indian
Khazana 158
Nirvanam 75-6
Tokyo Curry Lab 76

International Groceries
Kinokuniya 113
National Azabu
Supermarket 75

Italian
Selan Restaurant 115

Izakaya
Gonpachi 74
Kaikaya 97
Sakana-tei 97

Japanese
Irokawa 151
Komagata Dozeu 151-2
Sasa-no-Yuki 144-5
Ume-no-Hana 115-16

Japanese Noodles
Anpuku 136-7
Ippūdō 86-7
Keika Kumamoto Rāmen 126
Kyūsyū Jangara 113
Opippi 61
Sakata 61
Tajima 76
Ueno Yabu Soba 145

Kaiseki
Kikunoi 74
Ukai Tofu-ya 76

Macrobiotic
Chaya Macrobiotics 125-6

Okonomiyaki
Kiji 60

Robatayaki
Inakaya 74

Shabu-Shabu
Nabezo 97
Seryna 76

Shokudō
Honoji 113

Street
Ebisu-yokochō 86
Yanaka Ginza 145

Sukiyaki
Ibuki 126

Sushi & Sashimi
Daiwa Sushi 59
Sushi Kanesaka 61
Tsukiji Tama Sushi 158
Zauo 127

Tempura
Daikokuya 151
Edokko 151
Ten-Ichi 61
Tsunahachi 127

Tonkatsu
Marugo 60
Tonki 87

Vegetarian
Eat More Greens 73-4
Mominoki House 115

Yakiniku
Jomon 74

Yakitori
Akiyoshi 136
Birdland 59

000 map pages

Omoide-yokochō 126-7
Toriyoshi Dining 97
Vin Chou 152

Yoshoku
Rengatei 61

⭐ PLAY

Amusement Parks
Kōrakuen Amusement
Park 63
Tokyo Disneyland 52
Tokyo Joypolis 159
Tokyo Metropolitan
Children's Hall 101

Cinemas
Cine Amuse East &
West 99
Cinema Mediage 159
Cinema Rise 99
National Film Centre 63
Yebisu Garden Cinema 89

Clubs
Air 88
Club 328 79
Club Asia 99
Eleven 79
Harlem 99-100
Muse 80
New Lex-Edo 80
Unit 88-9
Vanilla 80
Vanity 81
Womb 101

Hot Springs
Asakusa Kannon Onsen
152-3
Jakotsu-yu 153
Ōedo Onsen Monogatari
19, 159

Karaoke
Festa Iikura 79-80
Lovenet 80
Smash Hits 88

Live Music
Abbey Road 78
AKB48 Theatre 62-3
Alfie 78
Billboard Live 78
Blue Note 78-9
Cavern Club 79
Club Quattro 99
JZ Brat 100
La.mama 100
Liquid Room 88
Loft 129
Milk 88
STB 139 80
Shibuya O-East 100-1
Shibuya O-West 101
Shinjuku Pit Inn 130

Lounges
Ruby Room 100

Onsen
Asakusa Kannon Onsen
152-3
Jakotsu-yu 153
Ōedo Onsen Monogatari
19, 159

Petting Zoo
Nekobukuro 137

Rakugo
Shinjuku Suehirotei 131

Spectator Sports
Jingū Stadium 116
National Stadium
116-17
Tokyo Dome 64-5

Swimming Pools & Gyms
Tokyo Metropolitan
Gymnasium 117

Theatre
Bunkamura Theatre
Cocoon 98-9
Kanze Nō-gakudō 100
National Nō Theatre 130
National Theatre 63
Session House 63
Shinbashi Enbujyō 63-4
Tokyo Takarazuka
Gekijō 65

Yoga
YogaJaya 89

🅖 SEE

Aquariums
Sunshine International
Aquarium 134

Galleries
21_21 Design Sight 67
Bridgestone Museum 45
Bunkamura Theatre
Cocoon 98-9
Design Festa Gallery 107
Ginza Graphic Gallery 45-8
Laforet Museum Harajuku
103
Mitsubishi Ichigokan
49-50
Parco Gallery 92
Tokyo Metropolitan
Museum of Art 141
Tokyo Metropolitan
Museum of Photography
84-5
Watari Museum of
Contemporary Art 107

Ikebana Schools
Sōgetsu Kaikan 71

Markets
Tsukiji market 13, 51-2

Monuments
Hachikō statue 92
Statue of Liberty 154, 165

Museums
21_21 Design Sight 67
Advertising Museum
Tokyo 50
Bridgestone Museum 45
Edo Shitamachi
Traditional Crafts
Museum 148-9
Ghibli Museum 15, 121
Hara Museum of
Contemporary Art 92
Idemitsu Art Museum 48
Kite Museum 48-9
Laforet Museum Harajuku
103
Meguro Parasitological
Museum 84
Mori Art Museum 67, 70
Musée Tomo 70
Museum of Maritime
Science 156
National Museum of
Emerging Science and
Innovation (Miraikan)
156
National Museum of
Modern Art 50
National Museum of
Western Art 140
National Science Museum
140

Nezu Museum 103
Ōkura Shūkokan 71
Ōta Memorial Art Museum
103-4
Seiji Togo Memorial
Sompo Japan Museum
of Art 120
Shitamachi History
Museum 140-1
Suntory Museum of Art
71-2
Taikokan (Drum Museum)
149-50
Tepco Electric Energy
Museum 93
Tokyo Metropolitan
Museum of Art 141
Tokyo Metropolitan
Museum of Photography
84-5
Tokyo National Museum
141
Watari Museum of
Contemporary Art 107
Yebisu Beer Museum 85

Notable Buildings
Akihabara 50
Fuji TV 156
Mitsubishi Ichigokan
49-50
National Diet Building
70-1
Prada Aoyama 106
Shiodome 50-1
Spiral Building 106-7
Tokyo Big Sight 157
Tokyo International
Forum 51
Tokyo Metropolitan
Government Offices
121-2

Tokyo Sky Tree 16
Tokyo Tower 72

Notable Streets & Districts
Cat Street 108
Golden Gai 14, 128-9
Kabukichō 120
Kichijōji 122
Love Hotel Hill 92
Naka-meguro 84
Nakano Broadway 125
Omote-sandō-dōri 103
Shibuya Crossing 93
Shimo-Kitazawa 95

Parks & Gardens
Hama-Rikyū-Teien 48
Imperial Palace East
Garden 48
Inokashira Park 122
Koishikawa Kōrakuen 49
National Institute for
Nature Study 84
Shinjuku-gyōen 121
Ueno-kōen 22, 138, 140-
1, 143, 175
Yoyogi-kōen 107-8

Planetariums
Sunshine Starlight Dome
134

Showrooms
Sony Building 51
Toyota Amlux 134-5

Temples & Shrines
Akagi-jinja 45
Asakusa-jinja 148
Benten-dō 140
Chingodō-ji 148
Dembō-in 148
Hie-jinja 67
Jingū-gaien 103

000 map pages

Kiyomizu Kannon-dō 140
Meiji-jingū 20, 30, 32, 103
Nogi-jinja 71
Sensō-ji 149
Tōshōgū 141, 143
Yasukuni-jinja 52

Zoos
Ueno Zoo 143

🏠 SHOP

Art & Antiques
Japan Sword 72-3
Kurofune 73
Tolman Collection 73

Books
Animate 135
Book Off 108
Jinbōchō 54-5
Kinokuniya 123-4
Mandarake 94, 125
Maruzen 55
On Sundays 110-11
Shibuya Publishing & Booksellers 95-6
Tora no Ana 58

Boutiques
Daikanyama 85-6
MISC 86
Shimokita 95
Shimokita Garage Department 95
Shimo-Kitazawa 95
Village Vanguard 95

Cameras & Electronics
Apple Store 52
Bic Camera 122, 135
Laox 55

Sakuraya Camera 124
Yodobashi Akiba 58
Yodobashi Camera 125

Comics & Action Figures
Mandarake 94, 125

Costumes
Haight & Ashbury 95

Department Stores
Decks Tokyo Beach 157
Isetan 123
Marui Young 124
Matsuya 55-6
Mitsukoshi 56
Odakyū 124
Parco 1, 2 & 3 94
Shibuya 109 95
Sunshine City 136
Takashimaya 56-7
Tobu 136
Venus Fort 157

Dolls
Yoshitoku 151

Fashion
BAPExclusive 108
Beams 122
Cat Street 108
Comme des Garçons 108-9
Hysteric Glamour 109-10
Isetatsu 144
Issey Miyake 110
Journal Standard 123
Laforet 110
Muji 56
Ragtag 94-5
Takeshita-dōri 111-12
Undercover 112
Uniqlo 58
We Go 112
Yohji Yamamoto 112

Furniture
Brunch 86
Claska 86
Misc 86
Moody's 86

Handicrafts
Japan Traditional Crafts Center 135
Kamawanu 86
Nippori Fabric Town 144
Oriental Bazaar 111
Takumi Handicrafts 57-8

Homewares & Novelties
Brunch 86
Claska 86
Condomania 109
Don Quijote 123
Kappabashi-dōri 150-1
Loft 94
Misc 86
Moody's 86
Muji 56
Three Minutes Happiness 96
Tōkyū Hands 96, 124-5, 136

Jewellery & Accessories
Atelier Magic Theater 108
Mikimoto Pearl 56
Pass the Baton 111

Markets
Ameyoko Arcade 143-4

Music
Disk Union (Shibuya) 93-4
Disk Union (Shinjuku) 123
Manhattan Records 94
Recofan 94
Tower Records 96

INDEX

Stationery
Haibara 54
Itōya 54
Muji 56
Sekaido 124

Textiles
Nippori Fabric Town 144

Toys
Hakuhinkan Toy Park 54
Kiddyland 110

Vintage Goods
Chicago 108
New York Joe Exchange 95
Pass the Baton 111

000 map pages